SO BY LEONARD KOPPETT

Thinking Man's Guide to Baseball

e New York Mets

24 SECONDS TO SI

A

A

T

24 SECONDS TO SHOOT

An Informal History of the National Basketball Association 1945-1970

Special Silver Anniversary Edition

by LEONARD KOPPETT

The Macmillan Company
Collier-Macmillan Ltd., London

To my mother,
who wondered where all that time was spent

All statistical material has been supplied by, and used with the permission of, the National Basketball Association.

Copyright © 1968 by Leonard Koppett
All rights reserved. No part of this book may be reproduced or transmitted in any form or by any means, electronic or mechanical, including photocopying, recording or by any information storage and retrieval system, without permission in writing from the Publisher.

The Macmillan Company
866 Third Avenue, New York, N.Y. 10022
Collier-Macmillan Canada Ltd., Toronto, Ontario

Library of Congress Catalog Card Number: 68-17200

Second Printing 1970

Printed in the United States of America

CONTENTS

PREFACE

It is astonishing, and even a little frightening, to realize that the National Basketball Association has reached its twenty-fifth year. For those of us who were part of its beginning, when our main assets were a capacity for hope and work, the time has passed too quickly. In a most vivid way, the adventures of the league's early days do seem like only yesterday. And yet, at the same time, the scope and stability of today's N.B.A. seem always to have been there, easy to take for granted as the natural order of things, so far removed from the kinds of problems that marked its infancy as to make that time dim and unreal.

Looking back over a quarter of a century, one is struck by the extent to which things have changed, not only in the N.B.A. and in basketball, but in all our lives. But living through it all, day by day, it seldom seems so dramatic. Problems are solved one by one, progress is made one step at a time, growth comes gradually, and every crisis and triumph is quickly displaced by the attention that must be paid to a new one.

Leonard Koppett first told the story of the N.B.A.'s development in *24 Seconds to Shoot,* two years ago. The many changes since then that are described in this special edition—and the proliferation of books about N.B.A. people and teams—only re-emphasize how we have continued to move faster and further from those uncertain beginnings. On the N.B.A.'s twenty-fifth birthday, it is still growing and developing, faster than ever; but a look backward adds to our feelings of accomplishment. It is too easy to forget how many people struggled to build it.

So the essential story, updated as it is, remains the same: how we grew from a vague idea in the minds of a few arena operators to our nation-spanning league with its audience of millions today. Tradition is important in all sports. Here, in compact form, are the elements of N.B.A. tradition, and everyone who had a hand in building it has a right to feel proud.

WALTER KENNEDY
Commissioner
National Basketball Association

INTRODUCTION

The National Basketball Association, which began life under the name of the Basketball Association of America in 1946, is the only professional basketball league that has fully succeeded in establishing itself as a permanent part of America's major-league sports scene.

This is the story of how it grew.

It is not, in any sense, a documented or even serious history. It is a description, an account, a narrative—a story, which tries to sketch the main steps in its development. The value judgments, interpretations of motives and trends, assertions about relationships, selectivity of material, are my personal views, formed through twenty years of newspaper reporting of the league's affairs.

Everything has been done in rough, broad strokes, with no attempt to be all-inclusive or too concerned with details. The aim is to present a wide-screen picture, a survey view of how this particular organization came into being and survived the problems that beset it.

The competitive details—records, facts concerning ownership and arenas, yearly leaders and individual team histories—are collected in an appendix which can serve as a rudimentary record book and outline of league history. For fuller details, other publications are available, and listed in the bibliography.

The focus of our story, however, is on the general development of the league and its principal figures. How problems arose, and what was done about them, while the annual succession of championships to be settled moved on without interruption—this is our main theme.

There were seven stages in this process, and our approach will be strictly chronological.

The first stage lasted from early 1946, when slowly percolating ideas about forming a pro league to cash in on the new popularity of intersectional college basketball finally crystallized into the Basketball Association of America, to mid-1948.

The second stage, which took a little over a year, consisted of arranging a merger between the Basketball Association of America, and the older, more orthodox (in its time) National League, which had the better players.

The third stage was the shaking out of weak franchises from the resulting merger, which brought seventeen teams into action during the 1949–50 season. It took until 1954 to get down to the bedrock of eight teams.

The fourth and fifth stages were simultaneous in time, but different in substance. In 1954, the 24-second rule was adopted, and it saved the game itself from the deliberate foul-trading and ball control that had been rapidly wrecking fan interest. While the game itself was being repaired, and a new, exciting style of play was being developed, the franchises were going through a series of stabilizations. Teams moved from smaller to larger cities, where they could play in larger arenas, and where ownership with greater financial resources could operate. This process continued through 1962, by which time all teams were in major cities and the league stretched from coast to coast.

The sixth stage, the arrival of stars of a new magnitude, overlapped the move into larger cities, and covered essentially the period between Bill Russell's arrival in Boston in December, 1956, and the entry of Oscar Robertson and Jerry West into the league in the fall of 1960. Wilt Chamberlain and Elgin Baylor came in between. Such players literally changed the nature of the game.

The seventh and final stage, reexpansion, began tentatively in 1961, when a new Chicago team raised the league's membership to nine for the first time since 1954. This team failed in Chicago and moved to Baltimore two years later. But in 1966, another Chicago team (which did catch on) gave the league ten clubs. Four more went into action in the next two years, and in 1970 three more made the total 17 again, this time organized into four divisions. The seventh stage, therefore, is just gaining momentum and is conclusive proof of how successful the passage through the first six had turned out to be.

That's our story—but it looks neat only in retrospect, from the vantage point of knowing how things wound up. It was a long time, from the beginning, before bare survival was assured, and both profit and prestige could be enjoyed. Uncertainty, a few touches of panic, frequent hysteria and very little sense of direction were the prevailing mood through most of the first decade—and memories of the first haunted the second.

Looking back, it is surprising how some of the precarious situations were survived at all, especially in the confusion that surrounded them. What these situations were, and how they were handled, form the main thread of this account.

1 THE IDEA

It all began because of a man named Ned Irish, although he really didn't want any part of it when it arose.

The idea of professional basketball on a stable, major-league basis was implicit in the runaway success of college basketball double-headers in large arenas. For this success, Irish was responsible. By promoting such double-headers at Madison Square Garden in New York, Irish had made his personal fortune, had shown the money-making potential of basketball, and had stimulated nationwide interest in the sport to an unprecedented degree.

A professional league, therefore, was of little immediate interest to Irish in 1946, when World War II had just ended and the public's craving for any sort of entertainment was moving towards insatiability. He was doing too well with his college programs to be concerned with new and risky ventures.

But the gold mine he had created was too promising to be left undeveloped by others. To understand why, and to see how Irish himself was drawn inexorably into the new orbit, one must consider the stage of development reached in 1946 by two originally distinct enterprises—commercial basketball and large-city sports arenas.

Like the game itself, professionalism in basketball had sudden and, in a sense, artificial origins. All other popular games—baseball, football, hockey, tennis, boxing, wrestling, fencing, and all the various types of races and field events—evolved gradually, through generations of informal practice. The final, familiar rules were distilled from countless trial-and-error experiments, long after the popularity of the activity had proved itself.

Basketball, on the other hand, was invented from scratch by James Naismith in 1891 in Springfield, Massachusetts. He had a very specific, and limited, purpose: to provide an athletic activity, more enjoyable than calisthenics, that could be engaged in during the winter months, indoors, when it was not possible (in New England) to play baseball or football (in any of its varieties).

Naismith's needs were specific, too. He was an instructor in physical education, attending the International Young Men's Christian Association Training School at Springfield, Massachusetts. His orientation was towards physical fitness. The competitive side of athletics was, for him, a stimulant that made exercise more pleasureable and attractive, not an end in itself—and certainly not the raw material for entertaining spectators. His ideals were those of the participant and the amateur, and his search was for an indoor game that groups of men could play with a great deal of exertion in a small place.

So, in his little gymnasium which had a running track circling the floor like a balcony, he hung two peach baskets, one at each end; he got a soccer ball; and he divided his class (18 men) into two teams. The idea was to throw the ball into the basket. The rules of play were almost automatically determined by the conditions. Purposeful blocking and tackling couldn't be allowed on a wooden floor, and would make progress impossible anyhow; but unopposed running with the ball in such a small space would make the offense unstoppable. Therefore, the ball had to be either bounced (dribbled) or passed to another player; and defenders had to devise ways of "guarding" that still permitted the offensive player enough freedom to throw the ball to a teammate or at the basket. Thus, the basic characteristics of the game—that undue interference by the defense was a "foul," and that artificial means (dribbling or passing) had to be used to advance the ball—were built in from the start.

The problems were built in from the start, too: exactly how much body-contact constituted a foul? When did a legal dribble slip over into "travelling"? When was the offensive player responsible for contact and a foul, and when the defensive player? These intrinsically borderline judgments, always affected by angle of vision and the subjective reaction of the observer, put a tremendous burden on the referee. His decisions, inevitably, had a greater effect on the outcome than in other games, and this feature of basketball has never been overcome with complete satisfaction.

However, as an exercise activity, with not too much attention to the score, it proved to be ideal, and an immediate hit with the participants. Within three years it had been introduced from coast to coast, by graduates of the Springfield classes and by active letter writing. Many who tried it immediately became addicts, and rules were quickly put into stable and standardized form.

By 1895, various Y.M.C.A. teams were holding regional tournaments, and basketball players were taking the game into high schools and colleges. To the participants, the sugar-coating had become the main course.

And it was this instant popularity that generated serious difficulties. Naismith had done far more than he had imagined. The game was so fascinating that its competitive aspects could not be kept under control. The good athletes who tried it became, like all good athletes, intent on winning, and tournaments added to the incentive. With victory prized so highly, the game became rough, since there were few experienced referees and no effective ruling body. It became too rough to be looked upon, by Y.M.C.A. administrators, as healthful exercise; nor could the presence of an increasing number of spectators, reacting passionately to their rooting interests, be fitted in to the Y.M.C.A. program. (Here again, at the beginning, was a foretaste of problems still with us: how to control tough play when the stakes become great, and how to handle unruly spectators.)

The Y.M.C.A., therefore, embarked on a campaign of deemphasis, only a few years after popularizing the sport it had invented. It discouraged the formation of club teams, and the conducting of tournaments.

But while the organization could draw back, the individual addicts could not—and would not if they could. They had learned how to play basketball, and were perfecting new items of technique and strategy every day. They had no intention of giving up their new love. If the Y.M.C.A. didn't want to run it, fine—that was the Y.M.C.A.'s business. The players would run it themselves.

And here, another built-in aspect of the game took effect. Teamwork, on an almost instinctive level, was the key to victory; that was obvious already. And the smoothest teamwork was achieved by having the same players work together in game after game. Therefore, the teams already formed—under Y.M.C.A. sponsorship, or representing clubs—tended to stay intact. When the Y.M.C.A. withdrew support from a particular team, it didn't disband. It simply changed its name and remained together on its own.

The main problem now became: where to play? There were no public arenas, and only a handful of school gymnasiums. Actually, any auditorium with enough floor space could be easily adapted to basketball—a dance floor, a stage, an armory would do, especially when the practice of enclosing the court in a wire or cord mesh (to keep the ball from going out of bounds) became popular. All such places, however, had one thing in common: rent. Sometimes the players could pay it out of their own pockets. Usually they couldn't. But a ready source of financing was at hand. The spectators—the same wildly interested spectators whose enthusiasm bothered Y.M.C.A. officials—would gladly pay to watch the games. And if enough spectators were interested, their money, in the form of admissions or post-game collections, produced a surplus beyond expenses. This surplus, naturally and almost unthinkingly, was divided among the players.

Imperceptibly, they had become professionals.

This process was complete before the turn of the century, well within the first decade of basketball's existence. Its significant feature was that it was unintentional. In all other sports, professionalism was the consequence of spectator interest: first the sport became entrenched among its followers; then, in order to have the best team, a team's backers offered money to the best players; when the best players and the best teams began drawing the largest crowds, the opportunity for profit was not lost upon the promoter-minded—and full-fledged professional teams and leagues were formed because it was obvious that a profit could be made. In basketball, there was no large preexisting audience guaranteeing interest, and no prior promotional intent: the players became professional in order to continue playing, before the best ones came into such demand that a business could be based on hiring them.

The importance of this difference is easy to overlook, but it proved relevant to what followed. In the earliest stages of organized professional baseball and boxing (the only two professional sports that mattered in the Nineteenth Century, aside from the totally different world of horse racing), command was taken by business men. These had the talents, outlook, experience and motivation of money-makers; they were capable in organizing, buying and selling, promoting. For all their mistakes and early failures, they were equipped to be business men.

In basketball, on the other hand, financial control remained primarily in the hands of players, coaches and non-playing promoters attracted more to basketball's appeal as an activity than as a potential business. In time, they became as eager as anyone to be commercially successful; but they were, by and large, different men, living on a lower economic and social level than the baseball and racing magnates, buffs first and entrepreneurs second.

It must be remembered that in those days, all professional athletic activity lacked full social respectability. The amateur ideals were still unchallenged, and the Puritanical disapproval of "frivolous" activities was still strong. Even baseball players were considered "rowdies," boxing (or more properly, "prize fighting") had just been made legal, and American football was being seriously attacked by the administrations of the colleges whose students were developing the game.

In this atmosphere, professional basketball had some special handicaps of its own.

The game itself had been sneered at as "sissy" by the football players, who yearned for uninhibited body contact, from the beginning. When it proved popular with girls (in a modified version, of course), this charge gained momentum. Anybody who played basketball knew better, but the noisier advocates of vicarious virility expressed their contempt (and still do).

More serious were the opportunities for abuse in the professional game's environment. In a game controlled so easily by skillful players, a "fixed" result was a constant danger (as it had been, notoriously, in baseball's early days, and has always been in boxing and racing). In the absence of firm leagues, strong administration, convincingly unshakeable referees and large-scale publicity, it was easy for the public to lack confidence in the integrity of the game, whether such doubt was well-founded or not.

Since seating capacities were small, opportunity for large profit, by businessman's standards, didn't exist. Yet the money being paid to individual players became, by personal standards, considerable. Consequently, players shifted teams frequently, and teams scheduled games on the basis of expediency. This created a self-damaging cycle: impermanence of line-up and unreliability of schedule limited fan interest to local die-hards, and the lack of accommodation for large crowds created the penny-pinching conditions that led to these shifting allegiances.

It was obvious that the answer to many of these problems lay in the formation of leagues. In 1898—only seven years after the game had been invented—a professional circuit was formed in Philadelphia, called the National League. It lasted for five years. In quick succession, other professional leagues sprang up, with essentially narrow geographic bounds. The usual pattern had several teams from different sections or suburbs of one large city, and a few members from satellite cities within a 100-mile radius.

The stronger teams, however, were more interested in barnstorming and touring than in formal league play. In the 1920s, when all commercial sports enjoyed a golden age, an American League, with teams in Cleveland, New York and Philadelphia, had a brief period of major-league aura, but very brief. The respected teams were basically independents—first and foremost, the Original Celtics of New York. They played, and won championships, in various leagues, but made more money and reputation by touring and taking on local opponents.

It was already evident that matches between top teams could draw large crowds. In 1921, games between the two top New York teams, the Celtics and the Whirlwinds, packed armories with nearly 10,000 spectators. And it was already clear that it was a good idea for an arena to town a team: the Whirlwinds had been organized by Tex Rickard, the boxing promoter who was principal operator of Madison Square Garden—at that time an aging building located in Madison Square, at 25th Street in Manhattan.

But none of this was systematized. Players kept jumping from team to team, league membership changed before a season could be completed, and outstanding professional players began to take jobs as college coaches while continuing to play. Intercollegiate basketball was growing steadily and modestly; on the high school level, it had become the number one sport for participants and spectators; but the pros were stagnating, primarily because there was no way to accommodate large enough crowds to generate consistent profits. More often than not, pro teams were sponsored by some business as a means of advertising that firm's name (as A.A.U. teams often do today).

At this point, other forces started to create large arenas.

In 1925, a brand new Madison Square Garden was opened, "uptown" at 50th Street and Eighth Avenue. It was designed to house, primarily, boxing, the circus and track meets. It could be adapted to almost any purpose, however, and could seat more than 18,000 people. This was the heyday of Jack Dempsey, and prize fighting was a thriving business. Championship fights in almost all weight categories were big events, and a tremendous number of small clubs flourished all over the country, feeding talent and publicity to the big arenas.

But fight programs, even in those days, would fill the Garden only once a week. The circus occupied a profitable six-week period, but that was all. Track meets were a handful. Other special events—six-day bike races, wrestling, horse shows, dog shows, rodeos, conventions—were only occasional. Obviously, a consistent tenant was desirable. A big expensive plant couldn't make money if it was not in use most of the year.

Into this vacuum, a new sport moved. Ice hockey, imported from Canada, was an instant success. The game itself was full of action, colorful, rough, fast, enhanced by the gliding movement over an ice surface. It could be played, at home, a couple of times a week. The big-city sports fan, indoctrinated by baseball to following long-season league-standing excitement, was all too ready to have the winter months filled with a similar interest. From every point of view, major league hockey was just the thing the new arena was looking for.

In other cities, the same process took place. Arenas built basically for boxing quickly found hockey and the other sidelines both profitable and necessary. By 1927, the National Hockey League had established itself as a permanent part of the professional sports scene.

Boxing, hockey, wrestling, six-day bike races, circus, other special events—that was the diet in the big-city arenas as the Golden Twenties ended and the Depression began. It was a rich program, in dollars and in variety, but it still left plenty of gaps. Ned Irish was the man who found the way to fill the gaps.

In New York, which had been crazy about basketball from the very beginning (the Y.M.C.A. clubs had championship tournaments there as early as 1893), college rivalries were at fever pitch. Basketball was indiginous to the city, the game kids could play with a passion in school yards and settlement houses, much as farm boys with more open space just naturally played baseball. With so many city-bred boys becoming first undergraduates and then alumni of New York University, City College of New York, Manhattan College, Fordham, Columbia and St. John's over in Brooklyn, it was not surprising that these schools frequently had outstanding teams which generated tremendous public interest.

None of these schools had a large gym. When climax games came up, they were played in armories, but many gym games were pretty climactic in themselves. Overcrowding was a constant condition, which increased the hysteria the actual games generated. Ticket scandals, with players involved as scalpers, arose repeatedly. In short, the spectators needed as much endurance as the players when teams with top records met—and the newspapermen who had to cover such games were exposed to madhouse conditions.

Irish was one of these newspapermen, a young writer for the *World-Telegram* who also had outside interests as a publicity man. From his experience, he became convinced that college games could be promoted in a large, adequate arena like the Garden. Occasionally, college games had taken place there; the pros, loosely organized as they were, played there from time to time. But no systematic approach had ever been tried.

His key innovation was the double-header. Irish realized that the general sports-attending public, which would have to pay major-league prices in a major-league setting, could not be satisfied with a game that lasted less than an hour and a half. It simply wasn't enough for an evening out. Baseball, hockey, the theater and even downtown movies had conditioned the regular spenders to a two-to-three-hour period of entertainment—and two basketball games would be just right. Besides, a double-header meant four teams instead of two, with four student and alumni bodies to draw from, and that many more individual stars to publicize.

And so, starting with an N.Y.U.-Notre Dame attraction in 1934 (when the Army-Notre Dame football game was New York's biggest annual event), Irish built a fantastically successful program. Soon the Garden season consisted of up to twenty double-headers, and its effects on all basketball were tremendous. Intersectional competition, sporadic up to then, became common: with the resources that Garden attendance was making possible, sizeable guarantees could be offered and the problem of travel expenses disappeared. Furthermore, appearance in the Garden meant instant fame, because New York was the hub of the communications industry, as well as the unchallenged center of glamor.

By 1938, the Metropolitan Basketball Writers Association—of which Irish was such a recent alumnus—sponsored the first championship tournament of national scope college basketball had ever had, an eight-team competition called the National Invitation Tournament. (It made so much money that the embarrassed writers promptly turned over the profits and the conduct of the tournament to college authorities, who have run it ever since). The next year, the National Collegiate Athletic Association, quick to recognize a good thing, launched its own "official" championship tournament, but it was almost a decade before this surpassed the National Invitational Tournament in prestige.

With such prizes to shoot for, basketball-playing colleges all over the country stepped up recruiting, and basketball coaches rapidly approached football coaches in importance on the college scene. And what could be done in New York could be done, if on a somewhat smaller scale, elsewhere. Large arenas in Chicago, Buffalo, Philadelphia and Boston promoted college basketball double-headers as well, and had a fall-out effect on the importance of basketball in their areas.

All this put new emphasis on the importance of pleasing the spectators, and hastened the trend to a faster type of game. The abolition of the center jump, and the consequent development and popularization of the fast break and one-handed shooting on the run, were stimulated by the Garden program. In turn, the new style stimulated wider spectator interest. Sectional rule interpretations and styles were subjected to a homogenization basketball had never yet enjoyed, because along with everything else the Garden established a communication center for coaches, fans, experts and players.

And all these trends combined to make Irish a rich and powerful man.

During World War II, the college basketball programs thrived as never before. Professional sports were decimated by the call to military service, but college basketball had some special privileges. Some of its greatest players were too tall to go into service, and this was the only major sport in which height was such an advantage. Furthermore, many outstanding athletes were still in college, although in service, because so many officer-training programs were in the hands of the colleges. Since basketball could be practiced so easily, and players blended together relatively simply, many such players could manage to play on varsity teams.

To the public, starved for the relaxations of entertainment in wartime, hemmed in by rationing and other restrictions, the Garden programs became a prime attraction. At the same time, wartime attitudes stimulated still further an always present facet of sports interest—the desire to gamble. Particularly in New York, where money was always plentiful for the leisure class, basketball betting appreciably increased both interest and attendance for the college double-headers.

Excessive gambling, excessively open, had obvious—inevitable—dangers. Sure enough, in 1945, with the war not yet over, there was a scandal. Some Brooklyn College players had been "fixing": rigging scores, if not actually losing games, since a bet on the losing team could still pay off if the final margin was "under" the point-handicap set before the game. (If a 10-point favorite won by 8, the bettors on the losing team won their bets). But this was quickly glossed over, and forgotten when a more serious fix scandal threatened the pro football championship game the next year. Everything was going too well, too profitably, for the Garden and for the schools; why worry?

Irish, by now, had become an important business executive. At first, the double-headers were his own promotion, under a sort of concession arrangement: he paid rent to the Garden, expenses and fees to the participating teams, ran the whole program and kept what was left over. When the profits became staggering, the Garden took him in: he became director of basketball, then a vice-president, active in other facets of the vast Garden operation, and without question the most influential single figure in the financial structure of basketball.

So this was the situation in 1946: the war over, larger crowds than ever flocking to all sports events, but particularly basketball; a firmly established "circuit," whereby college teams coming from the west could play in Buffalo, New York, Boston and Philadelphia on one trip; an unprecedented glut of spectacular players on dozens of college teams, as the naturally increasing talent supply was suddenly augmented by all the returned war veterans; and the electronic communications explosion just starting, with sports-on-radio developed to new heights and television just around the corner.

In many minds, in many places, the thought was insistent: if this game, in such a setting, could be so successful for colleges, why not for pros? Why should all these star reputations, nurtured by the new popularity of the college game, lose or waste their money-making potential after graduation? Why must the pros of that day—either in ill repute in the large cities, or playing in such inherently limited leagues as the National in the midwest or the American further east—remain so limited? Why not put on, professionally, college-style and college-atmosphere games, with college-developed players—and why not cash in on the economic advantages of an alliance between an arena and a promoter, the way Irish and the Garden did to their mutual benefit?

These ideas were in the air—but in a few specific minds they were not just a thought: they were an intention.

In Boston, a man named Walter Brown, and in Cleveland, a man named Al Sutphin, were about to join forces to bring into being what would eventually become today's National Basketball Association.

In New York, a man named Max Kase hoped to operate a New York franchise in such a league.

And in New Haven, Connecticut, a remarkable little man named Maurice Podoloff was about to take on the task of making this league a reality, although he didn't know it and had never given basketball a thought.

2 THE BEGINNING

Max Kase was the sports editor of the *Journal-American,* New York's largest afternoon paper, a part of the Hearst chain. He had been a baseball writer for a while, and had worked in Boston. There he had become friendly with Walter Brown, who was the president of the Boston Garden. This building was Boston's equivalent of Madison Square Garden and Brown's interests were, naturally, centered around the hockey Bruins that the Garden owned. But he was a man who involved himself in all the other activities that came through the arena, and was always receptive to new ideas.

In 1944, Kase had been involved in the promotion of a pro basketball game for war relief. It was played at Manhattan Center, a sort of assembly hall-auditorium with portable seats, on 34th Street in New York. It drew so large an overflow crowd that Kase became convinced pro basketball's future could be better than its present. He pressed the point informally, but persuasively, to Brown.

Nothing really happened, however, until the spring of 1946. With the war out of the way, Brown was eager to try a basketball experiment. By now, he and Kase—and many others—had discussed the subject thoroughly. Kase had already begun negotiating with Nat Holman, the most famous of the Original Celtics and then a distinguished and successful coach at City College, New York, to be coach of a New York team in whatever league was formed.

Brown had ready-made connections. Through the National Hockey League, he was already a sort of partner of the arena owners in New York, Chicago, Detroit and Toronto. The N.H.L. had close ties with the American Hockey League, the top minor league, and this included Cleveland, Philadelphia, Pittsburgh, Providence and St. Louis, where the hockey teams were prime tenants of arenas.

The operator of the Cleveland American Hockey League team was Al Sutphin.

By now, the arena operators had an even stronger tie. One of the biggest money-makers of all their attractions was the ice show, a music-and-skating extravaganza made popular by Sonja Henie in the 1930's. The ice show would come into the arena for two weeks at a time, and move on to the next arena. Its tour combined the fiscal advantages of the circus with a tinge of sports interest (since Olympic stars would move on into this profession). And since the ice show could play only in arenas equipped with rinks—not in theaters, ball parks or gymnasiums—the working relationship between the arenas and the ice show was particularly close. The big man in the ice show business was John Harris, of Pittsburgh.

As talk of pro basketball's possibilities swirled around at various meetings of the hockey leagues and the arena owners' associations, Brown and Sutphin became the leaders of a move to take action. They would start a league, and bring as many of their colleagues into it as possible.

Kase and Brown, naturally, were sensitive to each others' interests. Any major league would need a New York entry, as a matter of course. Kase was ready and eager to rent Madison Square Garden for a New York team, and had drawn up tentative plans for a league (with such matters as schedule, salary limits, etc., blocked out). The one difference in their viewpoints was that Kase was more oriented towards established pros, Brown towards the new crop of collegians.

To rent Madison Square Garden, Kase had to talk to Irish.

For himself, Irish could not have been less interested in embarking upon a new, unproven project. This was the spring of 1946. In the basketball season just completed, more than half a million spectators had paid their way into the Garden to watch the game. The attendance table is worth looking at, to realize what Irish had going for him:

21 regular-season double-headers:	380,346
National Invitation Tourney	73,894
N.C.A.A. Tournament	55,302
East-West All-Star Game	18,157
	527,699

The capacity of the Garden for basketball was 18,499. The *average* attendance for these 29 programs was 18,196, or 98 per cent.

Nevertheless, Irish was aware of pro basketball's potential, for the very reasons that had others interested. While he had no desire to look for a new world to conquer, he could not, realistically, allow someone else to move into the Garden and produce an eventual success.

Fortunately, he had something to fall back on. The idea of an arena-owned pro league had been discussed before Kase came up with a specific proposal. The arena owners had made an agreement, Irish explained, that if any of them went into it, all would go. The whole idea, after all, was that the teams *be* arena-owned. So although Irish wouldn't care to start one, if there was going to be such a league, the Garden would be in it, with its own team, just as it had the Rangers in the National Hockey League.

Therefore, when the first organizational meeting was finally held, Ned Irish, representing the Garden, had the New York franchise. Kase received, eventually, a cash settlement for his prior efforts—several thousand dollars—and the best evidence that it was a satisfactory settlement is that Kase continued as a sports editor for twenty years and never had any visible friction with Irish, whatever his private regrets.

Meanwhile, Brown and Sutphin were pushing their idea and rounding up support. First of all, they needed someone to take charge of organizational details: every organization must have a head. Since they intended to be club owners in the new league, neither could also be the central administrator. A president had to be found.

Brown suggested Podoloff.

Maurice Podoloff, about five feet tall, appropriately round, born in Russia, raised since infancy in New Haven, graduate of Yale, lawyer, banker and real estate entrepreneur, was at that time the president of the American Hockey League. He had come to that position because his family (father and brothers) had built the New Haven Arena before the Depression, and owned the New Haven franchise in the A.H.L.

Podoloff knew little about sports, including hockey, and never tried to hide the fact. But a league president doesn't have to play, coach or referee a game: he must handle legal matters, settle disputes and, above all, find ways to let (or make) the separate club owners live together. In a league, the franchise holders are in the unusual situation of being, simultaneously, bitter rivals and partners. Presiding over such a group takes special talent.

In his own way, Podoloff was a wizard at this sort of thing, and although his career turned out to be a stormy one, replete with criticism that sometimes bordered on insult, he proved to be an excellent choice. The league's success would not have been possible without his particular contributions, even though many of his specific actions were to be open to challenge. He was criticized for "minor league thinking," but it was precisely this shrewdness that enabled the young league to survive.

On June 6, 1946, the first meeting was held at the Hotel Commodore in New York, adjacent to Grand Central Station.

The league would be called The Basketball Association of America.

The charter members were:

The Boston Celtics, represented by Brown, who chose the name "Celtics" for its double associations to the most famous professional basketball team of the past, and to Boston's Irish population.

The Chicago Stags, represented by Arthur Morse, a lawyer who had connections with the Norris family which ran the Chicago Stadium and the Chicago Black Hawks hockey team (and which also had a hand in the Detroit Olympia and Madison Square Garden).

The Cleveland Rebels, represented by Sutphin of the Cleveland Arena.

The Detroit Falcons, owned by the Olympia. (The Detroit hockey team that James Norris, father of the clan, acquired in 1933 along with the Olympia, had been called the Falcons; Norris had changed that to Red Wings.)

The New York Knickerbockers, represented by Irish.

The Philadelphia Warriors, represented by Pete Tyrell, who ran the Philadelphia Arena and the Philadelphia Rockets of the A.H.L.

The Pittsburgh Ironmen, represented by John Harris, who along with his arena and general ice show interests was head of the A.H.L. Pittsburgh Hornets.

The Providence Steamrollers, represented by Lou Pieri, who ran the Providence Reds of the A.H.L. and the arena there, a close friend of Walter Brown.

The St. Louis Bombers, represented by Emory D. Jones of the St. Louis Arena and the A.H.L. team based there.

The Toronto Huskies, put forth by the Maple Leaf Gardens (which owned the N.H.L. Maple Leafs).

The Washington Capitols, represented by Mike Uline, who owned the Uline Arena, the biggest building of its type in the nation's capital.

All but Morse were members of the Arena Managers Association of America, the group that had made the "if any, all" agreement that shut out Kase.

Of the eleven, five were Podoloff's associates in the A.H.L. Five others were part of major league hockey operations, with extensive farm-club relationships to the A.H.L. Only Uline was not closely involved with hockey.

What was significant about this line-up was that it had no connection whatever with the existing professional basketball structure (with one partial exception that we'll come to in a moment).

This disassociation had several consequences. For one thing, it enabled the new league to deal with editors and reporters on a new basis. Whatever prejudices had grown up about pro basketball, the B.A.A. people could not automatically be saddled with them. Since they already had well-established contacts with their local newspapers through their other activities, they received a respectful hearing in the burgeoning battle for space in the crowded sports pages. They were free of any stigma previous pro teams may have accumulated, and were given from the start a degree of acceptance that would not have been available to "outsiders."

For another, it forced many of the teams into a policy that reflected the best feature of their idea—college players, with college reputations and the "clean" aura, and a college style of play. If the B.A.A. had been an outgrowth of the existing pros, not only would its psychology have been different, but many college players simply couldn't have held their own against older pros in the competition for jobs. This way, many experienced pros simply were not available: either they found the existing pro leagues profitable and satisfactory, or they weren't approached by a new league quite conscious of the supply of cheaper fresh talent. Thus the less-experienced mass of recent collegians had a chance to develop as a group, and to set the tone of the new league.

A third plus—and perhaps the most important—was that all the new owners had extensive experience in sports promotion and business methods. This had been lacking in all the other pro basketball organizations. The B.A.A. owners took for granted that their players would be full-time employees, like baseball players; that the schedule, and the authority of the league, would be basically tamper-proof; that the side issues of efficient publicity, concessions income and first-class travel were not really side issues at all, but fundamentals.

A fourth effect of the hockey experience was the concept, from the start, of championship play-offs at the end of the regular schedule. Nothing outrages purists more than this elaborate post-season competition, which reduces the whole long regular season to a jockeying for position; but nothing, in practice, is more essential to sports that have necessarily limited incomes (because indoor arenas can't be as large as ball parks) and that must generate some worthwhile prize money to keep player incentives functioning during a long schedule—which must be long to produce enough gross income.

There were negative consequences, too. Accustomed to the hockey pattern that a good fist fight peps up a game and brings back customers, many B.A.A. owners took much too lenient a view of rowdyism in the early days. Unfamiliar, for the most part, with the nature of basketball and with the tricks pro players quickly master, they never gave referees sufficient authority over abusive players and coaches, nor made sufficiently clear the type of game the referee was to call.

But their advantages greatly outweighed their disadvantages. They had the buildings. New players were plentiful. The audience was eager. Expenses, compared to other team sports, were moderate (because squads were small).

Then, one by one, these advantages were chipped away.

3 THE B.A.A.

On November 1, 1946, the Basketball Association of America began play. In Toronto, the New York Knicks defeated the Huskies, 68-66, even though Ed Sadowski, Toronto's player-coach, was high scorer with 18 points.

Both teams were in the Eastern Division, along with Washington, Philadelphia, Boston and Providence. The other five entries comprised the Western Division. Each division's standings were kept separately, but each team played all the other teams in both divisions the same number of times. The schedule called for 60 games.

Ironically, the Knicks were seldom able to use Madison Square Garden as their home court. The building that had started the whole chain of thought leading to the B.A.A. simply had no room for them. The college double-headers now numbered 28, not counting tournaments. These programs not only used up all the desirable dates, but were almost guaranteed sell-outs. Irish wasn't anxious to make room in the Garden's profitable pattern for an unknown quantity. So the Knicks had only six dates in the "Mecca of Basketball." The other 24 home games were played at the 69th Regiment Armory, which the Garden leased and outfitted with new seats. Nothing could symbolize more clearly the comparative importance of college and pro basketball at that time; the poor-relation status of the pros with respect to the flourishing collegians.

The best, and most experienced, pro players were still largely active in the National League, formed in 1937, and the American League. The National had teams in Rochester, Fort Wayne, Syracuse, Indianapolis, Oshkosh, Sheboygan, Anderson (Indiana), Toledo, Youngstown, Moline (Illinois), Detroit—and Chicago, which was most important of all because it had George Mikan, the six-foot ten-inch giant from DePaul University in Chicago. Mikan had been the most overwhelming, and the most publicized of the college stars. Literally a new breed because they combined real athletic ability with their extraordinary size, Mikan and

Bob Kurland of Oklahoma Agricultural and Mining had dominated the college scene in 1944–46. Kurland had chosen to remain an amateur, joining the Phillips 66 Oilers; Mikan had gone pro, but not with as much difference as the terminology implied. Most of the National League teams, like the industrial American Amateur Union teams, had businesses as sponsors.

The Chicago team that Mikan played for was called the American Gears, sponsored by the American Gear Company. The Fort Wayne team was the Zollner Pistons, owned by Fred Zollner's piston-manufacturing company. There were the Anderson Duffey Packers, and so forth.

The American League was an eastern circuit, a combination of earlier circuits named the Eastern and Metropolitan Leagues. Its activity was concentrated on weekends. It had been dominated by the South Philadelphia Hebrew Association team (the Sphas) coached by Eddie Gottlieb, and also had teams in Baltimore, Wilmington, Trenton, Jersey City, Brooklyn and New York. Among them were such famous pro-basketball names as the Brooklyn Jewels, the Visitations and the Celtics, once the "Originals" but then owned by Kate Smith, the singer.

While most of the National League players stayed with it when the B.A.A. was formed, much of the cream of the American League went into the new circuit—including Gottlieb, who took over as coach of the Philadelphia Warriors for Tyrell. Gottlieb soon emerged as the most important single acquisition of the new league—the exception mentioned in the last chapter—the one man who had lifelong professional basketball experience and background, with all the good and bad things that meant.

The fact that Mikan was coming out of college, in the spring of 1946, had been an appreciable stimulant to the formation of the B.A.A. The realization that there would be, eventually, other Mikans coming along, and that this Mikan might play for many years, certainly figured in the calculations of the arena men when they deliberated about their new business. That he did not choose to join them when they did organize was something of a disappointment, but by his mere existence he was helping them even while he played elsewhere. He created interest and excitement in the pro game, because he was playing it, and this helped spread seeds of interest embedded in a layer of respectability.

Nevertheless, it was an inescapable circumstance that few of the big-name college players cast their lot with the B.A.A. Mikan and Kurland had not. Many other stars, because of their returned-G.I. situation, still had college eligibility to play out. If any club owner had hoped for an immediate transfer of college glamor into the new pro league, he was promptly disillusioned.

Therefore a split in policy developed almost immediately, and it was to permeate the league's formative years. To have the best teams, competitively, it was necessary to rely on experienced pro players and, to some extent, on their rugged techniques; to have the shiny new product envisioned for long-term prosperity, it was necessary to cultivate the new college stars. In another sense, the two viewpoints boiled down to rate of growth: how quickly did competitive excellence have to be established, for a quick return at the gate? Or, how long could money be spent (and lost) to build for a sounder future, even if the immediate gate lagged?

Some owners went in one direction, some in the other, and the way they selected their original coaches was revealing.

In New York, Irish hired Neil Cohalan, who had coached Manhattan College and was well-known locally. In Chicago, the Stags landed Harold Olsen, who had just led Ohio State to a Big Ten championship and national prominence—and Chicago, of course, was the heart of Big Ten country. In St. Louis, the Bombers took Ken Loeffler, a scholarly sort whose college-coaching background included Yale. In Detroit, the Falcons came up with Glenn Curtis, whose Indiana State team had just gone to the finals of the small-college national championships.

Thus the three most powerful arenas (New York, Chicago and Detroit, with interlocking ownership through the Norris family) and the large (15,000 seat) St. Louis Arena went wholeheartedly for college flavor.

In Boston, Walter Brown seemed to get the best of both worlds. Honey Russell had been a famous pro player about a decade before, but also had college-coaching exposure.

However, in Philadelphia, Gottlieb was in command. In Cleveland, the coach was Dutch Dehnert, a famous member of the Original Celtics (and credited with the invention of the pivot play). In Pittsburgh, Paul Birch was another former Celtic, who had coached extensively in earlier pro leagues (and who had been a college star as a player at Duquesne). Toronto's Sadowski was an active prominent pro player.

These four, then, were building with hard-core pros.

The Providence coach was Robert Morris, who had been a prominent high school coach in Rhode Island for many years.

And the Washington Capitols, the organization that least fit the pattern of the others, had a twenty-nine-year-old local boy, who had never coached even a college team, fresh out of the Navy and known as pretty successful at the high school level. His name was Arnold (Red) Auerbach, and he talked Uline into giving him the job by persuading him that he could recruit a good team from fellow servicemen who had been playing plenty of free-lance pro basketball on weekends.

The rules of play, on the other hand, were agreed upon along college-style lines. With three exceptions, the college rules were taken over intact: the games were to last 48 minutes instead of 40 (to make it a long-enough show without double-headers); the limit on personal fouls was raised from five to six, in proportion to the increase in time played; and the zone defense, which tended to slow down action, was prohibited.

In the past, pro leagues had tried all sorts of different rules. There were two-handed dribbles, baskets without backboards, and, of course, the game inside a cage, where the ball could not go out of bounds so that action was continuous. Among other things, games played for money were understandably rougher than amateur games—and this roughness, in turn, promoted a sort of reciprocal consideration, a live-and-let-live policy by players who were often opponents one week and teammates the next. If one drove for the basket a little too aggressively, one was dumped a little too roughly—and the boys played nice after that. This sort of thing added to pro basketball's disrepute; but when the games were for blood the opposite became true. Experienced players could use little tugs, nudges, bumps and grabs that quickly took a game out of the referee's hands. Two of the goals implicit in "college style" ball, therefore, were the reproduction of enthusiasm of college players, and the physically cleaner and faster game.

It became pretty evident, right off the bat, that the pro approach was the correct one as far as winning was concerned. Coaches did not play, and did not even, in some cases, choose the players who made up the squads. But Gottlieb and Auerbach certainly had complete control of the personnel question, and they went heavily for men with previous pro experience.

What the coaches did do was reflect the approach of their managements, and in the Western Division, Olsen and Loeffler, for all their college backgrounds, quickly committed themselves to established players. When, in the cases of Boston and Pittsburgh, the management didn't get as good material, it didn't make any difference that the coaches were pro-oriented.

And so, almost as soon as the first season began, the Washington Capitols under the unknown Auerbach ran off and hid from the rest. A seventeen-game winning streak enabled the Caps to spread-eagle the Eastern division before the season was half over. In backcourt, Auerbach had Bob Feerick, his friend from the Navy, and Freddie Scolari, a West Coast friend of Feerick. Up front were Bones McKinney, a North Carolina All-American who was going to sign with Chicago until Auerbach side-tracked him; John Norlander and John Mahnken, an experienced pro. Another key man in backcourt was Irv Torgoff, who had been a leader of Clair Bee's Long Island University teams that started to thrive when the Garden double-headers came into being.

By the time the season was over, Washington had a 49-11 record (which was to remain unsurpassed for twenty years). Feerick and McKinney were first-team all-league selections, Scolari second team and Mahnken honorable mention. And Auerbach, whose talent as a coach was matched by the abrasiveness of his personality to non-intimates, was being down-graded as "a lucky stiff."

Fourteen games behind Washington, but with nothing to apologize for, were Gottlieb's Warriors. He had come up with the individual prize, a six-foot five-inch Kentuckian named Joe Fulks, whose shot-making ability was so unbelievable that people simply refused to believe it until they saw him.

In those days, a basketball player was still considered sensational if he scored 20 points in a game. It was a standard of achievement not unlike, in the sports fan's mind, hitting two home runs in one baseball game. In recent years, fantastic scoring totals had been posted by Mikan and a few others, but it was understandable—if marvellous or ridiculous, according to one's viewpoint—that an over-sized player could produce over-sized statistics by using his height near the basket. But Fulks wasn't all that big, and he wasn't scoring from close to the basket. So when fans read that Fulks *averaged* 23.2 points per game over a 60-game season, and that he had scored 30 or more in 12 different games (going as high as 41), they just couldn't swallow it.

"There must be something funny about that pro game," said countless reading fans, who hadn't seen for themselves. They didn't know what was "funny," but something must be. Perhaps pro defense was being cooperative. The years of suspicion and unrespectability couldn't be sloughed off so easily.

Yet, what Fulks was really doing was pointing the way to the future. His fantastic scoring was the result of fantastic scoring skill, pure and simple. The jump shot, properly executed, cannot be stopped without fouling; a defender can force the jump shooter to take the shot prematurely, or from an undesirable angle, but he can't do anything about the shot itself. Fulks was the pioneer of the shot that was to become pro basketball's primary weapon.

The opposition, and the relatively small crowds that saw Fulks in action, had no trouble appreciating him. He was the only unanimous choice for the all-league team, and as scoring champion he averaged almost seven points per game more than the runner-up (Feerick with 16.8). Not until 1962, when Wilt Chamberlain made all statistics meaningless (in a totally different style of game) did a scoring champion produce a bigger margin of superiority.

Fulks' teammates were Howie Dallmar, a brilliant all-around player from prewar Stanford; Angelo Musi, the backcourt scorer; Art Hillhouse, George Senesky and Jerry Fleischman. While not good enough to keep pace with Washington over the full season, they proved good enough to emerge from the play-offs with the first B.A.A. championship.

According to the play-off pattern settled upon, the first-place teams in each division met each other, the second-place teams played, and the third-place teams met. That was the first round. The division leaders had to play a best-of-seven set, which allowed the others, playing best-of-three, to play an extra round before producing a survivor to play for the championship.

The Western Division, during the regular season, had produced the closest possible race: a tie between Chicago and St. Louis. Chicago won the one-game play-off for first place (in overtime, no less)—and proceeded to knock off Washington, four games to two.

Olson's team had an all-star in Max Zaslofsky, a great outside shooter who had been at St. John's in Brooklyn before the War. It had Chuck Halbert, a prewar college star from West Texas State, at center, and Don Carlson, Tony Jaros, Marv Rottner, Jim Seminoff.

In beating Washington, the Stags reversed one of the first trends of basketball, the home-court advantage. During the regular season, the Caps had won 29 of their 30 home games, a lopsided proportion that was symptomatic of many of the difficulties that would follow. But in the play-offs, the Stags won the first two games played in Washington, by 16-point margins. They won the third at home, taking an insurmountable 3-0 lead, and ran out the series in six games.

Philadelphia, meanwhile, disposed of St. Louis by winning the third and deciding game on the other team's court. The other series, however, followed home court pattern completely: Cleveland won the first, New York the remaining two in the match between third-place finishers.

Now Philadelphia polished off the Knicks in two straight, and moved into the final against Chicago. It turned out to be the Warriors, in no uncertain terms: two decisive victories at Philadelphia, a split of close games in Chicago, and an 83-80 victory at Philadelphia to wrap it up.

And so, on April 22, the first season of the B.A.A. had ended. In the sense that it had been completed at all, and that outstanding players had proved themselves, it could be called a success. But its impact on the public, in its own cities, was still quite secondary, and on the general sports public nil. Financially, there was a great deal of wreckage.

The three trailing teams in the Western Division—Cleveland, Detroit and Pittsburgh—closed up shop. They abandoned the original conception because they didn't have the resources, or the will, to keep spending money. Whatever the salaries had been the first year—few players got more than $6,000—it was obvious that these would rise. The travel, by rail, in a league that stretched from Toronto to Washington and Boston to St. Louis cost an appreciable sum. Pittsburgh had a rich college basketball tradition and was "a good basketball town," but its arena simply didn't generate the kind of year-round income Madison Square Garden could rely on. Cleveland and Detroit, by and large, were not "good basketball towns."

In the East, Toronto and Boston had tied for last. Walter Brown, of course, had no intention of quitting, since he was one of the chief advocates of the league in the first place. But Toronto, with neither a fertile field for basketball in its area (although Naismith was born in Ontario), nor a winning team, pulled out. The Huskies had gone through a harrowing season, changing coaches three times. Sadowski, after only twelve games, had been traded to Cleveland as a player. The team finished the season under Red Rolfe, the former New York Yankee third baseman who was soon to return to baseball as manager of the Detroit Tigers, and then move on to a more serene life as a highly successful Director of Athletics at Dartmouth.

Those four defections left only seven teams, and a serious question of survival. In money, the B.A.A. hadn't done as well as the National League. Free-lance teams, especially the Harlem Globetrotters, were still the real money-makers, and while the sports world as a whole didn't pay too much attention, a world championship pro tournament held annually in Chicago was still a big event within the pro basketball sphere.

As the owners faced retrenchment and reorganization, what may be called political positions started to harden. Irish, who had gone into the enterprise with doubts which now seemed at least partially justified, was firmly committed to a sort of ruthless major-leagueism. He wanted things done with "class," he wanted a college-type game, and he was willing to go on losing money now to make it later—because the Garden had plenty of money. He had no patience with the struggles of less affluent promoters, or the traditional scrambling for a few extra bucks or a slight competitive advantage that characterized the older pros.

Some might call Irish's viewpoint admirable, and perhaps it was in theory. In practice, however, it simply antagonized most of his colleagues, who didn't have comparable resources behind them. Podoloff, as president, sided with the poorer members—out of political instinct, personal inclination and business experience. Podoloff bent his efforts to juggling disasters as best he could—overlooking a debt here, bending a rule there, trying to make decisions that would assist existence rather than perfection.

This way, there arose two camps: the Podoloff camp, characterized by any expedient for survival, and the Irish camp, pressing for big league standards and the devil take the hindmost. The reality of life made it inevitable that Podoloff's camp was always larger.

It was strange how Irish, whose avowed ideas were unassailable logically, became an increasingly isolated minority because of his lack of sympathy for illogical necessities. Irish also felt personal antipathy towards Podoloff, and not only didn't bother to hide it but often flaunted it.

In retrospect, it is easy to see that both attitudes were useful, and that the league eventually succeeded out of their synthesis. Without Irish's insistence that the original grand concepts not be lost sight of, the B.A.A. could easily have gone down the fruitless path of all the other pro basketball leagues. But without Podoloff's manipulations to let the weaker members stay in business, there would not have been any league at all to grow to maturity. But at the time, it often seemed that conflict polarized by Irish and Podoloff might rip the league apart.

The immediate problems, looking to the second season, were:

Finding enough teams to have a schedule.
Cutting back on expenses.
Bringing in a larger number of players whose college reputations would mean something to the fans in each city.

To answer the first, the seven survivors took in the Baltimore Bullets, who had been in the league that Gottlieb had abandoned. To balance the divisions, Baltimore and Washington were put in the "West" (with Chicago and St. Louis), while New York, Philadelphia, Boston and Providence comprised the East.

This arrangement, for the East at least, certainly cut down on travel expense. A cutback to a 48-game schedule also served this purpose. The teams played eight times against every opponent in the same division, and six times against the teams in the other division.

For the third problem, the B.A.A. relied on that great invention of professional sports promotion, the draft. By drafting the rights to graduating college players, the teams could avoid bidding against each other for the more desirable talent. By letting teams draft in reverse order of the previous year's standings, they could strengthen the weakest teams the most, and keep up the competitive balance on which close races depended.

To make maximum use of local interest, however, the B.A.A. added a gimmick called "the territorial draft choice." In the first round, a team could pick a player from its own area regardless of which turn it was entitled to, so that if a college star had made his reputation in Philadelphia, the Warriors would be able to get him and to cash in on his fame whether or not they finished low in the standings.

As an immediate gate-booster to teams trying to build public support from the ground up, the territorial draft was a fine idea. Eventually, it became unnecessary and was abandoned.

Still, the draft had one glaring weakness: it wasn't all-inclusive. There were still rival professional leagues, particularly the National. The A.A.U. teams were in a period of intensive recruitment, with offers of job security and even immediate income that rivalled pro salaries. In many cases, even after a player was drafted by the B.A.A. club, it took considerable persuasiveness and even (horrors!) bonus money to sign him up.

Nevertheless, the B.A.A. did succeed in bringing in a lot of attractive new faces for the 1947–48 season, and consolidation to eight teams had moved some of the first-season's regulars around to create stronger teams.

The situation in New York, so crucial to the league's search for an image and for press attention, was considerably improved.

Irish had hired a new coach—Joe Lapchick, one of the most famous Original Celtics, the first widely-known "giant" because he was six-foot-five (which was gigantic in the early 1920s), and now at the peak of his success as coach of St. John's, one of the regular Garden teams. Recently, Lapchick had come up with a true giant, six-foot-nine Harry Boykoff, the first New York area player of such dimensions. In 1944, St. John's had won the N.I.T. (by beating DePaul with Mikan) and had gone on to play Utah, the N.C.A.A. champion, in a uniquely publicized Red Cross benefit game. Gregarious, competitive, unpretentious, instantly recognizable and always willing to talk, Lapchick was as big a name and as popular a person as basketball had to offer.

One of the Knick players was Bud Palmer, a six-foot-four Princetonian with social-set credentials, who used an intriguing spin-around two-handed jump shot. His presence certainly supplied some of the Ivy League aura Irish wanted—and he could play, too. Another was Stan Stutz, who epitomized the headlong rush of Rhode Island's "race-horse" or "fire-house" fast break, which had taken the basketball world by storm a few years before. Another was Dick Holub, a big center from Long Island University. A new one was Carl Braun, a twenty-year-old Colgate drop-out who possessed one of the finest shooting touches anyone has ever had, before or since. With the season little more than a month old, he had a 47-point game against Providence, a league record.

In mid-season, the Knicks acquired Sid Tannenbaum, a great hero to the New York public while at New York University a couple of years before. He never became a star in the pros, but his presence added disproportionately to establishing Knick identity.

The Chicago Stags picked up two big local names, Andy Phillip and Gene Vance. Before the war, they had been the leaders of the famous Whiz Kids of Illinois, and although they failed to win another Western Conference Title when they returned to school as veterans, they were important. The Stags had also acquired Stan Miasek, who had been the all-league center the previous year, from the defunct Detroit club.

This enabled the Stags to send Halbert, their big center, to Philadelphia, appreciably strengthening the Warriors.

Red Rocha, an outstanding center at Oregon State, joined St. Louis and became a pro of the first rank right away. The new Baltimore team, led by player-coach Buddy Jeannette and other old pros, acquired the tough Paul Hoffman, from Purdue. The Boston Celtics, basing everything on Sadowski, acquired from the collapsed Cleveland franchise, were still getting "tone" from Saul Mariaschin of Harvard and George Munroe of Dartmouth. (They also had, for a few games, a Brooklyn Dodger farmhand named Chuck Conners, whose real future lay in becoming a movie and television star).

Nevertheless, the National League got at least as many prominent graduating collegians as the B.A.A., even though it, too, was going through wholesale reorganization. The Chicago team had folded, and Mikan had moved to Minneapolis, a new franchise, where the coach was John Kundla, of the University of

Minnesota. Some B.A.A. players, like Tony Jaros (who joined Minneapolis) moved over into the National League, and teams like the new Lakers, the old Rochester Royals and Fort Wayne were apparently more powerful than anything in the B.A.A. Boykoff went into the National League, with Sheboygan. Jim Pollard, a Stanford All-American, joined Mikan.

Meanwhile, all pro basketball was still very much overshadowed by the college scene and the forthcoming Olympics. Kentucky had one of the most glamorous college teams of all time, with Ralph Beard and Alex Groza in what amounted to an all-star line-up. There were 29 double-header programs scheduled for the Garden, 23 for the Memorial Auditorium in Buffalo, 15 in Philadelphia's Convention Hall, 15 for the Boston Garden, and 11 for the Chicago Stadium. In 1948, the first postwar Olympics were to be held in London, and basketball would be on the program, and the United States team would be chosen from outstanding college and A.A.U. teams—and the A.A.U. teams were loaded with recent college stars. To the annually increasing climax of N.I.T. and N.C.A.A. tournaments, then, the prospect of an Olympic Tournament was added. There was little reason—and little time—for the basketball fan to shift his attention to the new pros, even though Irish permitted his Knicks to play 11 of their 24 home games in Madison Square Garden.

Competitively, the 1947–48 season was a dazzling success: in the East, the Warriors took first place by only a one-game margin over New York; in the West, the finish almost defied probability, as St. Louis finished first by a one-game margin and the other three teams tied for second. Only Providence, last in the East with a 6-42 record, was outclassed.

And the marvellous balance continued right through the play-offs. To untangle the tie in the Western Division, Chicago defeated Washington, and then Baltimore defeated Chicago, so the Bullets were given second place, the Stags third, and the Caps found themselves fourth and eliminated from the play-offs.

Now the Bullets had to play New York, in the play-offs proper, and the Stags had to play Boston. Both Western teams won two out of three, and had to play each other again to reach the final. This time, Baltimore took two straight.

Meanwhile, the Warriors and St. Louis Bombers battled

through a seven-game series, which Philadelphia won. Thus the Warriors, defending champions, met Baltimore, the only new team, for the title—and Baltimore took it, in six games.

One couldn't ask for a better season—if one were a fan. If one were an owner, the picture was quite different. The 48-game schedule proved to be disastrous: it cut down on income far more than it did on expenses. And the competition for talent was serious: college players were playing off one league against the other in negotiation, and the pros themselves had somewhere to go if they wanted to move.

Another such season, Podoloff felt, might be the last.

Irish, as usual, did not quite agree. His Knicks had made progress, and a longer schedule meant finding more dates on a crowded calendar. "Be patient and build," Irish advocated. "I've got to do something, and quick," Podoloff felt.

And Podoloff knew what that "something" must be. One way or another, the cream of the National League must be brought into the B.A.A.

He found a way.

4 THE MERGER

Originally, Podoloff's office had been up on Madison Avenue, where the American Hockey League office was, but soon the central office of the N.B.A. was moved into the Empire State Building, on the 80th floor. This gave the league the highest office, and the shortest commissioner, in sports—an obvious sort of joke that was repeated frequently and that fairly represented the attitude of most of the sports world towards the two-year-old circuit. The older columnists knew, with the certainty of fossilized prejudices, that pro basketball "wouldn't work" and that basketball was a game either for "sissies" or "goons." The younger writers, exposed at high intensity to the exciting college scene, were predisposed in favor of the new venture—but repeatedly appalled at the bush-league aspects that were too glaring to overlook: the squabbling in public among owners, the abuse heaped upon referees by owners and coaches as well as players, the last-minute schedule changes, and the rapid turnover of franchises. Most of all, in New York, where so much opinion was formed, Irish's unconcealed lack of respect for Podoloff did little to enhance the league's dignity—and Podoloff's penchant for double talk in countless syllables didn't help either. The very technique of equivocation and filibustering, legitimately helpful in private when warring owners had to be reconciled for the sake of league business, was a damaging handicap when applied to press and public.

To handle the league's publicity, Podoloff had hired Walter Kennedy, who had come out of Notre Dame in the mid-1930s and had done social work, coaching and publishing. Kennedy was knowledgeable and energetic, but kept pretty much in the background in a setup that had the league president himself and various owners so much in the limelight.

Neither Kennedy nor Podoloff had the slightest suspicion, at the time, that Kennedy would eventually succeed Podoloff.

First-hand knowledge of Podoloff's maneuvers, however, was

giving Kennedy invaluable background, because Podoloff was really maneuvering.

The 1947–48 season had been an artistic success but a financial flop for the B.A.A. For the National League, operating on a smaller scale, it had been more successful financially, but a little disturbing artistically, since the Minneapolis team built around Mikan and Pollard threatened to become too strong for healthy competition. But the National League people had more reason for optimism than the B.A.A. people, despite—or perhaps because of—their less grandiose ideas.

During the summer of 1948, as both leagues prepared for necessary expansion, it was more and more obvious that a real battle for talent was around the corner. The returned G.I.s, now finishing interrupted college careers, were about to graduate in large numbers with bigger reputations than ever, older than most graduates, more prepared to be pros. The college tournaments had become so large, and so well-publicized (and attended), that nationally-known stars were being produced in unprecedented numbers—which made it all the more important for any particular team, or league, to get the half-dozen top names.

The underlying conditions for a merger were plain, if not quite irresistable: the National League had the players, the B.A.A. had the cities and the arenas.

But the real question was, merger on what terms, and into what?

Podoloff probed, in informal conversations, all summer. The Minneapolis Lakers, under Max Winter, were not particularly interested, since they were on the verge of establishing a dynasty in their own league. The second best team, year in and year out, was Rochester, loaded with hard-nosed pros and New York area products—but what would the B.A.A. want with a city the size of Rochester?

Yet, there had to be an entering wedge somewhere—and Podoloff found it in two men: Paul Walk of Indianapolis and Carl Bennett of Fort Wayne.

Walk was the general manager of the Indianapolis Kautskys, owned by a florist. Bennett ran the Fort Wayne team for Fred Zollner, the piston man. Podoloff convinced both, one way or another, that their future lay in the more prestigious big arenas, playing as much on the social-climbing (in terms of sports) inclinations of their owners as on logic. But there was logic, too: if they were in basketball for the publicity, obviously they'd get more of it in league with the biggest cities.

Indianapolis and Fort Wayne decided to jump to the B.A.A.

"Betrayal!" screamed the other National League clubs—with plenty of justification. But screaming was a reaction, not a policy. If the National League was going to break ranks, the Lakers would go along with the times. Winter and Ben Berger, the principal owner, decided to accept the B.A.A. invitation too.

But that left Rochester, in particular, out in the cold. Lester and Jack Harrison, who operated the Royals (with Lester as coach), simply weren't going to take that. They threatened, pleaded and argued—and the B.A.A. decided to take them too, without allowing questions of damage go too far.

It was a victory of staggering proportions. All of a sudden, almost on the eve of the 1948–49 season, the very players whose absence had become a reason to downgrade the B.A.A., were in it: Mikan, Pollard, Bob Davies and Arnie Risen of Rochester, a half-dozen lesser but visible lights.

In effect, the National League was dead, then and there, although it went on with eight teams: Syracuse, Anderson (Indiana), Hammond (Indiana) and Denver in one division, Oshkosh, Sheboygan, Tri-Cities (Moline and Rock Island, Illinois, and Davenport, Iowa) and Waterloo (Iowa) in the other. It still had Boykoff, and Al Cervi (one of the Rochester greats who had become playing-coach at Syracuse), Frank Brian and seven-foot Don Otten, out of Bowling Green—but the names of the cities were enough to brand it as inescapably minor league.

To the B.A.A., the bonanzas were Mikan and the near elimination of competition for next year's college stars. Wherever Mikan went, as a visiting player, he filled the house. In a league in which home teams kept all the receipts, that made him as popular as (and synonymous with) money.

To Irish, specifically, Mikan and the highly-regarded Rochester team meant something new to justify more Garden dates for his Knicks. He complained of the minor-league connotations of the names on the shirts—Minneapolis, Rochester, Fort Wayne, for heaven's sakes!—but he accepted the reality. In fact, a larger league than the eight-team circuit of 1947–48 seemed essential to one of his main precepts: in Madison Square Garden, he felt, the public had been conditioned to double-headers by the colleges, and double-headers it must have from the pros.

By double-header, of course, Irish meant two games involving four teams, and this created a scheduling nightmare. To have any double-headers at all, anywhere, meant abandoning any idea of a completely balanced home-and-away schedule. If all teams played the same number of double-headers, however, it would be possible to have an equal number of games at home and away and a set number of "neutral" games. But not all teams wanted double-headers, which were neither necessary nor desireable in smaller arenas which could be filled with one game, and not all wanted the same number. In order to provide a "first" game for a Garden double-header (or one in Boston or Philadelphia or Chicago), some other team would have to transfer one of its home games.

And this, in turn, meant that more games had to be scheduled in the first place, to provide extras for this "neutral pool."

This problem did not make its full impact immediately, but started to grow when the National League teams came in.

The twelve-team B.A.A. that played the 1948–49 season had a 60-game schedule, a return to the original number. Washington and Baltimore were now in the East, where they belonged, and the four newcomers were in the Western Division with Chicago and St. Louis. Washington, still coached by Auerbach and with substantially the same veteran club, won the Eastern race handily, by a six-game margin over New York with Baltimore, Philadelphia, Boston and Providence trailing in that order.

But in the West there was a surprise: even though Minneapolis and Rochester dominated the league, as the better-informed experts had expected, it was Rochester that finished first, by a one-game margin—despite the fact that the Lakers beat the Royals four times in six meetings, and the fact that the Lakers were 26-3 at home to Rochester's 23-6. Brains had beaten brawn.

The play-offs, however, were another story, and Minneapolis emerged as league champion. The play-off system had been changed. Now the first and fourth teams in each division played each other, and the second played the third. The winners met in semi-final series, and so a team from the East and a team from the West could meet only in the final. The Lakers started off by whipping Chicago two straight, did the same to Rochester in the next round, and overpowered Washington in the final, four games to two.

The year before, Chicago's Zaslofsky had beaten out Fulks for the scoring championship, but now Mikan took over. Even though Fulks raised his own average to 26 points a game, Mikan posted 28.3. (Zaslofsky was third with 20.6). Then in 10 play-off games, big George, elbows swinging and eyeglasses glittering, poured in 303 points.

Meanwhile, the emasculated National League went through the motions. Anderson won in the East, Oshkosh (in a close race) in the West, and both went through to the play-off finals, where Anderson won the title by taking three straight.

Barely noticed at the time, and certainly not fully grasped, was an incident whose full importance could not really have been foreseen. Out of N.Y.U., in the spring of 1948, came a twenty-year-old center named Adolph Schayes, about six-feet-seven-inches tall and on the skinny side. He had been a varsity player as a sixteen-year-old freshman, but was never as highly regarded as his teammates Tannenbaum and Ray Lumpp. Familiar to all the Garden fans, Schayes seemed a natural for the Knicks, but he certainly wasn't considered a sure-shot star.

The B.A.A. had instituted, from the beginning, a salary limit for first-year players. Schayes (and his father) wanted a little more. Syracuse, in the National League, offered it. The difference was about $1,000. Irish always insisted afterwards that he simply could not afford to break the salary rule, even though others might have done so, because the anti-New York feeling was already strong within league councils. More to the point, however, was the judgment that Schayes simply wasn't worth the trouble.

In any case, Dolph went to play under Cervi, under the toughest of old-pro conditions in the shrunken National League. He matured rapidly and by the end of the season was an acknowledged star. He went on to become one of the superstars of all pro basketball.

The importance of this lay in the Knick failure to get him. In the years immediately ahead, a Schayes added to the other Knick talent would have enabled the team to dominate the league. Such domination, on the floor, would have made Irish supremely powerful, and the whole direction of the 1950s would have been different. No one can say whether it would have been for better or worse in the long run, but it would have changed drastically the history that was to come.

As things stood, however, Irish was a still powerful but increasingly isolated voice. The four new teams had shifted the proportions of block voting—a shift that Podoloff could not avoid welcoming, since it strengthened his own position. There were now twelve teams and only half of them really stemmed from the original arena-owned, college-style concept. The immigrants from the National League, and Baltimore, had orthodox pro histories and viewpoints, and Washington had been a special case from the beginning. The problems and goals, as well as the ideas of how to operate, were quite different for owners in Minneapolis and Fort Wayne than for those in New York and Boston. The conflicts that arose in league meetings now, therefore, were no mere personality clashes—although Irish's characteristic aloof, imperious and humorless manner added to his difficulties; there were, now, authentic conflicts of interest.

Meanwhile, a peculiar facet of a much larger problem touched the basketball league: the color line.

So far—in the spring of 1949—there were no Negro players in the B.A.A. Traditionally, in pro basketball, all-Negro teams had competed freely against all-white teams, and the Negro teams often won championships; but integration within a team was rare. By this time, however, Jackie Robinson was playing his third season with the Brooklyn Dodgers, and baseball's stubbornly-held color line had been broken. On the college level, in all sports including basketball, it was being shattered more thoroughly every day. The B.A.A. owners were no more, and no less, enlightened on this question than other promoters of the time: they shared the same context of prejudice that pervaded American society, but as promoters they thought even more specifically and less idealistically. Whatever unconscious motivations may have been at work, on the surface they simply feared change. Would their predominately white audiences "accept" Negro stars, and "identify" with them? Today these seem to be naive, simplistic or insincere questions, but they generated real doubts at the time. Whatever else the sports promoters were, they were not social-engineering heroes, eager to take what they saw as a risk in their already shaky enterprise. In this, as in most things, they acted upon expediency as they understood it.

So the B.A.A. drifted on the color question, while outstanding Negro players went on to Olympic competition and joined A.A.U. teams, or free-lanced as pros.

But there was one special circumstance that made the pro basketball situation different from baseball's or football's. The most successful, in money, pro basketball team ever assembled was an all-Negro institution, Abe Saperstein's Harlem Globetrotters.

On sheer playing ability, the Trotters had been good enough to win world pro titles in the free-lance competitive pattern that preceded the B.A.A. Even now, passing into the 1950s, they were strong enough to battle the best league teams on even terms (as they were soon to prove). But they had become world famous, and had made millions of dollars for Saperstein, by clowning rather than by winning. They had developed comedy routines, incorporated into their games with the co-operation of their own "opposing" team (or without the cooperation of less skillful local teams). Even though they no longer concentrated on straight basketball—or maybe because of this—they were, without comparison, the biggest basketball attraction anywhere.

This meant that they could, and did, fill the biggest arenas, and that they were highly desirable tenants.

This meant, in turn, that the Globetrotters developed close, friendly relations with the arena managers who had launched the B.A.A.

This meant that the Globies were available, a couple of times a year, to stir basketball interest in any town they visited, to make a good pay day for the arena (even after the Globies got their cut), and to help bring in crowds to see a B.A.A. game by playing their own game as a preliminary. A spring tour against college seniors became a highly publicized annual series.

And this meant, of course, that the B.A.A. owners were not likely to raid the Globetrotters for experienced talent, even if they could afford to, which was doubtful.

And the Globetrotter management was not, understandably, bursting with impatience to see its stars offered a profitable alternative.

Finally, emphasizing how close these relationships were, there was the circumstance that the New York office of the Globetrotters (who were based in Chicago) was sublet from the B.A.A and located in the suite of rooms on the 80th floor of the Empire State Building.

Actually, the color bars were about to fall. By the fall of 1949, it was already clear that Negro players would be taken into the league for the next season. (The first one signed turned out to be Chuck Cooper, of Duquesne, by the Boston Celtics, but he didn't actually play any sooner than Nat [Sweetwater] Clifton did for the Knicks, who set a precedent by purchasing his contract from the Globetrotters.) In a short time, Negro stars were to become more numerous than in any other major league sport, but the beginnings were hesitant and humiliating.

The slowness of the B.A.A. in accepting Negroes was underlined by what happened in the summer of 1949. The inevitable formal merger with the remnants of the National League took place, creating a seventeen-team league, comprising about 200 players and a host of teams needing help—and even in this expansion, no place was found for a single Negro.

In those days—before the Supreme Court's school desegregation decision, before civil rights militancy was forced upon the attention of all—this aspect of B.A.A. policy received little notice. And, objectively speaking, the league had much bigger immediate difficulties on its hands.

By taking in the National League survivors (in August, 1949), the B.A.A. not only formally eliminated competition, but conclusively altered its own nature. It finished the process, at the top, of changing into an old-fashioned pro league with only vestiges of the arena-owned blueprint. Paradoxically, at the bottom, it was building a body of college stars and public acceptance that would, eventually, evolve back towards the founders' concepts. But for the time being, the forces of traditional professionalism had proved dominant.

The details of the merger were of staggering complexity, a conglomeration whose instability was obvious to the most casual fan as well as to those involved. This complexity generated new jokes, new disrespect and additional apathy among potential followers, especially since the rise of college competition was still accelerating. The one great advantage the pros had, for the average fan, was concise competition and familiar player identity. The college scene, for all its glamor, was too diffuse. But if the pros were to be diffuse too, the colleges had more fun to offer.

To begin with, the league adopted a new name: the National Basketball Association.

Then it gathered itself into three divisions. The real reason for this unwieldy setup was the insistence of the vintage B.A.A. members—like Irish—that there be the least disruption of the patterns the enlarged B.A.A. had developed in 1948–49.

Thus, the previous year's Eastern and Western Divisions were kept substantially intact, although the Western was now called the "Central." A new "western" division comprised most of the remaining National Leaguers.

But that wasn't all. Other franchise changes had taken place.

Providence finally gave up, and its owner, Lou Pieri, became a partner of Brown's in the Boston Celtics, who had also gone through three years of heavy losses. In the last two seasons, the Steamrollers had finished a deep last, winning only six games one year and twelve games the next. Their demise reduced the Eastern Division to five—New York, Boston, Washington, Baltimore and Philadelphia.

The Indianapolis Jets also went out of business, although another Indianapolis entry was in the wings. This reduced the old Western Division to five.

Four National League teams were being brought in: Syracuse, Anderson, Tri-Cities and Sheboygan.

Two other teams, Denver and Waterloo, had started the 1948–49 season in the National League but had not finished it. They were also admitted to the enlarged circuit.

The seventeenth team was unusual and important: it was the Kentucky team graduating en masse, going into business for itself as the Indianapolis Olympians.

The Olympians and five of the six National League newcomers comprised the Western Division of the National Basketball Association. Syracuse was moved into the Eastern Division, filling the gap left by Providence. But, for scheduling purposes, Syracuse was to play the pattern set for the Western Division—a triumph of illogic that typified much of the lack of realism that permeated the whole merger.

In short, what the B.A.A. had done was to invite the dying remnants of the National League to join in their own financial burial. It would have been more forthright (but perhaps sticky legally, on anti-trust grounds) to refuse to admit them. On the other hand, it is no one's right or duty to refuse to adult, competent business men a chance to lose money if they want to; that was the view of the B.A.A. That the end could only be further shaking down to stronger franchises, no one really doubted.

However, the merger did represent a historic accomplishment. For the first time, all players (or at least, all teams) with major-league pretentions were brought together under one organizational roof—except for Negroes, of course. Structurally, the consolidation that constituted an essential to growth had been effected, and if the character of the "only major league in basketball" was not quite what its formulators had foreseen, it did—at least and at last—exist. Its fourth season, and its first under its new name, was sure to be eventful.

5 THE SHAKEOUT

To keep up with what happened during the 1949–50 season, a basketball fan needed eyes in the back of his head, unlimited leisure and subscriptions to newspapers from more than a dozen cities. Few were that interested.

Those who cared, and settled for the limited view afforded from any particular city, could notice some distinct changes: hysteria was on the increase; home courts were becoming impregnable; more outstanding players were on hand than ever before; and the rough old-pro style was becoming more prevalent.

The schedule itself was a mishmash that violated all big-league traditions. The teams in the Eastern Division were supposed to play each other six times, the Central Division teams six times and the Western Division teams twice (to save on travel expenses, and so that the big cities wouldn't have to give up dates with the better-known old B.A.A. teams for the sake of these newcomers). The Central Division followed the same pattern: six inside the division, six with the East and two with the West. The Western teams were to play each other seven times, and everyone else only twice.

Right off the bat, that made a ridiculous imbalance. Here, in one league, were Eastern and Central teams scheduled to play 68 games, and Western Division teams scheduled for 62.

But the real joker was Syracuse. Its record would count in the Eastern Division standings—but its schedule would be that of the tacked-on Western group. So Syracuse would play only 10 games against the other teams in its own division, while all the others played 26.

Finally, just to keep things from coming out too even, Syracuse played two extra games with Indianapoils, and Tri-Cities played two extra games with Anderson, for no other reason than a little extra gate.

So here was a league where ten teams played a 68-game schedule, four played 64 and three played 62. And after all that, twelve of the teams would begin play-offs.

Such a schedule satisfied nobody, and results conspired to emphasize its ludicrous aspects.

Syracuse, led by Cervi and Schayes, ran off with the Eastern title. In reality, the Nationals (taking their nickname from their old affiliation) simply had an outstanding team, as they proved again and again as time went on. They didn't get credit for it, however, because of the crazy schedule. "They had an easy time with the Western teams," disgruntled New York and Philadelphia fans could claim, "and then they could be rested and 'up' for games with the stronger teams in the other division." The second part of the rationalization was necessary, because the Nats won nine of their ten Eastern games, splitting with Washington and sweeping everyone else. They also won seven out of ten from the toughest division, the Central, so there was nothing flukey about their success. But it *seemed* flukey to those who merely read the standings in the papers and saw the essential unfairness of unequal schedules. Nevertheless, Syracuse finished with a 51-13 record, thirteen games ahead of the second-place Knicks, and swept through the Eastern playoffs by knocking off Philadelphia in two straight and the Knicks in two out of three.

In the Central Division, the powerful Minnesota and Rochester teams finished in a flat tie, at 51-17, and had to play off for first place before they could start the play-offs. The game was played at Rochester on March 21 and the Lakers came from behind to win it, 78-76, as Mikan poured in 35 points. There was also a tie for third, 11 games behind the leaders, and in that play-off Fort Wayne defeated Chicago at Fort Wayne. Then the Pistons knocked out the disappointed Rochester team in the "regular play-offs" in two straight, leaving the Lakers a clear path. The Lakers polished off Chicago, Fort Wayne and Anderson (the Western Division survivor) without losing a game, to reach the championship series against Syracuse. There the Nats put up more resistance, but the Lakers took the series, four games to two, and were established as a "dynasty" with two straight titles.

Meanwhile, in the semi-ignored Western Division, first place went to the new glamor team, the Indianapolis Olympians. These were built around Alex Groza, the six-foot-seven center who proved himself second only to Mikan in scoring punch and effectiveness; Ralph Beard, a "little" man of incomparable ability; and Cliff Barker, Wah Wah Jones and Joe Holland, their Kentucky teammates. President of their club was J. R. "Babe" Kimbrough, a Lexington (Kentucky) sports editor who "graduated" with this great team. Barker was the "coach"—a coach and a rookie at the same time. Groza, Beard and Barker were listed as vice-presidents, Jones as Secretary and Holland as Treasurer. It was, without question, the best basketball-playing front office ever put together—and it was pretty tough by any standard. The Olympians won 39, lost 25, and finished two games ahead of Anderson, the previous year's National League champion.

The play-offs were another story, however. The Olympians had to go all three games to get past Sheboygan, while Anderson had a similar struggle with Tri-Cities, and Anderson then eliminated Indianapolis in another three-game set, taking the last one by two points, 67-65, at Indianapolis.

It was enough basketball—593 games decided, 94,952 points scored, 32,205 personal fouls committed—to make the most resolute fan bleary-eyed.

And yet, more than ever, it was overshadowed by a college scene of peak interest.

City College of New York, coached by Holman and loaded with spectacular sophomores, captured the imagination of the country by winning both the N.I.T. and N.C.A.A. tournaments at Madison Square Garden. In both finals, C.C.N.Y. defeated a favored Bradley team, and the feat—unprecedented then and forever unmatchable since—was seen as the ultimate triumph of the underdog. City was not only a municipal college, with only "local boys" to draw from, but traditionally over-matched in size. Here, just when the giants were becoming commonplace, a team associated with slickness and speed and skill swept to the top (even though, realistically, this Beaver team had a fair amount of size—and not by accident).

That, however, was only the climax, the capstone of the college season. For the fourth straight year, the Garden college programs (including tournaments) had pulled in more than 600,000 people. The N.C.A.A. had just announced that henceforth its championship tournament would be a "regional" affair, including sixteen teams, ten of whom would be qualifying automatically as conference champions. All over the country, new large field houses were going up at basketball-oriented campuses. Christmas-time tournaments of intersectional scope were springing up—the Dixie Classic at Raleigh, North Carolina, the Sugar Bowl tourney at New Orleans.

Significantly, almost all the millions of dollars being bet nightly on basketball games were concerned with the colleges. The pros were still, to confirmed bettors, suspect at worst and an unknown quantity at best. The college scene was intensively scouted, reported, analyzed and stable. And while serious gamblers were a minority of the audience, they reflected much more widely-held attitudes.

In this atmosphere, it was hard to sell a Sheboygan-Tri-Cities game as "big league"—or even a New York-Sheboygan game.

Long before the 1949–50 season was complete, therefore, it was evident that the death rate among franchises would be appalling. Sure enough, the summer brought the demise of six clubs and serious changes in a couple of others.

Sheboygan, Waterloo and Anderson were simply too small, in population and resources, to even dream of keeping up with the big cities. They folded. Denver was simply too far away at a time when air travel was not yet universal, nor so time-saving. It folded.

And, surprisingly, so did Chicago and St. Louis, two of the charter B.A.A. clubs. In Chicago, the Stadium itself had never actually taken command of the team, letting friends and associates run it (Arthur Morse and Judge John Sbarbaro) without really integrating basketball into the building's operation. In St. Louis, business just wasn't that good.

And, just as surprisingly in the other direction, Tri-Cities survived, along with Syracuse and Indianapolis. Syracuse had its championship team, a long-established natural rivalry with Rochester, and a growing rivalry with the Knicks to keep it healthy. Indianapolis had its Olympians, a sure-fire drawing card anywhere—as indicated by the fact that Indianapolis was the only Western Division team Irish had permitted to come to New York in 1949–50. The other five "home" games against those clubs were farmed out to neutral sites. Incidentally, it was this sort of hard-headed and hard-hearted business dealing that characterized Irish in this highly arrogant period of his life. There was no question of sharing gate receipts—home teams kept all—but certainly the last group of National League teams absorbed would have liked, and perhaps benefited from, a touch of the New York exposure. In dollars and cents, Irish may have been absolutely right, but his attitude didn't win him any allies among the owners who were struggling to stay solvent.

Going into the 1950–51 season, therefore, the N.B.A. was back to eleven teams, a wieldy number. New York, Boston, Syracuse, Philadelphia, Baltimore and Washington formed a compact Eastern division, with few travel and schedule problems. Minneapolis, Rochester, Fort Wayne, Indianapolis and Tri-Cities composed the Western Division, with more travel difficulties, smaller incomes, but excellent player strength and competitive balance.

The differences in playing facilities now emerged as a major question. The last two years had been devoted to merger and realignment, an obsessive struggle for survival. Now, at last, a viable major league seemed likely—but with a very distinct split in personality.

New York, Boston and Philadelphia, the only remaining representatives of the original hopes and concepts of the B.A.A., had large seating capacities, huge population areas to draw from, and a definite need for at least some double-headers.

Elsewhere it was another story. The Baltimore Coliseum, an old building, seated 4,000. The Fort Wayne Pistons played in North Side High School, with 3,800 seats. Rochester's Edgerton Park Sports Arena held 5,000. Syracuse played in the State Fair Coliseum, well out of town, where 7,500 could be accomodated. Washington's Uline Arena listed its capacity as 8,000, and the Lakers in Minneapolis claimed 10,000 at the Auditorium, although they had to use other local courts too. Tri-Cities played in the Wharton Fieldhouse, in Moline, where 6,000 could be handled.

Only Indianapolis, using the Butler Field House with 17,000 seats, could match New York and Boston in capacity, but this was not a commercial arena with the attendant advantages.

These others, then, had no need of double-headers. Nor could they hope to cash in on big attractions. Their only chance to make money was to play many games—a longer schedule, even if that involved diluting the quality and the excitement of any one particular game. Irish, whose interest it was to keep travel (and player fatigue) to a minimum while aiming at crowds of 18,000 for a hot event, was for a shorter schedule.

To no one's surprise, Irish lost again. The new schedule was set at 68 games, matching the maximum of the previous year.

Competitively, the seventeen-team league had provided some blessings, now being inherited by the eleven-team league. The two big benefits were: firm establishment of stars generally accepted by the whole sports public, and—after the winnowing down—a tremendous solidification of playing personnel for the teams that stayed in business. By now, almost all college hot-shots were coming into the pro league—and there was only one real league to go to. And the veteran pros, as some teams folded, became concentrated on the remainder, since only the best players were retained.

Mikan had finished first in scoring again, in 1949–50, with a 27.4 average, a trifle below the previous year's figure. But Groza, as a rookie, was not far behind with 23.4—a level reached before only by Mikan and Fulks. Going down the list, one came to, in order, Frankie Brian, Anderson's back court whiz whose name meant so much in the Midwest; Zaslofsky, completing his fourth year for Chicago; Ed Macauley, a skinny six-foot-eight rookie center for St. Louis, who had won All-America ranking while at St. Louis University; Schayes, Braun, Ken Sailors, Pollard; a bright rookie from West Virginia playing for Fort Wayne, Freddie Schaus; Fulks, Beard and Bob Davies of Rochester. In terms of identity, this was considerable progress. All the names meant something to basketball fans everywhere.

Mikan, Pollard, Groza, Davies and Zaslofsky were named to the All-League team—and no one could deny that those five, playing together, would overwhelm any basketball team the game had ever seen.

Coaching personalities were taking shape, too.

Lapchick, after three years with the Knicks, was still the best-known and most illustrious figure in the league, a magnet for endless stories about the old Celtics and a tireless advocate of hustle and college spirit from his players. His team had acquired Vince Boryla, whose background included Notre Dame, Georgia and the Denver A.A.U. team—a fierce competitor and fiercer negotiator, who was one of the first to wrangle a sizeable bonus out of the ownership for turning pro. Dick McGuire, who had played for Lapchick at St. John's, had come into the league now and led it in assists as a rookie. Harry Gallatin, a strong six-foot-six with the knack of rebounding against bigger men, had joined the Knicks in 1948–49, and had never missed a game—and wouldn't for ten years. Ernie Vandeweghe, who had made the East-West College All-Star game as a Colgate freshman in 1946 and had made a repeat performance as a senior in 1949, was now a medical student at Columbia and a part-time Knick. Ray Lumpp, the N.Y.U. hero who had led the old Indianapolis team in scoring as a rookie in 1948–49, was now back in New York. Connie Simmons, for whom the Knicks had traded Tannenbaum to Baltimore, was a slick offensive center. With this group, Lapchick substituted freely, kept everybody running, and played the "college-style" basketball the founders had envisioned.

Auerbach, after his success at Washington, had decided to ask for a three-year contract—and found himself out of work until he could take over the Tri-City Blackhawks with the season already on—while Bob Feerick, his Washington star, took over the Caps and finished under .500 with them.

But at the end of the 1949–50 season, Auerbach was hired by Brown to succeed Doggy Julian, who had gotten no further with the Celtics in the last two years than Honey Russell had in the first two. Auerbach now had to build from scratch.

Buddy Jeannette, still playing, was still coaching Baltimore. Gottlieb, increasingly active in the executive councils of the league, was known everywhere as he continued to coach Philadelphia. And Al Cervi at Syracuse was too colorful, as player and as coach, to escape full recognition for long. These three were the tough-minded "old pros," like Auerbach in a way, but without his psychological tricks and refinements.

Kundla, tall and comparatively quiet in manner, was always overshadowed by Mikan's presence—as everyone was—but as his Lakers kept winning his identity began establishing itself: a sort of sane gentlemanliness. Rochester's Les Harrison was, of course, owner as well as coach, at the opposite end of the scale of excitability from Kundla, and the league's master of the malapropism, a lifelong pro operator.

Going into 1950–51, Murray Mendenhall, of local high school coaching fame, had the Fort Wayne Pistons; Bones McKinney had succeeded Feerick at Washington; and Dave McMillan was the man on the spot in Tri-Cities. Barker was still in charge, nominally, of his teammates at Indianapolis.

All these coaches, during the summer of 1950, were deeply involved alongside their owners in settling the wholesale redistribution of experienced talent from the defunct clubs.

There were riches to be had.

In the college draft, in April, Paul Arizin, Bob Cousy, Bob Lavoy, Don Rehfeldt, Dick Schnittker, Bill Sharman, Charlie Share, Don Lofgran, Kevin O'Shea, Larry Foust, and Chuck Cooper were high-round choices, and these were names that carried immense weight with college-oriented fans.

A few months later, when it was clear which teams would not operate again, the following veterans had gone up for grabs: Zaslofsky, Phillip, Odie Spears and Leo Barnhorst from Chicago; Brian from Anderson; Macauley, Rocha and Johnny Logan from St. Louis; Bob Brannum and Noble Jorgensen from Sheboygan; and Boykoff and Dick Mehen from Waterloo.

Out of this shuffle came alignments that were to determine the shape of the league for the next fifteen years.

To begin with, Boston could have taken Cousy as a territorial choice in the draft—but preferred, in one of Auerbach's first decisions, to select the six-foot-eleven Share instead. From a technical basketball standpoint, Auerbach's choice was eminently sound, as the future would prove over and over; from a public relations point of view, it was a stunner, especially in so volatile a journalistic environment as Boston. Cousy, an All-American from Holy Cross, was indiscriminately admired throughout New England.

But others passed up Cousy too. Philadelphia had Arizin, the national scoring champion, from its own backyard, Villanova. Baltimore took Rehfeldt. Later, Schnittker was taken by Washington, Foust by Chicago before it dropped out, O'Shea by Minneapolis, Lavoy by Indianapolis, Lofgran by Syracuse.

Who did take Cousy? A man who had just hired, and fired, Auerbach: Ben Kerner, director of the obscure Tri-Cities franchise that had survived, so surprisingly, the great shakedown. The selection of Cousy, and its aftermath, was the first action that brought Kerner to the attention of fans all around the league. It put on the stage a character who would henceforth loom larger and larger in N.B.A. affairs.

Kerner was from Buffalo. He had been associated with Leo Ferris in program-publishing and other concession-like business, in promotion and publicity. Ferris had organized a Buffalo team in the National League, and had moved it to Moline during the 1946–47 season. Once the Blackhawks came into the merged league, however, Kerner had taken charge of the club.

In drafting Cousy, Kerner was reacting more to Cousy's exciting reputation than to any deep belief in Cousy's basketball greatness. Nevertheless, he managed to sign him (although Cousy had little enthusiasm for going to a place like Tri-Cities). Immediately, Kerner traded his new acquisition to Chicago, which was facing dissolution, for Frankie Brian, a star who really meant something. (Chicago had just acquired Brian in the demise of the Anderson club).

Meanwhile, as it became known that St. Louis was in trouble, Irish tried to buy the whole team (for $50,000) simply to acquire Macauley. A big center was the one piece missing from the Knick picture, and Macauley had captivated the Garden customers as a collegian. Irish's idea was excellent: it would have assured the Knicks of a championship team. But the other owners could also see how excellent an idea it was—for Irish. They refused to approve the deal. The St. Louis franchise was turned in to the league, and the players doled out—and Boston, as the weakest surviving team, was given Macauley. (Rocha went to Baltimore, Logan to Tri-Cities).

Suddenly, Auerbach's Celtics had their big center, and the need for Share was not so great. The Celtics never bothered to come to terms with the Bowling Green giant, who decided to play with the Waterloo team which, having fallen out of the N.B.A., went into something called the National Professional Basketball League.

That was in June. In October, about three weeks before the 1950–51 season was to start, Chicago gave up the ghost.

Now there was a real scramble for players. Barnhorst wound up with Indianapolis. Spears went into that N.P.B.L., with a team in Louisville (but wound up, a year later, with Rochester). Joe Bradley went to the Washington Caps.

But about the two big prizes, Zaslofsky and Phillip, there could be no agreement. New York, Philadelphia and Boston were equally insistent that the welfare of the league, not to mention of the whole Western World and perhaps the universe as we know it, depended entirely on being given the rights to Max.

Negotiation was getting nowhere. Podoloff, presiding over the argument, confronted three stubborn owners and had three names left on the Chicago roster: Zaslofsky, Phillip and, by default, Bob Cousy.

Three players, three claimants; Solomon-like, Podoloff made his decision: they would draw out of a hat.

Irish drew first. He got Zaslofsky, and gave way to ecstasy. A great scorer, a four-time league all-star, a native New Yorker, Jewish, spectacular—Max was just what Ned needed for his Knicks. At the agreed price of $15,000, he was a bargain.

Gottlieb drew second, for Philadelphia. He got Phillip, and wasn't too disappointed. Phillip was one of the great play-makers, a solid addition in every respect to a team that still had Fulks and was getting Arizin. At $10,000, he wasn't a bad buy.

That left Walter Brown with Bob Cousy and egg on his face, and $8,500 to pay to the league.

To begin with, he could have had Cousy for nothing, as a draft choice. Now he not only had to pay to get him, but he neither had nor needed the man he had drafted instead, Share. Furthermore, he would now have to expose Cousy to the Boston public, which idolized him so, after having rejected him—and, in fact, having been all but forced at the point of a gun to finally accept him.

And that's how the Celtics wound up with Cousy, who was to be more responsible than any other single player for giving the N.B.A. a positive image in the decade ahead, and who was to become the quarterback of the most persistently successful major league team on record.

Meanwhile, as its number two draft choice, Boston had taken Cooper, finally bringing a Negro to the league. A little later, when the attempt to get Macauley failed, Irish purchased Clifton from the Globetrotters to be his center (even though Sweetwater was really only six-foot-five).

These changes, and others, greatly strengthened the teams in the league below Minneapolis and Rochester, who needed little help. The Lakers, in 1949–50, had added two brilliant rookies: six-foot-seven Vern Mikkelsen, who joined Mikan and Pollard in what was physically the strongest front court ever put together; and five-foot-nine Slater (Dugie) Martin, a tough little Texan who had all the skills needed to feed those big men, and to defend against high-scoring guards. With the veteran Herman Schaefer and Bob Harrison in back court with Martin, and with Arnie Ferrin supplying extra punch up front, the Lakers had perfect balance.

So did the Royals, who weren't as strong but faster and slicker. Davies and Bobby Wanzer were deadly shooters, drivers and feeders in back court, Arnie Risen was the smoothest of centers, and Jack Coleman, and Arne Johnson took care of the corners, with Bill Calhoun and aging Red Holzman acting as top reserves.

These two teams, and Syracuse (which also got no help at all from the redistributions), were now not substantially stronger than their eight rivals. As the 1950–51 season started, therefore, there was every reason to expect better competition than ever, at a higher level of team skill (because of consolidation) and on a much sounder financial footing.

But no one even remotely suspected how completely pivotal a season it was to be.

6 SOLIDIFICATION AND SCANDAL

For the 1950–51 season, Irish had managed to squeeze in eighteen Madison Square Garden dates for his Knicks. Four of them involved double-headers. And it was really a squeeze: there were twenty-eight regular-season college double-headers scheduled, and the "circuit" was going full blast: the Boston Garden had eight college programs, the Chicago Stadium nine, the Cleveland Arena twelve, the Buffalo Memorial Auditorium twenty-one, Philadelphia's Convention Hall thirteen, the San Francisco Cow Palace eighteen, and the University of Pennsylvania's Palestra (where Penn and Villanova teamed up as the host teams) sixteen. Counting the various tournaments, just as many college games were being offered in big-league commercial settings as major-league pro games.

Then the college bubble burst.

In January, a Manhattan College player, Junius Kellogg, reported to the Bronx District Attorney that he had turned down a bribe to "shave" points—that is, not lose the game, but win by less than the margin set as a handicap for the gamblers. (This way, remember, a ten-point favorite, by making sure he won by only five or six points, gave the bettors on the underdog a sure thing, and yet didn't sacrifice the victory which was all that mattered to those who were indifferent to betting or pretended it didn't exist—that is, to coaches, school administrations, and non-betting fans.)

But investigation showed that a couple of his teammates had accepted such bribes, and had acted upon them.

Within a month, a parallel investigation by New York District Attorney Frank Hogan made the Manhattan College incident a minor aberration: the games had been crooked, Hogan discovered and the players confessed, on a vast scale.

City College's Cinderella Team of the previous year, the heroic double champions—all were implicated. So were the leading players from L.I.U., a perennial Garden power. Some N.Y.U. players were involved. St. John's players were accused but not indicted.

The shock that went through the sports world could only be compared to baseball's Black Sox Scandal of 1920, when it was revealed that the Chicago White Sox had conspired to throw the 1919 World Series to the Cincinnati Reds.

And all the revulsion focused on the Garden—and on Irish. He had made basketball big-time; he had created the large money stake that made schools recruit so uninhibitedly. (The City College kids, it turned out, had been recruited illegally, with some academic records altered to get them into school; L.I.U. had been built up, with little attempt at concealment, as a basketball foundry to be a "house team" for the Garden.) It was Irish who had made the game so popular that gamblers moved in; it was Irish who controlled the "commercial arena programs" that college administrators—who had been profiting from them for years and building up their own careers—suddenly found so dangerous and immoral. It was Irish who, somehow, had failed to police his preserve.

Remaining games were cancelled. Self-righteously, one conference after another declared the Garden "unsuitable" for college events. New York, as all right-thinking Americans knew, was the center of sin and corruption and Madison Square Garden was Sodom and Gomorrah, rolled into one.

And if the college boys were crooked, surely the pros must be too?

That question blew like a cold wind through the N.B.A. At that moment, its comparative obscurity was a life-saving blessing. There was no hint, from the underground gambling circles that were now a prime source of information for journalists, that pros *were* involved. Carryover suspicion of the pros, and the primacy of the college action, had kept betting on the pros on a relatively small scale. Treading on eggs, but for the time being untarnished, the N.B.A. finished its season in good order.

Well, not exactly in good order. The Washington franchise had collapsed on January 9, and the players had been redistributed (Freddy Scolari to Syracuse, Bones McKinney to Boston). But this was a bearable loss, since it balanced the two divisions at five teams apiece and eliminated another weak sister financially. Competitively, the team had deteriorated, losing twenty-five of its thirty-five games before quitting, and these results stood, so once again an unequal number of games was played. In the confusion, Boston wound up playing sixty-nine games but finished second to Philadelphia, which played only sixty-six, as did the rest of the Eastern clubs. Syracuse, playing a full Eastern schedule for the first time, fell below .500 and finished fourth, behind New York, lending substance to belief about the unfairness of the previous year's schedule.

Out west, the Lakers again had the best record in the league and finished three games ahead of Rochester. Fort Wayne beat out Indianapolis for third by one game and Tri-Cities, although it finished last, at least did finish.

By the time the N.B.A. play-offs were starting, in late March, the first shock was past. The college season had ended; the pros had not been implicated. The whole business, obviously, was a peculiarly New York evil.

Those New York gamblers, boasted Adolph Rupp, the Kentucky coach who had recruited and trained Groza, Beard and the rest, "couldn't touch my boys with a ten-foot pole." And Bradley University, party of the second part in C.C.N.Y.'s electrifying victories in 1950, self-righteously (and it hoped profitably) started a post-season tournament in wholesome Peoria, to counterbalance the terrible atmosphere of the Garden's National Invitational Tournament.

Nevertheless, faith in the validity of basketball results had been shaken. Some games, it was established, had been fixed, even with large crowds present and the spotlight on full. Any error, slump, or unusual play—innocent as it might be—could not help but start uncomfortable trains of thought in many minds.

In this touchy atmosphere, the N.B.A. went through an eventful set of play-offs. The Knicks, who had finished third, were the hot club (and it is quite likely that the New York players felt some extra inspiration from the slurs and abuse being heaped upon their city; after all, Zaslofsky, McGuire, Lumpp, Simmons and Vandeweghe were native New Yorkers, and their home area's honor was very much in question). At any rate, having finished third, the Knicks polished off Boston in two straight, while fourth-place Syracuse did the same to first-place Philadelphia. In a ferocious five-game semifinal, the Knicks had the odd game at home and won it by two points, 83-81. In the west, both Minneapolis and Rochester had to go three games to survive the first round, and then Rochester upset the Lakers, three games to one, as Mikan was partially hobbled by a bad ankle.

Now the Knicks and Rochester met for the championship, with all the New York games scheduled for the little Armory (capacity, 5,000) because the Garden had long since been occupied by its annual April tenant, the circus. For the first time, New York had a team in what was becoming basketball's equivalent of a World Series, but the big city was hardly aware of it, let alone interested, as the Yankees, Giants and Dodgers were all coming north. Rochester, quite properly, was heavily favored, and won the first two games, at Rochester, by one-sided margins (92-65 and 99-84). In New York, the Royals took the third game, 78-71, and they were leading by six points with eight minutes to play in the fourth game.

However, that close to elimination, the Knicks rallied. They pulled out that game, 79-73, then startled everyone by winning the fifth in Rochester, 92-89. In New York, with Zaslofsky gaining momentum, the Knicks evened the series, 80-73.

On April 21, at Rochester, a hectic final was won by Rochester, but only after the Knicks had fought back again to tie with one minute to play. In the records, Rochester had its championship, but the real appeal of the Knicks to New York—an appeal which was to have a great effect on the growth of the league in the next few crucial years—stemmed from the battle they put up in this series.

Meanwhile, back on March 2, another big step towards major league status had been taken. Walter Brown, midway through the season, before there had been any hint of scandal to weaken the college structure, had come up with a marvellous idea: an all-star game. It was held in Boston, on March 2, with ten top players from the Eastern Division (coached by Lapchick) playing ten from the West (coached by Kundla). The East won, 111-94.

The impact of that game on insiders is hard to recapture so many years later. For the general public, it had little impact, and not only because by the time it was played the scandal was exploding; the pro league as a whole still had limited prestige, and all-star games were all too common in baseball, football and college basketball.

But for the people in the N.B.A., and their fans—and especially for those who had longer contact with pro basketball—the gathering of the stars in the Boston Garden had special meaning. By its nature, basketball lends itself to all-star play better than most games, because the basic moves of great players can be blended almost instinctively, and because shooting is such an individual feat. Through all the barnstorming and free-lance days, the constant shifting of rosters constituted a sort of search for the all-star combination.

Now, on one floor, in one game, there they were: the twenty greatest basketball players living. George Mikan and Alex Groza—one the substitute for the other—and Ed Macauley and Red Rocha and Harry Gallatin actually outplaying them in the second half. Cousy, Dick McGuire and Phillip, all feeding them for the same team in turn—and feeding Arizin and Fulks, Schayes and Boryla. And, in the other backcourt, Beard and Brian and Davies—and Jim Pollard up front.

The basketball afficionado feeds on "match-ups," the fascinating duel of one great player facing another, aside from and along with the team struggle. What match-ups these were! And what shooting! And passing! And rebounding! As artificial, in a competitive sense, as all-star games must always be, they are most valid in basketball, and in this one the Basketball Association of America-born East, with its B.A.A. origins, really took to heart its victory over the National League West, led and symbolized by Mikan and Davies.

But these emotional values were for the already interested, as was the exciting Rochester-New York series. As both pro and college seasons receded into history, no sensational headway had been made by the N.B.A., now down to ten clubs. It seemed obvious that the Knicks would be used to fill gaps in the Garden schedule created by the defection of the morally upright colleges from other sections of the country, and the badly-burned New York schools—but this was a New York problem, or condition, or story; it didn't touch the N.B.A. as a whole too seriously.

Until the other shoe dropped.

In July, it was learned that the Bradley team had been crooked too.

Hogan's investigation had continued. Each interrogation of accused players turned up new leads. Toledo was in it, too.

And on October 19, on the eve of the 1951–52 N.B.A. season, after a charity all-star game in Chicago, two more players were picked up: Groza and Beard.

The Kentucky boys, it seemed, had not only been reachable by much less than a ten-foot pole. They had been the original fixers of the current cycle, going into "business" right after returning from the 1948 Olympics.

By the time Hogan's exposures were complete, the statistics were:

Games had been fixed in 22 cities in 17 states.

There was firm evidence against 33 players from 6 colleges.

On the record, 90 games between 1947 and 1951 had been discussed for manipulation, and 49 were actually rigged.

And no one with any sense of realism could doubt that this was only the visible tip of a very large iceberg. (In years to come, new investigations and new scandals were to touch a dozen more schools. The fixers had focused on the big arenas because that's where the games were; when the games were moved back to college gyms, the fixers moved there just as easily.)

Scandals of such scope put everything in a different light—including the N.B.A.

It was no longer a matter of bad old Madison Square Garden, and a New York problem. Large-scale commercialized college basketball had been dealt a body blow everywhere; the very idea of it was suspect.

Which meant that pro basketball had a golden opportunity. By a sudden twist, it was the more respectable of the two. As millions of words were written and read (and thousands of breasts beaten) in analysis of the moral breakdown of the colleges, one theme emerged again and again: huge profits in a supposedly amateur setting bred corruption—by promoting recruiting inducements (which were bribes offered by the colleges), and by flaunting the fact that lots of money was being made through the players' efforts, with none of it going to the players. The pros, simply because they were pros, were free of this temptation. They were hired openly, and their livelihoods depended on the integrity of their games. In one stroke, their competition (for attention) had been wiped out and their image (honest professionals instead of false amateurs) had been established.

College basketball's tragedy, then, proved to be the turning point for the pros. All the preliminary steps that had been taken under their own power—the merger, the consolidation, the building up of resources, the creation of stars and the establishment of a rudimentary tradition and following—could now pay off.

The immediate effects of the scandal on the N.B.A. were considerable, and troublesome. The Indianapolis Olympians, of course, were instantly wiped out as a gate attraction—although they did survive as an entity for two more years, and actually produced a better record without Groza and Beard.

Numerous potential pros, naturally, were cut off from careers because of their involvements as collegians, but two were particularly important. One of the L.I.U. fixers was Sherman White, a six-foot-seven center who had "all the moves" and was destined for stardom. The Knicks had been counting on him as their territorial choice in the spring of the 1951. With him, in the light of subsequent events, the Knicks certainly would have won some championships, and again, the shape of the league's development would have been different. The other was Bill Spivey, a seven-footer who had succeeded Groza as the big man at Kentucky. He, of all the thirty-three college players named by Hogan, insisted on his innocence, and was indicted for perjury. His trial, in January, 1953, ended in a hung jury, but he was sufficiently tarnished to be barred permanently from the N.B.A.

A dozen others, or more, had potential pro careers of the first rank aborted in this way, but in their effects on the league, White and Spivey were the most important losses. (Both went on to play out their careers in the Eastern League).

Another difficulty was the mood of disgust, disillusion and suspicion that swept through all basketball fans, and that stimulated again vague doubts about the pros as well. Adding to the climate of distrust throughout the sports world, was the West Point cribbing scandal, which wiped out the Army football team on the eve of the 1951 season. Furthermore, another war was on now, in Korea, which injected a solemn note into people's feelings without producing the somewhat desperate search for entertainment that the greater pressures of full-scale war had brought about during World War II. Emotionally, the times were not propitious for the microcosm of the N.B.A. as the 1951–52 season got under way.

And yet—the same ten teams that finished in 1951 were starting the new season, even though one of them had moved. Kerner took his Hawks from Tri-Cities to Milwaukee, where a brand new 11,000-seat arena had just been built in the middle of the city. This was certainly a step up in class, towards major league-ism, rather than a mark of failure. So for the first time, stability of ownership had been maintained over a summer.

In a positive sense, therefore, the 1951–52 season was uneventful—off the court. Syracuse, strengthened by the acquisition of Rocha and a brilliant rookie backcourt man in George King, finished first in the East, one game ahead of Boston, which now had a spectacular scoring trio in Macauley, Cousy and Bill Sharman, but weak rebounding and defense. In the West, Rochester nosed out the Lakers by one game, making season-long consistency overcome the fact that the Lakers won seven out of nine from the Royals hand-to-hand.

Neither first-place finisher, however, reached the final of the play-offs. The Knicks, who had finished third, again emerged as the hot club. They got by Boston by winning the third game in double overtime in Boston (on what Auerbach, to this day, insists was a "terrible call" which gave Vandeweghe two free throws at the buzzer), and disposed of Syracuse in what was to be a five-game set, three games to one. The Lakers polished off Indianapolis in two and Rochester in four.

Again, the final series went the full seven games, with the heavily-favored western team winning against unexpected resistance. This time the Knicks did not come quite as close, taking an 82-65 licking in the final game at Minneapolis.

Another all-star game was played in Boston, this time a month earlier, on February 11. The East won again, 108-91, as Arizin poured in 26 points for the team coached by Cervi, against Kundla.

Arizin performed the still more remarkable feat of dethroning Mikan as scoring champion, averaging 25.4 points a game (to 23.8 for big George and 21.7 for Cousy). Asthmatic, six-foot-four, with uncanny ability to "hang" at the top of his jump, Arizin was bringing the jump shot beyond the point Fulks had reached, even as Fulks was still playing alongside him.

A similar structural stability endured through the 1952–53 season. Again the same ten teams started and finished the season. Again Minneapolis defeated New York in the final round of the play-offs, although the Lakers needed only five games to do it this time, winning four straight after losing the first. Since both the Knicks and Lakers had finished first in their divisions during the regular season (the Knicks by half a game over Syracuse and one and a half over Boston, the Lakers by four games over Rochester), this was the "truest" world-series type championship the league had had so far.

The Knicks had been strengthened by the return of Carl Braun, after two years in the Army. Philadelphia, weakened by Arizin's departure for military service, finished with the worst record in the league, 12-57—but came up with a new scoring champion, an angular six-foot-eight center with a lantern jaw and a remarkable hook shot, Niel Johnston. He averaged 22.3 points a game to Mikan's 20.6, and finished second only to Mikan in rebounding, 1007 to 976.

Over this apparent tranquility, however, hung clouds. The apprehension, and trials, of players and gamblers involved in the college scandals kept making the papers, and an atmosphere of unease continued. The Grand Jury that had started hearing the basketball cases in February, 1951, was not discharged until April 29, 1953—three weeks after that year's N.B.A. play-offs had ended.

And at one point, the N.B.A. had been touched directly. It came out, during the 1952–53 season, that one of the league's referees, Sol Levy, had received $3,000 in bribes to affect the outcome of three games in 1950. Fortunately for the N.B.A., everyone seemed to take Levy's immediate dismissal in stride, without projecting further suspicions. But it was a subject that could not be brushed aside.

Other troubles were building, too, behind closed doors. The deceptive serenity and solidification of 1951–53 was about to be shattered on three fronts—the game itself, financial problems, and gambling, all coming to a head in the 1953–54 season which seemed to be starting so calmly and optimistically.

To see them in context, however, we'll have to stop for a moment to examine the type of basketball that had evolved in the early '50s, which can be called the Mikan Era.

7 THE MIKAN ERA

Rough.

That's the word for the brand of basketball evolved in the N.B.A. during its first eight years.

It was a combination of college philosophy and old pro technique. The B.A.A. founders had insisted upon, and had succeeded in planting, the collegiate enthusiasm, the uncompromising standard of maximum effort at all times that so many previous pro leagues had lacked. But the individual principles of established pro play were clearly the most effective—especially when added to such heightened motivation.

The result was a bruising, body-contact type of game. With so many large men moving quickly in a confined space, there was enough legitimate reason for accidental collision. But there were three distinct causes of collision-on-purpose, as well.

The first, and foremost, was test of manhood: as soon as possible, pros "put the question" (as Lapchick liked to say) to all newcomers. How much guts did the newcomer have? How much pain and risk was he willing to undertake to complete the path to the basket when it opened up? Could he be made to lose his temper, and therefore control of his own game? What happened to his normally accurate shooting if he could be made to anticipate a solid belt immediately afterwards? And if he passed all these spiritual tests, how much could he be worn down physically, over the course of forty-eight minutes or a season, by being made to fight back?

Establishing respect, therefore, was necessity number one for every new player—respect from the opposition, and from his own teammates for the way he responded to the opposition's pressure. And the only way to establish respect was to hit back, promptly and effectively—to give as good as one got. This led, naturally, to a considerable amount of contact that a referee's whistle or a subsequent free throw did not deter. In context, the test of manhood was more important than the particular play; and since new personnel was involved so frequently as each class of collegians came into the league, the testing was frequent and constituted an appreciable percentage of the deliberate roughness.

The second basic invitation to rough stuff was strategic. Obviously, the referees couldn't see everything, and couldn't call everything they did see. If they did, the whole game would quickly become a parade to the foul line, nullifying the very thing the owners were trying to sell—high-speed, college-style basketball. Referees who had worked with pros before knew how to be "intelligently selective"; those recruited from college ranks learned quickly, or went back to college games. But if the referees were being "selective," there were obvious advantages to being systematically rough. If you went ahead and grabbed on defense ten times, and got away with it six times, you were gaining more than you were losing. The same was true if you barrelled into someone on offense, since the referees were more inhibited about calling offensive fouls than anything else. And in rebounding, as much seemed fair as in love or war—anything at all. Possession really seemed to be nine-tenths of the law in the battle under the boards.

For this condition, the owners were responsible. By being afraid to insist that the referees call a tight game because "it would slow up the action," they were encouraging their players and coaches to do more and more of the body contact that made slowing up the game inevitable. After all, if you gained an advantage by getting away with six belts out of ten, you gained still more by getting away with twelve out of twenty, or eighteen out of thirty. In practice, the percentage of "getting away with it" was much higher than that.

The third factor was embedded in the rules, and was as much of a problem in college and amateur basketball as in the pros: as a close game came nearer and nearer to the final buzzer, there were substantial tactical advantages to fouling. The fact that a basket was worth two points and a free throw only one made it worthwhile to try to trade a foul—which could cost one point—for a chance to score two points.

Among pros, then, such tactics took on greater value. On a pro team, almost every player was expected to be able to make his free throws under pressure—so if the defense decided to "give a foul," it might as well be a healthy enough whack to leave the victim a trifle shaken as he stepped to the free throw line. A few such "tactical" exchanges quickly led to emotional ones: tempers rose, retaliations became progressively rougher, and the referee's task became impossible.

For that matter, the referee's task was impossible to begin with. As the smaller towns came in, with single-minded fan support, the sense of being physically threatened by a mob was hard to shake. Coaches and home-team players systematically incited the crowd with gestures and words, to make this pressure more intense. And the one person who could ease the situation—the owner—as often as not sat on the bench and added his screams to the rest. Since referees were, and are, inescapably human, they were affected—not, in the vast majority of cases, by yielding to threat, but by the commonsense approach of keeping all decisions to a minimum. Few referees compromised their own sense of objectivity by favoring either team (consciously, that is). But all, sooner or later, realized that fewer total calls meant fewer unpopular ones, and neatly rationalized this by telling themselves "they were letting the players play," and "giving the public what it wants"—meaning "owners" when they said "public."

And the referees were right: if an owner, who is actually paying your salary and freely complaining about you to the press and in the privacy of league meetings, is actually on the bench during a game, jumping up and shouting insults, waving his fist in the air, stomping out into the court itself—if an owner acts this way, the message is hard to miss. He wants you to "let things go" (for his side only, of course) and he is, when all is said and done, the man who is paying the freight. So if you want to keep your career as a referee thriving, you give the man what he wants —not "favorable" calls, which would be dishonest, but a minimum of whistles, which is fair, honorable and even conceptually defensible.

This approach applied, most of all, to the boards. Even theoretically, the ball doesn't belong to anyone once the shot goes up. Fine. When the shot is missed, let him get it who can. The referee's conscience is clean. It became virtually impossible to get a foul called on a rebound. One would have to pull a knife or a gun—and there's little opportunity to conceal a weapon in a basketball suit. The area near the boards was no man's land. This was where two, three or even four huge bodies crashed together in pursuit of the rebound, and where someone wound up hitting that unyielding wooden floor with a reverberating "thwack."

The other great danger was driving, full speed, for the basket. A well-timed hip, shove or trip could send the driver hurtling into the crowd, or wooden seats, or metal basket supports, or concrete flooring just beyond the court proper. Here there was much more likelihood of getting the foul called—but you might not appreciate the justice of it until you regained consciousness.

(In Syracuse, thick iron piping formed the base of the basket supports, with a crossbar about five inches above the floor. Once Harry Gallatin, driving in, went sprawling and got his head wedged under the pipe. It looked exactly as if he had been guillotined, for a few horrible moments. Then it seemed power tools would be needed to cut him out. But eventually he managed to unwedge himself—and stay in the game.)

This ruggedness has to be stressed for two reasons—because it had such great effect on the reforms that were to follow in a few years, and because the charge of "sissiness" or "a game for goons" rankled so much. For plain physical punishment, the pro basketball player did not have to apologize to the football or hockey player. Wooden floors are harder than turf, and the basketball player does not wear padding. When hockey players collide, they are on ice, and the slippery surface nullifies much of the impact. Football players, by and large, either come together from a standing start (in the line) or can brace themselves (or relax themselves) for the impact of an open-field block or tackle. In both hockey and football, the armor worn is considerable. But the basketball player, when knocked to the floor, most of the time is not braced for collision, since he is moving on the assumption that full contact is not allowed. Usually, he will get knocked down while jumping helpless with both feet off the ground, and will come down hard on the wooden floor on a bare elbow, knee, back or head.

In addition, basketball players did much more running, starting, stopping, jumping and shuffling than football players, and hockey players sit out, usually, four of every six playing minutes.

Men who are merely tall, therefore, have no place in so athletic a game—and they didn't in the N.B.A., from the beginning. Those who were exceptionally tall were also tough, determined, muscular, well-coordinated, and blessed with endurance. Without these qualities, they couldn't last out a season.

And this was the factor that finally determined the style of play N.B.A. teams produced: an abundance of big men who were not merely big, but talented athletes.

At the beginning, in the B.A.A. days, the "big man" was only the center. Every team had someone in the six-foot-eight to six-foot-ten size range, but men between six-foot-five and six-foot-eight could operate effectively at that position. (Gallatin was six-foot-six, Groza six-foot-seven, Miasek six-foot-seven.)

When Mikan came along, he was the biggest of the centers, in bulk as well as in height, but he represented a difference only in degree. He was still the only really outsized man on his team.

The forwards, in those days, ranged from six-two to six-six, and were still fundamentally what their name implied, the front line of offense. The idea was still to get as close to the basket as possible for a lay-up or an easy shot, so forwards did a lot of driving and helped with the rebounding.

The guards included many men well under six feet tall. (Slater Martin was five-nine; Red Holzman, Ralph Beard, Freddy Scolari, Ernie Calverly and Ken Sailors five-ten, Al Cervi and Bobby Wanzer and Dick McGuire five-eleven.) A six-two guard was considered tall, six-four a freak. The guards also still had classical functions: shoot from outside, deliver the ball to the forwards, drive in when possible.

Defense was essentially an individual matter. Since the zone was outlawed, none of the fancy prearrangements so dear to the hearts of college coaches were possible. In effect, zone principles were employed by proper switching when offensive men crossed, and it would take, in any case, congressional action and implementation by U.S. Marines to make any self-respecting center give up his territorial claims right near the basket. But for the most part, one man guarded another as best he could, and got help from one teammate when his own man did get by.

The centers scored almost entirely from the pivot, by hooking or wheeling in, or on tap-ins and other rebounds. The good shooters among the guards still used the two-handed set shot as a primary weapon, but even one-hand shooters "set" themselves as often as they fired on the run. The new breed, the jump shooters a la Fulks, were almost always the corner men.

Among alert and determined pros, a fast break could be contained pretty well because the defense dropped back quickly, and because the rebound (which must trigger the fast break) was vigorously contested. Besides, a team that had expert ball-handlers, good outside shooters and feeders who knew how to hit the big men didn't have so much to gain from fast breaking; it made better scoring opportunities for itself by operating slowly and purposefully for an opening—which also made it less vulnerable to fast breaking by the other team.

In this era, then, teams developed distinct personalities.

The Rochester Royals were, in a sense, the most perfect team. Davies and Wanzer could hit from far out, and drive. Risen could pivot, hand off, move and rebound at center. Arne Johnson could hit the boards, and Jack Coleman could do that and score too. Holzman, like Davies and Wanzer, had the full complement of backcourt skills. All were reliable from the free throw line. But their biggest assets were balance, ball handling and court sense. Their scoring was evenly distributed, they really looked for one another, and they were alert to all openings. In the six seasons between 1949 and 1954, the Royals won 266 regular season games while the Lakers won only 267, and the Royals actually finished ahead of them twice.

What made this so remarkable was the one Rochester deficiency: size. The Lakers, especially when they added Mikkelsen to Mikan and Pollard, simply overpowered the Royals in a showdown. Over those years, the Lakers defeated Rochester 38 times (including play-offs) and lost only 28 times—and that was enough to make it the Mikan Era instead of the Royals' Era. Against other teams, not so over-matched physically, Rochester won even more often than the Lakers did.

The Minneapolis game was simple, and to many ardent fans, unattractive. Mikan, Mikkelsen or Pollard would clear the defensive board when the opposition missed. The Lakers would bring the ball up slowly, waiting for the lumbering Mikan to get into position in the pivot. Then they would concentrate on getting the ball in to Big George, whose huge left elbow would open a swath as he turned in towards the basket. Since the opposition was concerned almost entirely with trying to stop Mikan somehow, or to keep the ball from going in to him, plenty of opportunities arose for Pollard, Mikkelsen, Martin, or any one else, to operate individually. And what anyone missed, one of the front three was likely to tap in.

It was simple—and it was effective. Mikan was simply too big in bulk to be blocked out. He couldn't jump very high, but didn't have to. He couldn't run, but didn't have to. But he had tremendous competitive fire and pride to go along with his size, and excellent timing, and knowledge of his assets. Determination was one of his most important characteristics. Just because a man is bigger than his opponent, it doesn't mean he's free from pain when they do collide, and Mikan took his share of the lumps in the battles under the boards.

Along with his size, Mikan had an outgoing, friendly personality, the right amount of humility, wide-ranging interests (he was studying law), a stubborn streak and a capacity for hard work. A man in his position could have been hated, or at least disliked; his size automatically created resentment in ordinary people (and in the six-foot-six opponents who, against George, suddenly considered themselves "ordinary"). But he was so good-natured—and obviously so good for the financial welfare of the whole sport—that he was generally well-liked around the circuit. What frictions he had (and everyone has them) arose more often within his own team than with opponents.

Everything, therefore, revolved around him. He scored more than anyone ever had, but not so much more as to distort statistics (as Wilt Chamberlain would in later years), because the slow-moving offense made the Lakers a relatively low-scoring team.

What Mikan was really proving, as the championships piled up, was the inescapable importance of possession of the ball. The well-schooled basketball people had always known that, of course; but now, even the casual fan couldn't miss it. The only answer to a team with Mikan on it was to get enough bigger players to attain an even break in rebounding—somehow, somewhere. People Mikan's size weren't easy to find, and some who were—Don Otten, Charley Share, Larry Foust—never matched Mikan's abilities. More plentiful were players of comparable height who were considerably thinner, but perhaps more agile; and players in the six-foot-five to six-foot-eight range who could really leap.

So Mikan's presence intensified the search for "big men." A big center was no longer enough. Now you needed at least one rugged six-foot-seven forward—to handle Mikkelsen, for instance.

And a bigger back court man became useful too, since one of the ways to combat the big forwards was to maneuver them away from the basket to let the little men operate. Once the little men got inside, the six-foot-two man had the same advantage over the five-foot-eleven man that the six-foot-eight had over the six-foot-five: he could take him into the pivot.

By the end of the Mikan era, then, at least two men who would have been centers at the beginning of it were standard equipment for every team, and back court men in the six-foot-three range were becoming common.

The Lakers and Royals dominated the league, but other winning teams had identifiable styles. Syracuse was an offshoot of Rochester, since Cervi had come from the Royals, but was more aggressive and scrambling while equally devoted to team balance. The Nats had no board strength to match Minneapolis, and not as even a scoring distribution as the Royals, because they depended too much on one man, Schayes. Dolph grew into an unusual problem for the opposition. He filled out to a heavier six-foot-eight, but he could drive, move and handle the ball like most men half a foot shorter—and he had a fine, two-handed outside shot besides. He worked out of the corners, and constituted a complete team offense in himself.

The Knicks, under Lapchick, had no comparable size, no inbred finesse and no individual superstar. What they did have was hustle and balance, and they played a running game—in relays. It was Lapchick's idea that you couldn't lose a game, irretrievably, in the first twelve minutes. So, often, he would start two or three members of his bench, and shoot in fresh regulars at the start of the second period. In reality, what he had was a squad of eight players who were all "regulars." The Knicks hoped to counteract bigger and stronger teams by running them into an equalizing state of fatigue. Gallatin and Sweetwater Clifton did remarkably well rebounding, considering their size. Braun could shoot on the run, or any other way. Dick McGuire was the ultimate playmaker (but poor shooter), Ernie Vandeweghe the perfect floater, ball-hawk and "garbage man" near the basket. When Zaslofsky came (just as Braun went into the Army for two years), he became the chief scorer. Boryla, six-foot-five, with little jumping power but solid as a rock, possessed a long set shot as well as pivot skills. Connie Simmons could run as well as hook. In a sense, the Knicks, although they never won the title, were pointing towards the future, when everyone would play a running game.

And perhaps the best demonstration of the emerging pattern was seen in Boston, by contrast. When Auerbach took over the Celtics, he had in his mind all the ideas about fast-break basketball that would eventually make the Celtics champions—but making them work was something else. Cousy could pass and score with the best; Macauley and Sharman were as deadly on offense as anyone could be. They were all but unstoppable—once they had the ball. But they couldn't get it often enough, and they couldn't put up enough defense against powerful forwards or driving backcourt men. So the Celtics often finished second during the regular season, but never reached the later rounds of the playoffs, because they couldn't get past the Knick depth (in some years) or Schayes (in others).

Philadelphia, meanwhile, was the team that had high scorers, year after year, starting with Fulks. The Warriors worked on the perfectly sound proposition of finding the hot man and feeding him. The progression would go from Fulks to Arizin to Neil Johnston to Chamberlain. With this system, when other good players were available, a championship could be won; when the rest of the talent was thin, the team could easily be last and still have a scoring champion.

For all teams, however, roughness and fouling were the central problems, precisely because getting possession through a rebound was so important, and so difficult when there was a discrepancy in size.

The owners recognized the problem. There was much talk about devising ways "to counteract the big man"—but what was really involved was counteracting the deliberate fouling used against the game the big men created, since it was perfectly plain that the stars of the future would be bigger and bigger—and better.

The closer the game, the worse the problem. Just when excitement should be reaching its peak, a tight battle deteriorated into foul trading. The team that was ahead by a few points, confident of its ability to handle the ball, (since these were pros), did not try to score; it sat back and tried to run out the clock. If the trailing team fouled, to try to trade one point for two, the leading team fouled right back. Yet, the trailing team had to keep fouling and hope for a miss, since there was no other way to try to win.

For the 1950–51 season—the first "shakedown" season after the merger, when the league was down to eleven teams—a new rule was tried. In the last three minutes of the game, there would be a jump ball after every successful free throw (but not, naturally, after the first try of a two-shot foul). This meant a team couldn't be sure of getting possession even after the free throw, so that "trading one for two" took on an added element of risk.

It helped a little—but only a little. All it really did was push up the foul-trading segment to before the three-minute mark. And it didn't really deter. For instance, in the third game of the final round of the play-offs, at the 69th Regiment Armory in New York, the Royals had a six-point lead over the Knicks with four and a half minutes to play. The Knicks rallied, and cut this margin to 62-61 just as the three-minutes-to-play point was reached.

In the next seventy seconds, the Royals shot—and made—seven consecutive one-shot fouls. They won the game 78-71.

For the next season, 1951–52, the jump-ball rule was applied to the last two minutes, instead of three. But a more important change was made, this one aimed directly at the big centers and specifically at Mikan. The free-throw lane, the area in which an offensive player is not allowed to be for more than three seconds, was widened from six to twelve feet.

This meant that Mikan (or anyone else) had to take up his pivot position further from the basket—six feet away instead of three feet away. It meant an extra step in wheeling in, and a changed trajectory on hook shots—and a much better shot at the rebound for the defensive team. It also meant that the alley for driving was opened up. In every respect, this was a progressive change, which proved permanent, although it failed partially in its primary objective: Mr. Mikan adjusted quite well. His scoring average did drop from 28.4 to 23.8, and the scoring championship did go to Arizin (with 25.4), but Mikan and the Lakers did win the play-offs, which they had not done the previous year. They won the next two championships, too, although Mikan's scoring totals continued to drop—as much in response to better balance among the Lakers and the acceptance of the percentages, as from any "impossibility" created for the big man.

By now, the tireless and fertile imaginations of the pros had found a new flaw in the jump-ball rule. The jump was between the man who was fouled and the man who committed the foul. All you had to do, then, was to have your big man foul their little man, and the chances were you'd get the ball after the jump. So, for the 1952–53 season, the rule was changed: now the jump would be between the man who was fouled and "the player whom the fouled player was playing immediately before"—in other words, the normal match-up.

None of this was having much effect, and game after game was ending in shambles. The players and coaches complained, the referees suffered, the owners squabbled about which team was getting an advantage in which game—and the customers showed their disapproval in the most convincing fashion, by walking out and not coming back. Early in the 1950–51 season, two particular games focused attention on the inherent weaknesses in the rules.

On November 22, 1950, at Minneapolis, the Fort Wayne Pistons defeated the Lakers—19-18. Among their other advantages, the Lakers had a home court that was shorter and narrower than normal, which made their bulk all the more effective and their lack of speed less significant. The Pistons, who were a pretty rugged bunch themselves, simply held the ball out.

Less than two weeks later, in Rochester, the Royals played a five-overtime game with Indianapolis, the longest every played in the league. What could be more exciting? Lots of things. In this one, during each of the overtime periods, the team that got the tap merely held the ball for one last shot. Even the rabid Rochester fans, with their team on its way to a championship, first booed and then walked out in droves while the game was still on. Finally, the Olympians won, 75-73.

Bad as things were during the regular schedule, they were much worse in play-offs, because the stakes were greater. The tighter the game, the more fouls; the more fouls, the more bickering about the ones that weren't called; the more bickering, the more frustration for all concerned—no dignity in winning, a feeling of being cheated in losing.

At this point, the referees were living under siege, permanent villains no matter what they did. From time to time they would need police protection in leaving an arena. The rough play led to frequent fist fights among players, which in turn incited the court-side fans and added to the hysterical atmosphere.

For the 1953–54 season, the most gimmicky rule tried yet was adopted. In an attempt to reduce fouling, each player was limited to two personals committed in any one period; if he committed a third, he had to sit out the rest of the quarter—although his game limit was still six.

Nothing helped. In one of the 1953 play-off games, Boston and Syracuse battled through four overtimes, before Boston won, 111-105. In that game, Bob Cousy scored 50 points—with only 10 baskets and 30 free throws. For all the play-off games that year, the *average* was 80 free throw attempts per game (40 for each team).

In such circumstances, the stronger teams were virtually unbeatable on their own courts. The Lakers, for the six years of their dominance, posted home records of 26-3, 30-1, 29-3, 21-5, 24-2 and 21-4. Rochester had similar figures, Syracuse and Boston only a less extreme. In 1951, when Philadelphia finished first in the East, it was 29-3 at home. Fort Wayne, that year, finished four games under .500—despite a 27-7 home record. The Pistons were 5-29 on the road. That year, 75 per cent of all games were won by the home team.

The Knicks had a certain disadvantage. When they played at the Garden, their home-court edge was reduced, for three reasons: referees were totally free of intimidation, because the Garden crowd often included much vocal support for the visiting team; visiting teams were always "up" when playing in the famous arena and in the publicity spotlight; and the Knicks themselves seldom practiced there. However, the Knicks also played many home games at their Armory, where they had as big a home-court edge as anyone. But even the Knicks, in these years, thrived at home, with 22-5, 21-4 and 21-4 in the three years that they went to the finals.

What was happening, then, was all too clear. For all the improved financial stability, the shaking out of weaker franchises, the opportunity for attention afforded by college basketball's burst bubble, the influx of new stars and the traditions already established, the N.B.A. was starting to fail in its one crucial aspect—the product. The game itself was going the way so many pro leagues had taken it in the past, towards oblivion.

But the owners, now more involved in acting like rabid fans than like business men, weren't ready to face up to the facts. The 1953–54 season would force them to.

8 THE BRINK OF DISASTER

The N.B.A. owners, who called themselves the Board of Governors, had every reason to feel optimistic as they looked ahead to the 1953–54 season—as long as they were willing (and stubbornly eager) to ignore the deterioration of their game on the floor.

During the previous season, the Dumont Television Network had televised fourteen Saturday afternoon games. Now N.B.C. was ready to step in with a larger program, and this was Podoloff's pet. He might still not know too much about the technicalities of basketball, but as a businessman he certainly grasped the importance of nationwide television exposure. Pretty soon, the bustling little figure of Podoloff, moving up and down the sidelines during televised games and being interviewed polysyllabically whenever possible, was to be a familiar sight on home screens.

And what would the expanded audience see? A compact nine-team circuit in which all the teams had at least four years of continuous identity behind them. Indianapolis had finally dropped out, but that was a small loss, since Groza and Beard had been caught. Syracuse, Fort Wayne and Milwaukee had bright new arenas, municipally built, to play in. The league structure was certainly in the best shape it had ever been in.

The players were a dream. So many exciting ones were coming out of the college ranks that the effects of the scandals were all but forgotten. Clyde Lovellette, of Kansas, the giant of the college season of 1952, had decided to join Minneapolis as Mikan's heir apparent after spending a year in the A.A.U. ranks. Another star abandoning the A.A.U. was George Yardley, joining Fort Wayne.

Coming out of college was Walter Dukes, a seven-footer who had led Seton Hall through an undefeated season. From Columbia, there was six-foot-seven Jack Molinas, who had performed a similar feat for the Lions in 1951 as a sophomore. There was Bob

Houbregs of Washington, and Richie Regan of Seton Hall, Ernie Beck of Pennsylvania—and, again after A.A.U. detours, Ernie Barrett of Kansas State, Don Sunderlage of Illinois, and Walt Davis, a six-foot-eight Olympic high jumper from Texas A. & M. There was also Ray Felix, a skinny six-foot-eleven L.I.U. product who had not been touched by the scandals because, as a sophomore, he had been simply left out of the deals.

However, there was a booby trap in each of these promising elements.

The television program languished. The individual owners couldn't look beyond selfish interests: who was to get more money by having his team make more TV appearances? Who wanted to schedule a Saturday afternoon game when a Saturday night game would draw more at the gate? Instead of pulling together and making the televised games as attractive as possible, they bogged down in bickering for small advantages. Here, again, the basic conflict of interest showed itself. Irish, with the Knicks now the most important feature of Garden basketball, had little interest in the small fees television could bring. He wanted the big live crowds. For the shoestring operators in smaller cities, on the other hand, no fee looked small and every little bit of exposure was welcome. Podoloff, siding as usual with the have-nots, never succeeded in arranging a TV schedule that gave the uncommitted audience the best available games instead of the games particular owners wanted most to sell.

On the matter of franchise stability, a cruel trick had been played on one member, through no fault of his own or of the league. When Kerner moved from Tri-Cities to Milwaukee, it was a major step up in class, even though Milwaukee could hardly be considered a hotbed of basketball interest. Still, he had brought a major league sport to a city that didn't have any such representation, and that resented being in Chicago's shadow. With a new, 11,000-seat arena to play in, he had all the building blocks of a success, and during the first year there had done well.

Then, without warning, in March of 1953, the Boston Braves moved to Milwaukee. Suddenly, Milwaukee was a major league baseball town, wild about its new status, commercially committed to giving baseball every support. Suddenly, Kerner and the N.B.A. were forgotten and ignored, small potatoes no matter how you looked at it in the presence of big league baseball. The financial position of the Hawks was compromised from that moment on.

Since the Baltimore franchise was also struggling, and Philadelphia was having lean years, one-third of the league wasn't as solid as it had seemed a few months before.

And a snag developed on the player front, too.

The Knicks, having finished first in the East, with a record second only to Minneapolis', did not rate a high draft choice—but they were confronted with an embarrassment of riches. Under the territorial draft rule, they could pick Dukes, Molinas or Felix, generally regarded as the three most desirable properties. Felix, in fact, had been out of school the previous year and actually on a Knick payroll, playing for a semi-pro team. Dukes was clearly a better player, but known to be an independent thinker and the object of competitive offers from the Globetrotters. Molinas seemed to be the most talented of the three, but his ability was considered somewhat unproven because he had played in the despised Ivy League.

Irish chose—characteristically—the one with the biggest reputation, Dukes. Baltimore, picking first in the regular draft, grabbed Felix—because Clair Bee, who had been the L.I.U. coach, was now coach and president of the Bullets. (Philadelphia, with a worse record than Baltimore's, was permitted to take three local stars as territorial choices: Beck, and Jack George and Norm Grekin of LaSalle.)

The next pick was Milwaukee's, and Kerner took Houbregs. Then Fort Wayne took Molinas.

It soon appeared that Irish had guessed wrong all around. Again characteristically, he refused to meet the $17,000 bonus that the Globetrotters gave Dukes, and wound up with nothing. Felix, who would have been grateful to join the Knicks on any terms, went on to become the rookie-of-the-year and the number five scorer in the league—ranking between Schayes and Mikan—under Bee's tutelage.

And Molinas, in the first half of the season, proved himself a real find, all doubt about his talents dispelled. He had the shots, the mobility and the size to be a major-league star for many years.

But he also had something else: a desire to gamble.

In late December, the news broke. Through Ike Gellis, sports editor of the *New York Post,* Podoloff had been informed that there were rumors about Molinas. An investigation led to direct questioning of Molinas by Podoloff and Zollner. Molinas would admit only that he had bet small sums, occasionally, and only on his own team to win. Even this, however, was enough for Podoloff to act upon. The player contract specifically prohibited betting of any sort on any game played by an N.B.A. club.

Podoloff acted promptly, and was backed up unanimously for once. Molinas was barred, period. Further investigations were conducted and nothing was turned up to indicate that any other player had been involved. ("A personal psychiatric aberration," Podoloff called it, and years later no one could deny that Molinas had his own strange attitudes about the subject. After becoming a lawyer, and striving repeatedly for reinstatement, Molinas was found in the fixer's role in a new wave of college scandals, and actually went to prison.)

There was no mistaking the shudder that went through the N.B.A. at this point.

For the first time, the scandal had touched the pros directly. Was it just Molinas? Had the cancer really been caught in time and cut out? Only time would tell, but at that moment it took considerable faith in the essential goodness of the universe to feel confidence in the N.B.A.'s future.

As things turned out, however, the Molinas case was a turning point. Because there was no terrible aftermath, because no further incidents cropped up, and because this one had been faced frankly and investigated instead of glossed over, faith in the league's integrity took firmer root than it might have otherwise.

Meanwhile, an immediate improvement of image was needed, something to counteract the ugly thoughts. Fortunately, it was at hand.

The 1954 All-Star Game had been scheduled for January 21 at Madison Square Garden. This was indicative of the change in Irish's position after the college scandals. The number of Knick double-headers at the Garden had gone from four the year the scandals broke, to eight to fourteen in 1952–53. This year, the double-headers were cut back to nine, but only because first games were hard to find, and because Minneapolis, Rochester and Syracuse had become attractions that could stand on their own. After the first two All-Star games in Boston, which were Walter Brown's personal productions, the third had been played in Fort Wayne (and won by the West, 79-75, with Mikan the outstanding player).

Now this extravaganza was to be put on, for the first time, in the most appropriate setting, that Mecca of Basketball that still had such glamorous connotations for all players and most of the public.

And the boys really put on a show.

Ray Felix, the skinny, awkward rookie whose reflexes were never first-rate, played Mikan—and played him even most of the game. Pollard, meanwhile, made six baskets in the first half en route to a 23-point total, high for the game. Davies and Wanzer on one side, Cousy and McGuire with Sharman on the other, set off backcourt fireworks that had the crowd of 16,478 ecstatic.

The East led, 28-25 at the quarter and 48-44 at the half. Mikan and Pollard got rolling in the third period, and the West took the lead. With seven minutes to play in the game, the West was ahead, 73-69. But the East roared back, led 76-73, was caught, and went into the final minute with an 82-80 lead.

Lapchick sent in Cousy, to kill the remaining 50 seconds by dribbling—but Davies stole the ball, drove and tied it up with 33 seconds left. Cousy, biding his time for a final shot, sent up a long one-hander with only 3 seconds to go, and made it, for an 84-82 lead. But the West was able to call time out, then get the ball in to Mikan, who wheeled on Felix—and was fouled.

With the clock showing one second to play, George calmly stepped to the line and sank the two free throws, sending the game into overtime.

In the extra period, Cousy went wild. He hit from outside, he drove in for a three-pointer, and then sank five more free throws as the game ran out, a 98-93 victory for the East, all the while dribbling to kill time and passing perfectly.

But the ultimate moment, to the pros themselves, had been Mikan, under the pressure of all that pride, making those two free throws to save the game at that point. That's what they identified with most completely.

This spectacular game gave the basketball world something to talk about for weeks, when something positive and exhilarating was most needed.

For the rest of the season, close pennant races maintained interest. The Knicks finished first in the East again, but didn't clinch first until the next to last day of the season, as Syracuse and Boston tied for second, two games behind. In the West, the Lakers beat out Rochester by a two-game margin also. Neil Johnston won the scoring title again, with a 24.4 average, but no other player in the league succeeded in averaging 20 points or more. In fact, the team average of 79.5 points per game was the lowest since 1947–48, the league's second year. This decrease in scoring was a symptom of the increased roughness and orientation toward fouling.

Then came the play-offs.

Shambles.

One of the worst ideas ever to come out of the councils of the Board of Governors was the play-off pattern for 1954. When the Indianapolis team had folded, leaving the Western Division with four teams, it was no longer possible to have four teams qualify for the play-offs. To accommodate three teams in the first round, a round robin was devised. Having just completed a 72-game schedule, the top three teams in each division would now play a six-game round robin, each pair playing once at home and once away—to eliminate one of the three. The two survivors would then have a two-out-of-three semi-final, and the usual seven-game final would follow.

Although this was as silly a procedure as one could find, it wasn't, in itself, the cause of the shambles. Fouling was.

Once again, one game symbolized things out of proportion. The Knicks, having finished first, were crushed by the Celtics in the first game of the round robin at home, then beaten at Syracuse. In between, Syracuse nipped Boston in overtime.

That meant that the Knicks had to win at Boston to stay alive, since Syracuse already had two victories. This could be Boston's second, and it would leave the Knicks with only a meaningless game to play against Syracuse if they lost.

It happened to fall on Saturday afternoon, March 20—on national television. The game encompassed all the repulsive features of the grab-and-hold philosophy. It lasted three hours, and the final seconds of a one-point game were finally abandoned by the network. The arguments with the referees were interminable and degrading. What had been happening, as a matter of course, in dozens of games for the last couple of years, was shown to a nationwide audience in unadulterated impurity.

Boston won, 79-78. The round robin was completed, with Syracuse beating the Knicks and Boston again—and then Syracuse beat Boston two more times in the next round. In the West, the Royals and Lakers followed the same cumbersome procedure to get rid of Fort Wayne, which had finished third anyhow, and then the Lakers took two out of three from the Royals.

In the final round, Syracuse managed to push the Lakers through a full seven-game series before yielding. The Nats had no physical means of coping with Mikan, Lovellette and Mikkelsen, even though George was slowing down. He was now thirty years old and thinking of retirement. But it was all anticlimax now. A Syracuse-Minneapolis final—"minor-league cities"—was not calculated to absorb the American public in early April, with the baseball season starting.

The identity of the cities involved in the final, the foul-filled style of play, the touch of scandal—all these things represented the final triumph of the "old pro" context represented by the old National League over the "college-style" idea with which the B.A.A. started. Two-thirds of the nine-team league now had nothing whatever to do with arena control, even indirectly. Of the original three, the Knicks had prospered but had been touched most closely by the college scandals and had not succeeded in bringing home the big prize, a play-off title; the Celtics, too, had never become quite good enough and had cost Brown hundreds of thousands of dollars; and the Warriors had passed entirely into Gottlieb's hands, making him an owner-coach like Bee and Harrison. And although few people put it in such terms, it was a fact that no league in which three of the nine teams have owner-coaches can have big-league aura or reality.

The original dream, it seemed, was gone, and not only that—the whole league might go. As the 1954 season ended, the ostriches on the Board of Governors could no longer escape confrontation with their weaknesses. They were being vilified on all sides as "bush league," and whatever merit there was to such a charge, the attitudes that invited it could not be separated from the unsatisfactory quality of the games themselves.

Something had to be done. Promptly.

Something was.

9 THE NEW RULE

Devising new rules for basketball was a mental exercise and parlor game that had absorbed basketball people for years. From veteran coaches through teen-age fans, everybody knew there was something wrong with the game, and everybody had some sort of remedy in mind. Everyone agreed that "big men" were a problem (except, of course, the big men themselves and those coaches fortunate enough to have them). Dozens of proposals had been in the air for a long time—raise the basket, lower the basket, widen the free-throw lane, let the fouled team keep possession after the shot whether it was made or missed, reduce the limit on personals, change the relative values of field goal and free throw—and so on, and so on, and so on.

The difficulty was a real one, and had been building for nearly twenty years.

Originally, there had been a jump ball at center court after every score. Theoretically, this was absolutely sound. But when "big men" (like Lapchick in the 1920s) started to appear, the team with the taller center had an overwhelming advantage. It would get possession of the tap most of the time, as well as getting most of the rebounds. Once such a team got ahead, it could freeze the ball very effectively, and if it did lose it and the other team scored, chances were it would get the ball back anyhow. On the other hand, if it did score, it still had a better than even chance of getting the tap and increasing its lead.

This was one motive for eliminating the center jump. (Another was simply to speed up action.) Now the team that scored automatically gave possession to the other team, and play continued.

Theoretically, this sounded like an equalizing process—but practice quickly proved otherwise. Now, once a team was ahead, there was little incentive to try to increase the lead. If you did score, you automatically gave the other team a chance to match it; if you tried to score and missed, the other team might close the gap. Obviously, it was better to sit on the lead and let the clock run out. On the other hand, the trailing team faced a self-perpetuating problem in trying to catch up. Every time it cut its deficit by scoring, it gave the other team a chance to get the two points back; the only way to make progress was to attack aggressively before the other team could shoot—which meant more and more fouling, either accidentally in a sincere effort to get the ball, or deliberately to trade one point for two, or indifferently, hoping for the best.

There was the crux: the game of basketball had no way of assuring teams of equal ability roughly equal opportunity to score. In baseball, each team had a stipulated number of innings in which to bat. In the tennis-family games, service alternated. In football, a team could keep possession only by earning ten yards every few tries, so that strong defense was rewarded by forcing the other team to give up the ball. In the hockey- and soccer-type games, with goals so few, there was a constantly fluid offense-defense situation that was inherently fair and equal. But not in basketball. Once the game broke a certain way, once a team had the lead in a game played by the clock, it became not only possible but just plain sensible to let time run out by withholding the ball from play, one way or another. It was the attempt of the trailing team to prevent this, and the counterattempt of the leading team to resume it, that promoted excessive fouling.

One radical idea was in the air, but less often discussed than most others: a time limit on one team's possession of the ball without attempting a shot.

On April 22, 1954, the N.B.A. owners met. The play-off fiasco had come to an end only ten days before. The Molinas case still sent shivers of apprehension through many minds. The financial problems in Milwaukee and Baltimore were acute. The television ratings—and income—had been unsatisfactory. And from all sides, criticism of the leagues games and "bush league qualities" was reaching new intensity.

At last, a radical solution found fertile soil. At last, the owners were ready to admit their difficulties weren't trivial. They decided to put petty pursuits of minor advantages aside and to really seek something better.

Danny Biasone, of Syracuse, got behind the time limit idea. He proposed a 24-second rule: each team would have to take a shot at the basket within 24 seconds of getting full possession of the ball.

That Biasone would suggest it was significant. This short, somewhat dour, rather unpolished man had come in through the National League merger. He wasn't given to making long speeches, but when he did speak, he said exactly what he meant, his Italian origins a trifle audible in his vowels—and then lived up to what he said.

He represented no major financial power. His city was not essential to the league. He was not one of the arena operator originals, with prior associations with Irish, Brown, Podoloff or Winter. He was not an independent millionaire like Zollner. In the acrimonious rivalries that marked those years, he had insisted on his right to sit on his team's bench, to root and to bait referees. When the Nats and Knicks had some of their bitter battles, he had been singled out by Irish—to the press—as the sort of "small town" owner that the league didn't need.

Underneath, however, those who came to know Biasone better found a man with intense loyalties and great common sense. In this crisis, his common sense and sincerity proved priceless.

Biasone had arrived at 24 seconds as the time limit by the simple method of dividing the number of shots taken in typical games into time played. Twenty-four seconds meant 120 shots a game—60 per team. In the season just completed, each team had averaged 75-80 shots per game. Obviously, the new rule would not be too restrictive. And 24 seconds was a long time. A team had to get the ball past the center line within 10 seconds anyhow; usually this took only two or three. And the average basketball play, with a couple of cuts off the pivot and other maneuvers, seldom took as long as 10 seconds to execute. Without a limit, the N.B.A. had averaged about one shot every 18 seconds. The new rule would be reasonable.

It was adopted.

But it wasn't enough by itself, they could see that.

A time limit, by itself, might encourage more fouling. If the offense had to shoot within 24 seconds, it might be a good idea to foul it first, and give up one point instead of two. Some way had to be found to nullify the strategic advantage of fouling.

The answer was: a limit on team fouls. Up to now, the only limitation in basketball had been applied to the individual player: six personals, and he was out of the game. Now the fouls would be charged against the team as well as against the man—and only six team fouls per quarter were to be permitted. After that, every additional foul committed would cost an extra free throw: if on an ordinary one-shot foul, an extra free throw for an extra point; if on what would be a two-shot foul (in the act of shooting, for instance), three chances to make two points.

In this way, an extra foul would be too great a price to pay deliberately. Once the quota of six was used up, a foul would mean a near certainty of two points (among the good pro foul shooters). Since one didn't *have* to foul to get possession—the 24-second rule took care of that—it was better to try to force a missed field goal than to give up two free throws.

This combination, the time limit on shooting and the team limit on fouls, saved the N.B.A.

Literally.

The game that resulted was so superior that, in retrospect, all concerned were soon willing to admit that without this change the league would have died. That the basic idea was sound was soon confirmed by the fact that international amateur rules (including the Olympics) were changed accordingly (to a 30-second shooting limit).

Two important refinements went along with the new rules. Since the whole purpose was to reduce or eliminate strategic fouling, offensive fouls could be punished differently. The team that already had the ball had nothing to gain from committing a foul; offensive fouls were always overzealous attempts to score. Therefore, the penalty was changed as follows: the individual player was still charged with a personal, towards his own limit of six, but the team was not; and the victimized team did not get a free throw, but only possession of the ball out of bounds. An offensive foul, made in an attempt to score, was thus more properly punished by the deprivation of a chance to score—and the long walks to the foul line at the other end of the floor, which used to be the annoying aftermath of offensive fouls, were eliminated.

The other refinement was the backcourt foul, meaning anything beyond the center line. This automatically called for two shots now—so there was no sense fouling a man before he got into scoring range, to save seconds in the closing moments.

In that one meeting, the N.B.A. owners accomplished more than they had in eight years, although the magnitude of their achievement was not seen at the time, even by them.

Over the summer, as special 24-second clocks were designed, built and tested, they looked ahead to the 1954–55 season with trepidation as deep as the unjustified optimism they had experienced the year before.

Various administrative changes had taken place. On the eve of the 1951–52 season, Kennedy had suddenly left Podoloff to go with the White Tower hamburger chain. His replacement, needed on short notice, came right out of the Globetrotter office that was sharing Podoloff's quarters—Haskell Cohen, a publicity man from Pittsburgh whose knowledge of basketball and its playing personnel exceeded Kennedy's and Podoloff's tenfold. As a publicity man for the league, Cohen was to have his difficulties—especially with Irish, and with the New York press; but as a knowledgable basketball figure behind the scenes, he proved invaluable to Podoloff, and, through the president, to the league.

From the beginning, there had been a permanent staff of referees, supplemented by others used more seldom. These had been put under the supervision of Pat Kennedy, the most flamboyant and most famous referee of his day, whose reputation had been made in the Garden college programs. Kennedy, himself, was a great referee, but was too individualistic to do much supervising. Now, in the summer of 1954, he was replaced in this capacity by Jocko Collins, a veteran basketball referee and Philadelphia Phillies baseball scout, with a self-effacing personality quite the opposite of his predecessor's.

Zollner had made the most startling move of all. After firing Paul Birch, who had coached his improving Pistons for three years, he hired Charley Eckman—one of the referees, with no major coaching experience. Everyone thought it was a joke, but Eckman was to have the last laugh.

Mikan, deciding to retire as a player, became general manager of the Lakers, as Winter stepped out. Leo Ferris, Kerner's partner originally, was now running Syracuse under Biasone. Bee in Baltimore, Gottlieb in Philadelphia and Harrison in Rochester were owner-coaches.

And a strange thing had happened to Ned Irish. The super-cold business man was carried away with his fan's interest in his Knicks.

He had been a fan from the start, but while the colleges were still the bigger operation, his emotional involvement with the pro team stayed somewhat under control. It was a precious hobby, but a hobby. Once the college situation collapsed, however, the Knicks became everything to him. They would be his vindication, in a business sense by prospering for the Garden, and competitively to prove his basketball acumen.

Unfortunately, Irish was walking into a trap on both counts. For all his business skills, he was simply unqualified to make athletic judgments. Unqualified, that is, by professional standards. Like any fan, he saw only the obvious, and was swayed by unreasoning likes and dislikes, and by reputations. When the team came so close but didn't win a championship, he could not restrain himself from second guessing Lapchick, and thus started to undermine his most valuable possession. In the meantime, those other owners and general managers who did have first-hand knowledge of the game on the floor—Gottlieb, Auerbach, Harrison—took advantage of Ned's high opinion of his own opinion. At the same time, on a strictly business level, Irish often generated opposition to his best proposals by his generally unyielding attitudes and personal aloofness—and thereby made himself less effective than he deserved to be. His impatience for big-league trappings and full acceptance for the N.B.A. provoked him into stiffening the opposition to his measures.

The 1954 draft had produced two big prizes. Baltimore, picking first, took Frank Selvy of Furman, the most fantastic scorer the world had seen to date, a six-foot-four marvel of versatility who had once scored 100 points in a single game. Milwaukee, choosing next, grabbed Bob Pettit, a six-foot-nine center from Louisiana State University. Philadelphia went third and took Gene Shue, a remarkably sound (and defensive minded) player from Maryland.

Since Dukes was still with the Globetrotters, and since Bee was in desperate need of money at Baltimore, Irish was able to buy Felix for the Knicks. But Syracuse picked up a center in the draft who was to mean much more—John Kerr, a skinny redhead from Illinois with a lively sense of humor and a tireless, observant, perceptive mind.

And finally, one more new dimension was coming into N.B.A. life at this time. More and more travel was being done by air. In the old pro leagues, including the National, many of the trips had been made by private car. Otherwise, almost all travel was by train, and neither pullman berths nor day coach seats had ever been designed for a six-foot-eight basketball player. Since the schedule called for one-night stands (unlike baseball, there were no three-or-four-game series in one town, and unlike football, it wasn't a once-a-week proposition), the travel was pretty wearing. Cities like Syracuse and Rochester, Fort Wayne and Minneapolis, did not offer too much choice in train schedules, and when it snowed (which was often), trains ran late more often than not. Syracuse to Philadelphia or Boston meant eight to ten hours, after either a mad dash or long wait to make connections. A trip to Milwaukee or Minneapolis for an Eastern team meant changing in Chicago, and vice versa. Even the New York to Boston run took five hours. A tremendous proportion of the time, therefore, was spent in transit, and in discomfort.

But by 1954, air service was expanding unbelievably, and apprehensions about flying were disappearing. Baseball teams were already using chartered flights occasionally. Commercial air service, to the Eastern cities, was shifting from the little, reliable-but-slow and bouncy DC-3s (which had been the primary means of transport during World War II in their khaki garb as C-47s), to the roomier, faster (250 miles an hour) Convairs. For longer jumps, four-engined DC-4s were starting to give way to Constellations and DC-6s, and for the flights to Minneapolis, Northwest Orient Airlines had those fascinating big-bellied Boeings with the lounge one flight of stairs below the main cabin.

Because winter weather was so unreliable, even air travel meant repeated delays, misdirections and other difficulties. To be sure of arrival in time to meet the demands of the crazy quilt schedule, it was still necessary to rely on trains most of the time. But even a few plane trips could help ease the fatigue.

The hotels used by most clubs, in most cities, were first-class. The arena facilities ranged from disgraceful (in Philadelphia, where bare rooms with a few folding chairs and no soap for the showers were the rule) to beautiful (in the new buildings). Radio broadcasts of the games, piped back from the road to the home city, were standard. All in all, the basics of big-league conditions were gradually becoming established.

That was the picture as the N.B.A., largely unaware of how completely new an era it was entering, went into the 1954–55 campaign.

10 STABILIZATION

On Saturday, October 30, 1954, the first day of the new season, Boston played at Rochester in a nationally televised game. Rochester won, 98-95. In New York, the Knicks defeated the Lakers, 94-83. Fort Wayne won at Milwaukee, 91-72. The high scores were an omen.

In preseason exhibitions, the 24-second rule had worked without a hitch. A 24-second violation came up once a game, if at all. And, more than anyone expected, the game could be played honestly right down to the last minute. A team with a six-point lead could afford to kill a couple of 24-second periods during the last two minutes, perhaps. But with a smaller lead, it couldn't, and with a larger lead it didn't have to. The offense went about its business—trying to score; the defense went about defending, with relatively few opportunities for fouling on purpose.

One thing, it had to be admitted, was gone along with the destructive tactics: a set, deliberate offense, of the sort the Lakers had used. If a team moved into position slowly, to set up someone like Mikan, there really wasn't enough time left to run a play or two. The new rules definitely favored a running club, and anybody who didn't have a good fast break had better think about getting one.

The Celtics had one. In their first home game (their third of the season), they defeated Syracuse 107-84. Forty-five more times that season they would go over the 100-point mark. For the season, the Celtics *averaged* 101.4 points scored—and 101.5 allowed.

But Syracuse could run more effectively, because Schayes, Rocha and Kerr got the ball off the defensive board more often than Macauley could, with only the high-jumping but relatively small (six-foot-five) Don Barksdale and the aging Jack Nichols to help.

And Fort Wayne could run, because Coach Eckman had no set plays to use even if he wanted to. Uninhibited, profane, with inexhaustible imagination and good humor, Charley kept his boys relaxed and ready to put out—and he had some boys who knew what to do. The Pistons had wound up with Zslofsky, Phillip and Brian, an all-star back court; plus Foust, Yardley and Mel Hutchins (a 1952 All-American from Brigham Young)—and Houbregs.

In mid-November, Bee gave up his struggle in Baltimore and turned the team over to Al Barthelme, his publicity man. After three more games, on November 27, the Bullets folded, their record 3-11, and their players were distributed among the remaining eight teams. That's how Houbregs got to Fort Wayne—but the big prize was Selvy, who went to Milwaukee to join Pettit.

No one would have wanted to bet on it at the time—but the Bullets turned out to be the last team ever to fail in the N.B.A.

The eight survivors, all fairly strong now, went on through a season in which the full possibilities of the 24-second rule were just being tentatively explored. Syracuse won handily in the East, by five games over the Knicks. The Pistons won in the West, by two games over the Lakers, who now had Lovellette instead of Mikan at center. The Royals, suddenly old, were caught at the wrong stage of their careers and couldn't cope with the running required by the new style. They won only 29 games and lost 43, and held off the Milwaukee Hawks by only three games to save third. The Warriors, with Arizin back to supplement Johnston, finished last in the East with a 33-39 record, four games better than Rochester's.

The balance of power was starting to shift, from West to East, and the play-offs confirmed the fact. For the first time since the merger, an eastern team won when Syracuse took a seven-game final from Fort Wayne. (The East also won the All-Star game, 100-91, held at the Garden again.)

The really significant items, though, were the nature of Syracuse's victory, and the league's statistics. In the early rounds of the play-offs, there had been three overtime games, and four other close ones. None were marred by game-end stall-and-foul tactics. In the final round, Syracuse won the first two by margins of two and three points. Fort Wayne (playing its home games in Indianapolis) took the next three, by seven, seven and three. Syracuse, back home, won the sixth game by five.

In the final game, the score seesawed throughout the last

quarter. There were 12 seconds to play when George King, another of those superlative backcourt men who seemed to blossom under Cervi, sank a free throw that gave Syracuse the victory, 92-91—and then stole the ball to preserve it.

A series between teams named "Syracuse" and "Fort Wayne" got little national attention, but the lesson wasn't lost on the basketball world. That a championship game, with so much at stake, could go down to the wire with nothing but straight basketball being played, was nothing short of a miracle. The new rules had triumphed beyond their sponsor's wildest dreams—and Biasone, the sponsor, had a title to enjoy besides.

Statistics told the rest of the story.

The average score, per team, had jumped to 93.1—an increase of 13.6. This wasn't as surprising as it seemed, since the 24-second rule effectively added to the amount of time played in which someone was actually making an effort to score. It insured 48 minutes of action and effort, instead of unofficial subtractions for rest or strategy accomplished by holding the ball out.

At the same time, despite the greater activity, the number of fouls committed dropped slightly.

Johnston, repeating as scoring champion, actually scored less, 22.7 per game. But right on his heels were Arizin, Cousy and Pettit, all scoring over 20, and Selvy with 19.0.

The first season under the 24-second rule had not yet revolutionized play—that would take about three years, while old habits were abandoned and new techniques explored. But it did, instantly, eliminate the bad taste that had been building up for so long. Finally, the emphasis had settled on where it always had to be if a league was to succeed—on the players and the games.

It was with a sense of fitting tribute, therefore, as well as mischievousness, that the Metropolitan Basketball Writers Assoccіation arranged a little surprise for Podoloff when he spoke at their annual dinner in Leone's restaurant. Right above the speakers' table on a balcony, where it would be visible to the whole audience but not to the speaker, they placed a 24-second clock. As Podoloff began to talk, the writers started the clock. The audience started to laugh, and Podoloff could hear a loud click every second, but couldn't see or imagine what was happening. At the 24-second mark, the buzzer went off, sounding astonishingly loud in the relatively confined space. In 24 seconds, of course, Podoloff had managed to utter approximately 18 words, with a total of at least 72 syllables.

It was a memorable joke, but even the owners (and Podoloff) who laughed at it so heartily refused the suggestion that the clock be instituted at all future league meetings.

Considerable excitement was building on the college front, too. The scandals, while all but killing big arena double-headers, quickly provided some unforeseen benefits. Once the shock wore off, the scandals were seen as simply too small a fraction of total basketball activity to spoil anything, and with the resulting decentralization of the big-time circuit, fan interest grew larger than ever and wider in scope. The tournaments were bigger, and Christmastime tourneys were proliferating, making more and more college stars better known. To top it off, the stars themselves were more remarkable in size and ability each year.

In the spring of 1955, the crop coming out of college was the most attractive so far.

Philadelphia, as a territorial choice, got Tom Gola of LaSalle, a six-foot-five, selfless playmaker, scorer and rebounder who was being hailed as the finest all-around player of the age.

The Lakers, also exercising territorial rights, took Dick Garmaker, a great shooter from Minnesota.

Kerner, who already had Pettit as a center, chose Dick Ricketts, a six-foot-seven corner man who had led Duquesne to an N.I.T. title. That allowed Rochester to take the man who proved to be the best and most admirable player of the group, Maurice Stokes, who had made people aware that there was such a school as St. Francis of Loretto, Pennsylvania. A well-muscled, strong and remarkably agile six-foot-seven, Stokes could rebound, score and defend with unsurpassable smoothness. Even the Knicks, picking sixth, were able to get as fine a player as Kenny Sears, a painfully thin six-foot-nine with a delicate shooting touch that men a foot shorter would envy. Sears was out of Santa Clara, where Feerick was now the coach.

The Knicks also acquired two other important players—Dukes, who finally abandoned the Globetrotters (but with two years of accumulated bad playing habits from their clowning routines), and Shue, purchased from Philadelphia during the previous season.

It was plain to see that each of the eight teams was stronger, and that the difference between the best and worst was the smallest it had ever been—the ideal situation from the league point of view. There were now two or three individuals on every team, sometimes more, that basketball fans would pay to see in action regardless of context. On the competitive level, major league quality had become so thoroughly established as to be taken for granted.

Financially, though, there were still difficulties. In midsummer, Kerner gave up the struggle in Milwaukee and moved his all but bankrupt franchise to St. Louis—a move that proved to be one of the most brilliant in the history of sports promotion. St. Louis had lost its baseball Browns (to Baltimore) only the year before, and the city's sports public was in exactly the opposite state from the euphoric Milwaukeeans. Their pride had been hurt at the blow to their "major league image," even though the Browns had been perennial tail-enders and the Cardinals were still there (and in a promising condition now that Gussie Busch had bought them).

In Rochester, the Harrisons were having a tough time. They never had had much capital, and their fine teams had not been able to earn large surplusses because of the tiny arena. Now a shiny new 10,000-seat War Memorial was ready in downtown Rochester, but it was too late. They wanted to move, but for the present they had to stay.

In St. Louis, Kerner had a 9,000-seat building—Kiel Auditorium—and the largest population in the Western Division to draw upon. This meant that seven of the eight buildings in the league had capacities of 9,000 or more—and Syracuse's 7,500 wasn't bad for a city its size. At last, the physical potential for economic health existed, if the promoters could sell enough tickets.

The 1955–56 playing season helped sell some. The competition was closer than ever and, thanks to the new rules, adequately limited to straight basketball instead of brawling.

Not that there wasn't still plenty of turmoil. The change in rules had not changed the characters or the tempers of the men involved. The referees were still subject to inexcusable abuse from coaches as well as from players and owners. Auerbach screamed systematically, believing that you had to intimidate to get an even break (and never really willing to settle for an even break, but seeking an advantage). Cervi was of the old school, and gave the impression that he might throw a punch. Gottlieb was, of course, a member of the Board of Governors, coaching. Lapchick's screams were more of anguish than rage, but he had just learned to abandon the habit of tossing coins on the floor (implying something or other about the referee's integrity). If one listened carefully to the low decibel remarks of Kundla, one might be shocked. Harrison had turned over the coaching of the Royals to Wanzer, who was still playing, and Bobby was rather well-behaved (since he had the psychic release of actual combat)—but Harrison retained his sideline yelling rights. Eckman could hardly pick on his former colleagues, the referees—but he was such a volatile cheer leader that it was hard to tell whether he was complaining, urging or raving. Only Kerner's coach, Red Holzman, was an essentially quiet man—and he, like Wanzer, had his owner to do the raving for him.

The referees, especially with the new rules, were becoming more and more oriented to the "no-harm-no-foul" philosophy, which seemed reasonable until one tried to define what constituted "harm." At any rate, the game remained as rough as ever, with two mitigating factors: the fouls now, by and large, were sincerely accidental, and the increase in running made man-to-man roughness less feasible (while, by the same token, making the game more taxing for each player).

The fans, encouraged by their teams, remained on the hysterical side, and feelings during traditional rivalries—New York-Boston, New York-Syracuse, Rochester-Syracuse, Fort Wayne-Minneapolis—continued to run high.

All in all, however, it was now possible to play in a fairly civilized manner, and the future began to look just a trifle brighter.

Philadelphia turned out to be the championship team. Gola didn't make the difference all by himself, but he was the key. With Johnston scoring from the pivot and Arizin from the corner, Joe Graboski and Walt Davis helping with the rebounding, Jack George playing backcourt with a year of experience under his belt, and Beck sharpshooting as a reserve, Gola provided the "cement" as the other starting guard. Too big to be handled by the opposing guards of his day, with quick hands that enabled him to steal the ball so often on defense, he was also a first-class feeder. Most of all, though, he provided extra rebounding strength from a backcourt position. In effect, the Warriors with Gola were a team using four "big men"—the front three and an oversized guard.

And so were Eckman's Pistons, who finished first in the West even though they finished only two games over .500 with a 37-35 record. Yardley provided the explosive jump-shot scoring from one corner, while Mel Hutchins (whose sister Kay had gained her own fame by winning the Miss America contest) took care of rebounding and scored a lot too. Foust was huge and experienced at center, while Houbregs could make hook shots from fantastic range. The young men in backcourt—Corky Devlin, Chuck Noble —were six-foot-four or more. When Eckman started using Hutchins in backcourt, with all the traditional backcourt duties in the hands of Phillip, he had four big men out there at once.

What's more, Eckman made the lesson flamboyantly clear in the all-star game, which was played in Rochester's new arena. Eckman was the West coach, Georne Senesky—to whom Gottlieb had turned over the bench coaching reins at Philadelphia—the East. The East was heavily favored, since now it had the preponderance of stars. But, in an example of how short-sighted the owners could be, they allowed a Philadelphia-Boston game, involving six of the ten East players, to take place the night before. These men were tired and disgruntled by the time they got to Rochester for the league's "showcase" game, and obviously not sharp. Nevertheless, the East led, 24-17 at the quarter, when Eckman turned loose his four big man offense, with Hutchins operating from backcourt with people like Pettit, Yardley, Foust, Lovellette and Mikkelsen up front. In the second and third quarters, the West outscored the East 67-40, and wound up with a 108-94 victory. Gola despite his size, was thought of as a backcourt man in style; Hutchins showed that a "forward" could be used there too.

Shortly after this game, which was played on January 24, 1956, Lapchick resigned as Knick coach, removing the most distinguished old-time basketball name from the league's roster. His friction with Irish had been growing for two years, and when a statement to the press by Irish amounted to a vote of no confidence, Joe left quietly and amicably. He helped break in, as his successor, Boryla, who had always been a personal favorite of Irish's. The Knicks finished with a 35-37 record, tied for third place with Syracuse, and lost the one-game play-off for third. Thus, for the first time, New York was out of the play-offs. It was to become a habit.

In Minneapolis, too, there were signs of deterioration. When the team lost 15 of its first 20 games, general manager Mikan decided to make a comeback as a player. "An overweight ghost," one newspaper story called him, to his chagrin; but although he could (and did) get himself back into physical condition, he simply wasn't equipped for the 24-second game. The widened foul lane he had been able to handle; the constant running he could not. He played in 37 games and averaged 10·5 points, but the best the team could do was win 33, lose 39, finishing under .500 for the first time in its history.

That record was good enough for a share of second place, however, and the fact that St. Louis tied the Lakers for it was a major accomplishment for the transplanted Hawks. Kerner had worked hard at selling season tickets, and his team had, in a sense, made good for its customers. Selvy had gone into the Army after a few games, but Pettit blossomed, under Coach Holzman, into the league scoring champion. He was now a forward much of the time, with Charlie Share playing center. Coleman and Jack McMahon had been obtained from Rochester, and Bob Harrison, who had helped the Lakers to championships, was also a hard-driving backcourt man. For spot duty in front court, Kerner also had a six-foot-seven, balding thirty-year-old Californian named Alex Hannum, who had put in five years with Syracuse and Rochester before coming to Milwaukee the last year the Hawks were there. His presence would prove important.

At Rochester, Stokes took over as if born to it, scoring 16.8 a game, placing second only to Pettit in rebounds, and leading the team in assists—from center! Twyman scored a lot at forward, but had defensive problems. Ricketts, obtained from the Hawks for Coleman, never made it big. Most of all, however, the backcourt was overmatched with a combination of kids and the rapidly aging Wanzer. The Royals finished last.

The play-offs were, fortunately in a sense, uneventful, or at least routine. The Hawks, in what was a major triumph for them, knocked off Minneapolis (116-115 in the third and deciding game at Minneapolis) and pushed Fort Wayne through a five-game maximum semifinal. Syracuse upset Boston in a bitter series, and also pushed Philadelphia to the limit before yielding the fifth game, 109-104, at Philadelphia.

But in the final round, the Warriors were really rolling. They lost only once (the second game, by one point, at Fort Wayne), and closed out the series, four games to one. Gola was spectacular, and Arizin averaged 28.9 points for the ten play-off games.

Thus the 1956 season ended on a note of consolidation, and there were new stars on the horizon. The success in St. Louis was a big step towards stability, an omen and a blueprint of future moves. The 1956–57 season would start with the same eight teams, in the same eight cities—something that had never happened before. One could dare to speak of the N.B.A. as "major league" without automatically drawing derision or the accusation of "narrow outlook," even if only a small portion of the sports public still accepted the designation unquestioningly.

The next year would change all that—and many other things—forever.

11 ENTER MR. RUSSELL

The fact that 1956 was an Olympic year, and that the games were to be held in Melbourne, Australia, had strange consequences for the N.B.A. Because Australia is in the Southern Hemisphere, where the seasons are reversed, the competition was scheduled for November, running into the first few days of December.

The N.B.A. season was to start on October 27.

What did one thing have to do with another?

William Felton Russell.

Bill Russell was a six-foot-nine, thoughtful, strong willed, thin, wiry Negro who had established himself as the most important college basketball player in the country. With him at center, the University of San Francisco had won fifty-five games in a row and two straight national championships. Because Russell's scoring statistics were relatively modest (more than thirty other college players averaged more points per game), there was a large class of doubters about Russell's real ability—a class composed of those who had never really watched him play. Even the statistics readers could have drawn the right conclusion from the fact that San Francisco led the country in defense in both seasons.

Professional scouts were not misled about Russell's ability. There were large questions, however, about his intentions. The Globetrotters were talking publicly about offering him $50,000 and more—but privately offering him what they had given Dukes. But even before the pro draft came up in April, two things had been established: Mr. Russell would come high, by the money standards of the day; and that whatever else he did, he would play on the United States Olympic basketball team first.

That meant he wouldn't be available for N.B.A. play until the season was two months old, whoever got him.

Three teams had particular interest in him: Rochester, which was entitled to first choice; Minneapolis, which was seeking a successor to Mikan; and Boston, which had Auerbach making the basketball decisions and Brown backing him up all the way. Always informed, tirelessly curious, a one-man scouting organization who did his most effective work by relying on the evaluations of people he had come to trust, Auerbach was only too aware of what Russell could represent: the man who could get the ball, the man Boston (and so many others) had sought so long who could turn the offensive talents already at hand into invincibility.

In Rochester, Harrison simply didn't have the money (around $25,000) that Russell demanded. Anyhow, Harrison did have Stokes already. He could pass up Russell and survive. When it came time to draft, the Royals took Sihugo Green of Duquesne, who had been such an effective backcourt partner of Ricketts.

Second choice belonged to Kerner in St. Louis. He, too, couldn't afford Russell, and he did have Pettit.

Boston's turn would be sixth.

So Auerbach called Kerner. Would he make a trade? Would he take Macauley, whose return to St. Louis would mean so much at the gate, in exchange for Russell?

It was a fateful call. Chances were that Kerner couldn't take Russell anyhow, for himself—and that Russell would not want to play in St. Louis, which was still not the most hospitable town in the world for a Negro in 1956. If Kerner passed him up, the Lakers, whose turn was next, could deal with Russell (who had already decided he didn't want to go there, but no one knew that). On the other hand, a chance to get Macauley was exactly what Kerner did need, promotionally and competitively. Not only would the sentimental fans of St. Louis respond to "Easy Ed's" popular presence, but a front line of Pettit, Macauley, Share and Coleman would be something to contend with.

Nor was Auerbach being magnanimous. He was going to lose Macauley anyhow. Ed had been ill, and was tired, and wasn't far from retirement. He didn't want to go back to work in Boston. In St. Louis, he would have a new lease on life—but in giving him up, Boston wasn't really giving up so much.

But Kerner, weighing all these factors, didn't jump at the offer. He insisted on getting more, correctly gauging Auerbach's eagerness for Russell. He demanded, and got, a throw-in—a six-foot-four rookie forward named Cliff Hagan, who had been All-

American at Kentucky on an undefeated team before going into the Army, which had just released him. Hagan's equally brilliant college teammate, Frank Ramsey, also belonged to the Celtics, and Auerbach had prided himself on drafting them ahead of time, knowing military service would intervene. Now he had to give Hagan (and Macauley) to get Russell.

Auerbach did.

But could he afford to make such a deal for a man who wouldn't even show up until the season was so far under way? In terms of the long run, Auerbach could; but even for the short run, he had little problem—because the Celtics also had a territorial choice coming, and in their territory was Tom Heinsohn, a six-foot-seven center from Holy Cross who was as exciting offensively as Russell was defensively.

In addition, Auerbach had picked up Risen the previous year, when Rochester got Stokes, and Arnie was still effective if not played too long at one stretch. Jack Nichols, who had done so well for Auerbach at Washington and Tri-Cities, had been a Celtic now for a couple of years. And to back up Cousy and Sharman, Auerbach had signed Andy Phillip, no less. Fort Wayne had decided Phillip was expendable when it acquired Gene Shue from the Knicks.

All this added up to a team of exceptional strength and versatility, and it started to prove itself right away. Heinsohn did heavy duty rebounding from the start, and at last Auerbach's favorite conceptions could be put into practice. After splitting the first six games, the Celtics ran off ten straight victories. By December 5—just as Russell was leaving Australia to go home to Oakland to get married—they had a 13-3 record and a five game lead in the standings.

Auerbach's ideas were simple, and in principle, not original. With the 24-second rule in effect, the old theory (expounded twenty years before) that the more shots, the more baskets, was truer than ever. The best way to get a lot of shots was to fast break. The two keys to a good fast break were possession (the rebound) and an expert quarterback who could receive the first pass out and direct the rest of the play. In Cousy, now a six-year veteran and generally accepted as the best passer-scorer-ball handler the game had, Auerbach had the perfect quarterback. In Sharman, as well as in Cousy, he had maximum capability in shot-making. As soon as Heinsohn got the ball, therefore, the sequence could start.

But Heinsohn, brilliant as he was, was neither big enough nor a high-enough leaper to assure board control for a 72-game season. After the winning streak, the Celtics started to level off. When Russell reported for action, finally, on December 22, Boston's record was 16-8. He played 21 minutes, got 16 rebounds, scored six points—but it took baskets by Sharman and Heinsohn in the last ten seconds to defeat St. Louis, 95-93.

Already, the Celtics were pulling in large crowds. Now, with Russell making his debut in one city after another, they drew full houses. Few of his debuts were spectacular because, remarkable as he was, he was very green compared to the experienced pros facing him, and he was not in top competitive shape, coming in so late. Nor had there been a chance to blend his play with that of his teammates in practice, since once the N.B.A. schedule started, opportunities for practice sessions were few.

What made Russell so great, however, began to show itself after a few weeks. He had fantastic timing, the knack of going up and getting the ball at the right instant. The combination of height, spring in his legs, lightning reflex and alert intelligence was unique. Besides getting the defensive rebound with such regularity, and firing the ball out to Cousy so productively; besides operating almost as neatly on offensive rebounds; besides his ability to guard the other centers in the league effectively; besides these things, Russell introduced a new and devastating dimension —the blocked shot.

His quick reactions, and his court sense, enabled him to block the shot of a man going in for a lay-up. He could bat it away before it actually approached the rim, but a little after it left the shooters hand. He didn't have to succeed in doing this very often to create a perpetual mental hazard for all shooters. After all, the whole idea of basketball, from Naismith on, had been to work the ball as close as possible to the basket. The domination of the big men had been based on the fact that they were closer to the basket to begin with. Now here came Russell, acting like a hockey goalie, and negating the basic thought: the shot that should be the clearest, the lay-up, was being stuffed down the shooter's throat.

This was not merely demoralizing to the shooter: it also set up the Boston fast break even better than an ordinary rebound, because when Russell blocked one, the rest of the opposing team was still on offense mentally, and moving towards the basket. At the same time, it freed Cousy and Sharman, who weren't the greatest defensive players in history anyhow, from absorption with defense. If they lost a man, they could turn to offense themselves immediately because Russell would be there to block the shot or grab the rebound.

After about a month, Russell had found himself. On January 13, Boston's record was 24-14, and its lead over Philadelphia three and a half games, over New York four. For six weeks, the Celtics had been playing .500 ball. Now they ripped off another winning streak, of eight games, and were never threatened again, partly because Ramsey finally arrived (from service) on January 4. They finished with 44-28, six games ahead of Syracuse, which closed with a rush to finish second.

Meanwhile, all sorts of things had been happening elsewhere. On November 26, Cervi resigned as coach of Syracuse and was succeeded by Paul Seymour, an equally aggressive back court man who was still active. It was under Seymour that Syracuse finished strong.

Just before the season had begun, the Knicks had traded Dukes to Minneapolis for Slater Martin. (Without the hot big man, the Lakers could spare their expert feeder). On December 10, the Knicks passed on Martin to St. Louis for Willie Naulls, a phenomenal shooter, six-foot-five from U.C.L.A. (The Knicks could have drafted Naulls on the first round, but didn't, and the Hawks took him on the second).

Just as Russell was the missing piece in the puzzle for Boston, Martin was for St. Louis. What he had done for Mikan all those years, Slater was now able to do for Pettit—even better, because this was now a running game and therefore more fluid for Martin's passing and driving.

Still, the Hawks didn't jell, and on January 7, Kerner dropped Holzman as coach. The team's record was 14-19, too disappointing in what Kerner had advertised as "the year." Actually, no better coach than Holzman was immediately at hand. So Kerner made Martin player-coach.

This lasted for just eight games (of which the Hawks won five). Then Dugie (as his teammates called him) asked out. Combative, fun-loving, intense, the thirty-one-year-old Martin wasn't ready for the responsibilities of coaching: he had too much to give as a player, and wanted to concentrate on that.

This was January 21. Experienced basketball coaches are not floating around loose on such a date. Kerner looked for another player-coach, and found him on his own bench: Hannum. Outspoken, forceful, full of theories and, more important, gifted with the indefinable quality of leadership, Alex was prepared for his opportunity. But he didn't produce any overnight miracles, either. Under him, for the rest of the regular season, the Hawks went 15-16, which wasn't so different from what they had done under Holzman.

But it was good enough. The whole Western Division finished under .500, while all the Eastern teams did better. The Knicks, with 36-36, finished last in the East and didn't make the play-offs. The Hawks, with 34-38, found themselves in a three-way tie for first place with Minneapolis and Fort Wayne.

The Hawks had won the season series from each of them, 8-4. Thus they were entitled to home court for the dissolution of the tie. They polished off Fort Wayne first, 115-103, and got by the Lakers, 114-111. After the Lakers took two straight from the Pistons in the first round of the playoffs proper, the Hawks beat the Lakers again, in three straight (although the third was double overtime).

And so Ben Kerner, the gypsy—"Benny the Boob" they had called him when he had decided to move to St. Louis, he liked to point out—Ben Kerner was in the final round of the play-offs, "the World Series of basketball," against a Boston team already being described as the "best ever assembled."

The Celtics had swept Syracuse in three games in the semifinals. They had won seven out of nine from St. Louis during the regular season. They had scored 100 or more points in 55 of their 75 games. Heinsohn had been named rookie of the year, but Russell, who had missed the first third of the season, was fully appreciated. Cousy was "the best small man in the history of the game" (although not everyone would call six-foot-one "small"). Sharman, who had set a record by sinking 52 consecutive free throws during the season, popped the ball into the basket like coins into a slot machine. Ramsey, six-foot-three and quick, could and did play any role on any sector of the floor. Phillip and Risen, league All-Stars only a couple of years before, were spot substitutes. Jim Loscutoff, a rookie, was a rugged rebounder and defender, and Lou Tsioropoulos—number-three man on the Ramsey-Hagan Kentucky team—a useful reserve.

Such a team had no reason to fear the Hawks; that is, the fans and experts saw no reason why the Celtics should fear the Hawks. (The players and coaches involved saw things more realistically.) When the four-out-of-seven series began at Boston on March 30, Boston was an overwhelming favorite.

There was nothing neat or dignified about the series that followed—and no championship series could have been better competitively.

The first game, in Boston, went into overtime—and into another overtime. With 30 seconds to go and the 24-second clock running out, Coleman heaved one at the basket and it went in. St. Louis won, 125-123. Pettit had scored 37 points, Sharman 36.

Boston breezed through the second game, 119-99, and the series shifted to St. Louis for the next two games.

St. Louis won again, 100-98, and could have taken a decisive lead in the series by winning the fourth game, too. But Cousy took command and Boston evened it at 2-2 with a 123-118 victory.

Then Boston took the fifth game, 124-109 in Boston, and it was obvious that the gallant Hawks had shot their bolt.

But they hadn't. Two days later, in St. Louis, Hagan scored in the final second and the Hawks had a 96-94 victory in what was truly a defensive battle.

So it all came down to one game, in Boston, on Saturday afternoon, April 13.

By now the N.B.A. had the attention of the sports public to an unprecedented (in the league's experience) degree. The tempo of the 24-second game, now established, was exciting—but the savage intensity of rebounding, when players like Pettit and Russell went up against each other, was also higher than ever. Auerbach and Kerner, exchanging insults, almost came to blows; but while both sides moaned about "officiating," the fact was that the referees were in command, doing unbelievably good work under the circumstances. McMahon and Martin, against Cousy and

Sharman, were displaying prodigies of defense. In short, to anyone who liked basketball, the show was terrific, and also spiced with controversy and heroes.

Most of all, though, it now said "St. Louis" and "Boston" on the shirts—names associated with "major league" since the 1880s, thanks to baseball. What was of local interest in Boston and St. Louis spread out to the rest of the country, through established wire service channels, more thoroughly than from Syracuse or Fort Wayne.

And April 13 was the Saturday before the opening of the baseball season. Those teams, and the writers and columnists who followed them, had come north. It was as if the entire sports public was suddenly poised and receptive. What about these St. Louis upstarts, with that tiny Slater Martin and that remarkable Pettit? Could they really beat the Boston team so overloaded with talent?

It was a perfect moment, in terms of public relations, for some spectacular happening—and it happened.

Six times, the Celtics took what seemed about to become a commanding lead. Certainly it was time for the Hawks to bow to the inevitable. But six times the Hawks rallied, and actually took the lead with a minute and a half to play. But, with 13 seconds to play, a free throw by Cousy gave Boston a 103-101 lead. Now, surely, that was it.

No it wasn't.

A few seconds later, Pettit sank two free throws, and the struggle for the championship went into overtime.

Again, in the closing seconds, the Hawks averted defeat when Coleman hit a jump shot. A second overtime period began with the score 113-113.

The see-saw continued. With a minute and a half to go, Boston led, 122-121. Med Park, a St. Louis substitute (and Pettit's roommate), tried to drive—and Russell blocked his shot. Ramsey put up a jump shot, and it was 124-121.

The remaining 72 seconds of play took about 10 minutes to complete. There were substitutions, interceptions, missed free throws. The Hawks closed to within 124-123. With only two seconds to play, Loscutoff sank a foul shot to make it 125-123.

But Hannum had some ammunition left, a play the Royals had used. Taking the ball out of bounds at one end of the court, he tried to hit the backboard at the other end, because the clock would not start to run until some player touched the ball in bounds. If the heave could hit its target, and if Pettit could get the rebound, there was time to tie it again.

Hannum threw. He hit. Pettit went up, and did get the rebound. He put the ball back up. It hit the rim and came off. The buzzer sounded.

The Celtics were champions. By the margin of the metal hoop, no more than five-eighths of an inch thick, a dynasty had been established.

It would be saved by that margin at least twice in the future.

12 THE DYNASTY BEGINS

The sensational Boston-St. Louis series of 1957 was another major milestone in the N.B.A.'s history. In the publicity that followed, and the verbal replaying of the games, important shifts in attitude took place. The innate attractions of championship competition at the highest level, in games that could be played "straight" down to the final seconds, were irresistable to sports fans. The league's status went up several steps overnight, and continued to grow. It had succeeded in exactly the area it had failed in for so long—the quality of the product.

For the first time, all the regulars of the championship team, and of the runner-up, had acquired distinct personality in the mind of the sports public at large. Cousy, Russell, Pettit, Sharman, Macauley, Martin and Heinsohn—these were no longer merely top basketball players, but sports figures. In the endless flow of wire-service feature, radio and television interview, magazine profile, they were interviewed, explained, displayed.

The struggle for existence had been won, and the deepest satisfaction belonged to Brown, who had launched the B.A.A. and who had maintained enough faith in his Celtics to invest every bit of his own money in them as the frustrating years piled up. He had almost gone broke. Now he had not only a money-maker, but a team worthy of the famous name he had given it. Within a short time, all connotation to the Original Celtics would be wiped out of the consciousness of sports fans, and this in itself was a symptom of how the modern pros had succeeded.

More changes were coming rapidly, but they were in a different context now. The atmosphere was one of growth and entrenchment, not desperation.

As the 1956–57 season was ending, Zollner announced that he was moving his team to Detroit. After it ended, the Harrisons made a deal to move from Rochester to Cincinnati. These, like St. Louis, were large cities whose major-league identity was almost a century old. Furthermore, the Pistons would play in the

Olympia, and the Royals in the 14,000-seat Cincinnati Gardens. Now six of the eight teams were in the big arena housing the B.A.A. had first envisaged—with the advantage, minimized then, of being in the hands of experienced and interested basketball owners.

In Minneapolis, the original owners sold the Lakers to Bob Short, a boyish-looking trucking firm executive who had boundless ambition and energy. Short promoted Kundla to general manager and made Mikan coach. Attendance in Minneapolis had started to shrink even while the Lakers were winning, perhaps out of boredom; but a losing Laker team, after what had been, held no appeal at all. Short was willing to try any sort of promotion to stir things up—and had a bigger idea at the back of his mind: California.

Philadelphia had suffered during 1956–57 because Gola had gone into the Army, but Gottlieb wasn't really worried. Gola would come back, as Arizin had. But even that was secondary. Philadelphia's Overbrook High School had produced a phenomenal athlete back in 1955. His name was Wilt Chamberlain, and he was seven feet tall by the time he graduated. A hundred colleges had sought him, and he had chosen Kansas—but Gottlieb had chosen him first. No college player could come into the N.B.A. until the class with which he entered college graduated, so Wilt would not be available, even theoretically, until the fall of 1959. But Gottlieb, back in 1955, had persuaded his colleagues to let him claim Chamberlain as a territorial choice for the 1959 draft then and there, while Wilt was still in high school. Chamberlain was as big, proportionately, as he was tall, weighing over 250 pounds. He was taller than Mikan, just as strong, and far superior as an all-around athlete, able to run the 220 in top college competition. His qualities were well known to the basketball set, because he played during the summers at Kutshers, in the Catskills, where many N.B.A. players and collegians mingled in summer basketball activity while working as bellhops and waiters. (His coach there was Auerbach, of all people, and they developed a mutual distaste for each other early).

In 1956–57, Chamberlain, at Kansas, had blotted out the memory of Lovellette and had incited the whole country to apprehension at his size. He was only a sophomore, and his team was beaten in the N.C.A.A. finals by Frank McGuire's North

Carolina team (in triple overtime), but pro fans were already muttering "Chamberlain will wreck the game; he'll be unstoppable some day."

So Gottlieb could draft Lenny Rosenbluth, a six-foot-five scorer from undefeated North Carolina, and wait patiently.

The most publicized of the college seniors in 1957 was "Hot Rod" Hundley of West Virginia. Cincinnati, with first choice, took him and traded him to Minneapolis for Lovellette. But none of the 1957 first-round draftees were to become stars in the N.B.A., except the last one: Sam Jones, taken by the Celtics.

The 1957–58 season, then, began with a feeling of unprecedented promise. Perhaps the best indication of the prosperous outlook was that the players, as employees, were restless. They wanted a pension plan, and other communal benefits, and were getting a runaround from Podoloff (who was not getting any authorization to spend money from his owners). There was talk of striking before the 1957 All-Star Game, which had been moved back to Boston again, but Podoloff's promises prevailed.

The Globetrotters were fading out of the picture, too. Almost all the top Negro players were now N.B.A. bound, and accepted by fans and players—although some owners still worried about keeping within a quota. The Negro player who was not quite star material was not likely to be hired unless he was decidedly better than his white counterpart for a reserve role. Nevertheless, the rapid integration of the N.B.A. was making the Globetrotters less important at the gate in the big arenas; so was overexposure of the Trotters, who had been on television and were making a movie; and so was the increasingly independent prosperity of the N.B.A. teams, who needed the Globies less as a tenant.

Travel, now, was more and more by air, and having Cincinnati and Detroit in the league certainly simplified matters in this respect. The TV program wasn't all Podoloff had hoped it would be, but it was still functioning and providing indispensable nationwide exposure.

All in all, it was possible for the owners, as well as the fans, to concentrate on their on-court activities, and this was a sign of health.

Both the Celtics and the Hawks, with substantially the same teams strengthened by a year's experience and togetherness, won their division titles handily. (Selvy, returning to the Hawks from service, simply couldn't crack the Martin-McMahon backcourt, whose function it was to feed the Pettit-Macauley-Hagan front court, which now averaged 60 points a game. Selvy's wanderings in the next few years underlined the drastic upgrading of N.B.A. playing standards).

Yardley, called "Bird" by his teammates for the way he "flew" while hanging at the top of his jump, emerged as scoring champion and broke Mikan's record for points scored. He finished the year with 2,001, publicized as "the first 2,000-point scorer in basketball history," but of course his average (27.8) did not match Mikan's best (28.4) because it was a 72-game schedule now. Still, the attention Yardley received added to the league's fund of hero images.

Scoring in general, of course, was going sky-high, as the implications of the 24-second rule took hold. (The implications were: practice your shooting, and get your shots off quickly, and that's what all the most talented players worked on). In 1956–57, the average score per team game had gone to 99.6. Now, in 1957–58, every team in the league averaged well over 100, offensively and defensively—and would from now on.

In the play-offs, Boston and St. Louis quickly reasserted their superiority. Each breezed through the semifinal by winning four out of five. This time, there was more anticipation of competition in their confrontation, but Boston was still heavily favored. It began almost as a replay of the previous year: the Hawks sneaked off with an opening game victory in Boston, 104-102, and then absorbed a solid beating in the second game, 136-112.

St. Louis won the third game, again, at home, 111-108—but something happened that was more important than the result. Russell injured his ankle.

Even without him, the Celtics were able to even the series, 109-98, and the Hawks were kicking themselves for letting their big opportunity slip away. Such self-criticism had its effect, because the Hawks did win the fifth game, at Boston, 102-100. Now they could win the championship at home without having to go back to Boston for a seventh game.

They did it. Russell tried to hobble around for a while, but it didn't matter. Without Russell, the Celtics had no way of contending with Pettit, who scored 50 points, including 19 of the last 21 scored by St. Louis as the teams battled through the fourth quarter. His final basket, a tip-in of a shot by Martin, established a three-point lead in the last few seconds, and a final goal by Sharman didn't matter. The final score was 110-109 and the Hawks were champions.

For Kerner, the sweetness of the victory was every bit as rich as it had been for Brown the year before. But it was also a lesson, by example. Kerner had gone from last place to championship in three years with a good deal of luck as far as the breaks of the game went; but as he went from near bankruptcy to affluence, luck had nothing to do with it. It was hard work, shrewdness, the nerve to take risks and the conscientiousness to deliver on promises. Kerner was flamboyant, noisy, liable to lose his temper, restless and at times crude—but he had the capacity to recognize and admit mistakes, to analyze problems, find imaginative solutions and grasp the true role of publicity in promotion. He was the one who showed how twenty-four-hour effort and a forward looking attitude could build a basketball team into a profitable organization. Irish, Brown, Zollner, Short and even Biasone all had other important business interests, however dedicated emotionally they were to their teams. For Kerner, Harrison and Gottlieb, basketball was it. Gottlieb, succeeding in his own way, never outgrew the strictly private "office in my hat" approach; no one could knock it, because he made it work in his case—but it was no guideline for anyone else. The Harrison brothers (Les the coach, Jack the office man) were shrewd in their way, but lacked Kerner's vision and were really the products and the prisoners of old-time pro ball. Only Kerner showed what could be done when a man with promotional talent devoted himself wholeheartedly to this business. In this aspect, he was the counterpart of baseball's Walter O'Malley.

From his fellow owners, Kerner elicited a human reaction: now that he had a champion, now that he was making money, his word carried much greater weight in the inner councils. What he had to suggest gradually drew more and more respect. In the early days of struggle, he and Podoloff had been natural allies. Now they could be more effective partners, with Kerner offering ideas and Podoloff delivering the votes.

In another way, too, Kerner's success had its effect. Whatever Irish had proposed, or had actually done in his own operation of the Knicks, others felt he had special advantages because of the Garden's vast resources. Thus, no matter how good or practical or even necessary a procedure Irish suggested, other owners could easily rationalize their own failure to follow suit. "It's fine for him," they'd say, "but I'm not a big organization like him." They could not say that about Kerner, however; he had started as far down as any of them, and now if he advocated a policy, it had to be considered. (Kerner was secretly proud of his role as an advisor to other owners, but their reactions weren't always ego-boosting. One time, Harrison, who was an inveterate advice seeker, called Kerner to get an opinion on a player. The phone was answered by Kerner's mother, a vigorous lady in her seventies, straight out of a Sam Levenson anecdote, who rooted cheerfully for her son's teams and was a well-known figure to everyone in the league. She called Ben to the phone, and Lester asked his question, and Ben gave his answer. It wasn't quite enough for Lester. "Ask your mother what she thinks," said Harrison.)

What Kerner came to stand for, within the league, was "big league image" as a goal. Irish had always fought for this, but lost; Brown had always been eager to go along with it; Gottlieb had felt it was overrated; Zollner always considered his team a very private proposition. The others had always been too busy fighting for survival and fighting each other to worry about such long range refinements. Now Kerner saw the importance of it, and helped shift the balance of power within the league towards this outlook.

Between outlook and accomplishment, however, was still a long journey.

External events, meanwhile, were changing the face of large portions of the league. A tragic illness struck Stokes during the play-offs: encephalitis put him into a coma, and complete paralysis resulted. It would be years before he could even talk. The personal tragedy was so deep that even the most callous basketball people—and there were some who could be pretty callous—never brought themselves to talk of "the loss to basketball," or to the Royals. Twyman, his young teammate, with a wife and baby of his own, began to devote himself to looking after Stokes, to raising money for his medical care, and so forth. Over the years, as the story of Twyman's friendship and Stokes' courageous battle against his infirmity became known, more people began to help, and eventually an annual benefit game for Stokes was established at Kutsher's. As a model of one human's feeling of responsibility for another, the Twyman-Stokes story deserves its own book.

At the same time, another star was on the way. His name was Elgin Baylor, and he had the can't-miss tag. The Lakers, who had finished last, offered him enough to turn pro immediately, although he did have another year of eligibility at Seattle (where, however, his entering class had graduated). Elgin was six-foot-five, strong, a great scorer and powerful rebounder. He had a slight twitch, a jerking head movement, that didn't bother him in the least, but gave him an added identifiable characteristic.

Baylor was the vanguard of a new generation of college stars. On the All-America team with him that year were Chamberlain and Bailey Howell of Mississippi State, juniors, and a sophomore at the University of Cincinnati named Oscar Robertson. Less prominent for the moment was another sophomore at West Virginia, where Freddie Schaus had gone to coach. That one's name was Jerry West. Such players, well identified as pro prospects from high school on, were now as often the subject of conversation in the N.B.A. world as the men already playing.

Going into the 1958–59 season, the biggest changes on the N.B.A. scene were in coaching.

Hannum, although he had won the championship, couldn't come to terms with Kerner for the new season. (Kerner's intense interest in every aspect of his club's operation often shaded into interfering with the coach, and Hannum—like Auerbach at Tri-Cities years before—was too strong-willed a man to take that.) So Kerner hired Andy Phillip—who set some sort of record for not being able to get along with his boss. During preseason training, Kerner was already sure he had the wrong man—not because Phillip couldn't handle the strictly basketball aspects of the job, which he could, but because Phillip could never be the type of promotion-oriented, personal-appearance, devoted, quotable coach Kerner felt he needed. By mid-November, after only ten games played, Kerner changed again—to Macauley, who was exactly what he wanted in every respect.

In Cincinnati, the Harrisons had sold the club to a local group in which Tom Grace was the activist. The new owners started the season with Wanzer, but dropped him after the team lost fifteen of its first eighteen games and made Tom Marshall, a young player, the coach. The Royals had hopelessly inadequate personnel; Stokes was, after all, irreplaceable, and Lovellette had been traded to St. Louis (in one of Kerner's coups). This was now strictly a holding operation until Oscar would arrive.

In Minneapolis, Mikan had lasted only half a season, and Kundla had taken over the team again.

In Detroit, Zollner had dropped Eckman early in the first season there, and had brought in Rocha.

In New York, Boryla showed his business acumen by persuading Irish that he, Boryla, could be an absentee general manager operating out of his home in Denver. He turned the coaching over to Fuzzy Levane, who had played with Rochester, coached at Tri-Cities, and had been serving as Boryla's assistant with the Knicks.

In Philadelphia, Gottlieb had hired Cervi, who had been out of basketball since leaving Syracuse, to replace Senesky.

That made Auerbach and Seymour (in Syracuse) the senior coaches in point of continuous service.

Once the season began, both Boston and St. Louis ran away with the division titles, Boston by twelve games (with a 52-20 record), St. Louis by sixteen (with 49-23 in the weaker division).

Late in the season, just before the preplay-off trading deadline went into effect, a deal was made that set the competitive pattern for the next few years. Syracuse acquired Yardley from Detroit (for Ed Conlin, a journeyman forward) and thus became immensely stronger. The net effect was to condemn the Knicks to the Eastern Division cellar for some time to come, since now Syracuse and Boston were out of their class and Philadelphia would be as soon as Chamberlain arrived.

Chamberlain, incidentally, had left Kansas at the end of his junior year, and spent 1958–59 touring the world with the Globetrotters. But there was no question about his joining the Warriors as soon as he was eligible; as competition for talent, the Globetrotters were no longer a factor.

Baylor, in his rookie season, exceeded expectations. He averaged 24.9 points a game (fourth in the league) and took down more rebounds than anyone but Russell and Pettit. The year before, the Lakers had been able to win only nineteen games. With Baylor, they won thirty-three, good enough for second place in the West. In the all-star game, which was played in Detroit, Baylor had shared Most Valuable Player honors with Pettit, as the West scored a 124-108 upset.

Then to top it off, he led the Lakers to a surprising victory in the semifinals of the play-offs, eliminating St. Louis and preventing another Boston-St. Louis final. Things seemed under control for the Hawks when they won two of the first three games, but the Lakers took the fourth in Minneapolis, the fifth in overtime at St. Louis, and the sixth by two points in Minneapolis.

This was an achievement for the Lakers, but a disappointment to the public. Another Boston-St. Louis final would have been dramatic and exciting, especially since Pettit had broken all scoring records by averaging 29.2 points a game. The television games had been shifted from Saturday afternoons to Sunday afternoons, and were pulling a bigger audience, so that the glamorous Celtics and powerful Hawks were thoroughly familiar to a coast-to-coast public. The TV program was getting about 15,000,000 viewers, the ratings said, and arena attendance had pushed past the 2,000,000 mark. This was no time for anticlimax, but that's what the Laker upset led to.

The Lakers, since Mikan's day, had been unable to cope with the Celtics at all. On February 27, in Boston, the Celtics had beaten them 173-139, the highest score anyone had ever heard of—so high that Podoloff carried on a discreet investigation to find out if there had been anything fishy about it. (There had not.) That was the seventeenth consecutive time the Celtics had beaten Minneapolis—and the Celtics made it eighteen before the regular season ended.

In the play-offs, Syracuse, with Yardley, had extended Boston the full seven games. But the Lakers would be no match for Russell, Cousy, Sharman, Heinsohn, Ramsey and the gradually improving Sam Jones. Everyone could see that.

Everyone was right, too, for a change. The Celtics swept the final in four straight, the first time that had ever happened.

In a way, however, the anticlimax had its value. It set up, by its very one-sidedness, the run of championships that was to enable Boston to bring permanent distinction to the league.

13 ENTER MR. CHAMBERLAIN

It was ironic. With the long-awaited arrival of Wilt Chamberlain—the Boston dynasty took its firmest root.

As the 1959–60 season neared, anticipation on the part of fans and owners reached new heights; a level enjoyed by baseball every spring but as unfamiliar as it was welcome to the N.B.A. The fans couldn't wait to see Chamberlain in action, to see more of Baylor, to see what would happen when Chamberlain and Russell went up against each other, to lavish more worship on Cousy and Pettit, to see what would happen to the Celtics now. The owners couldn't wait for a much simpler phenomenon: Wilt's ability to sell tickets. He would fill their arenas as never before, and would double their television potential. In anticipation of this attraction, N.B.C. had already expanded its coverage to include both Saturday and Sunday afternoons for the coming season.

The day of the supreme star had dawned. In Minneapolis, Kundla had gone back to college coaching and Short hired young, inexperienced John Castellani—who had been Baylor's coach at Seattle. It was a move that advertised Short's intention to simply keep Elgin happy (in a way that was, really, both an insult and an injustice to Baylor). But it made the point as to who was important.

Gottlieb, in Philadelphia, had found that everything didn't run so smoothly with a strong coach like Cervi (who might have become just a mite old-fashioned in his thinking, too). Besides, Gottlieb had another problem: Chamberlain was going to take Neil Johnston's job away, especially since injury had made Johnston miss two-thirds of the previous season, and Johnston had given Gottlieb so much. There was an easy solution: make Johnston coach. Gottlieb did.

Gottlieb also had strong ideas about what he wanted Chamberlain to do: score. This giant, who felt he had polished his dribbling and outside shooting during his Globetrotter tour, was to play every possible moment and to be fed by his teammates as much as possible (which, after all, had been the Philadelphia pattern going back to Fulks).

And to make sure everyone could take advantage of the new prosperity, the schedule was lengthened to seventy-five games, an increase of three.

This brought criticism, from players and journalists, but it was hard to avoid. Chamberlain was getting, it was reported, the unheard of salary of $65,000. Cousy, Russell, Baylor, Pettit, Sharman, Lovellette were all getting big money, although not that much. The earning power of the basketball star had been raised drastically, and the money had to come from somewhere. The longer schedules and the longer play-offs were inevitable.

It all worked like a dream—at first. Chamberlain did pull people in. He did break all scoring records. He did make Philadelphia a powerful team. Yet, something was wrong. At the moment of peak potential, something was starting to stagnate. Nobody would pay attention to it for a while, but it was there, and the measure was an indirect one: the 1959–60 season, the most successful professional basketball had ever enjoyed, wasn't as successful as it could or should have been—and it was hard to see why.

On the surface, though, there was only cause for self-congratulation. The Celtics and Hawks were better than ever, so the league had two strong champions and Chamberlain too. Boston now had K. C. Jones, Russell's friend and partner from the University of San Francisco and the Olympic team, along with Sam Jones as the second-string back court for Cousy and Sharman—a second string that would eventually be a devastating first string. Gene Conley, the six-foot-eight baseball pitcher, had come back to basketball to provide exuberant rebounding strength as relief for Russell or Heinsohn. And Loscutoff was still on hand, to provide more backboard muscle and some surprisingly accurate shooting when needed.

Such a team could handle Chamberlain or anyone else. It ran off a seventeen-game winning streak and went on to finish first by ten games, with a 59-16 record to Philadelphia's 49-26. Then they beat the Warriors (who had ousted Syracuse) in the play-offs, four games to two, and were ready to face the Hawks again.

For the Hawks, Pettit, Lovellette and Hagan had averaged 71.7 points per game. Johnny McCarthy was sharing the back court now with the aging Martin, and this was strictly a feed-the-bigmen type of operation. In the Western Division, the Hawks won the pennant by sixteen games, although their 46-29 record was three games worse than Philadelphia's, and only one better than Syracuse's.

The final wasn't as close as it looked. It did go seven games, but the Celtics were in command in the seventh, which ended 122-103. The Hawks had disrupted the home-victory pattern by winning game number two at Boston, but the Celtics had come right back to win number three in St. Louis and the home teams ran it out from there.

Nothing these teams could do that year, however, could really take the spotlight off Chamberlain.

He had averaged 37.6 points per game—*averaged* it. Seven times, he scored 50 or more in a single game. He took in more rebounds than Russell. He played 48 minutes of almost every game. He never fouled out. He dominated the boards, of course, and scored on tap-ins and "dunks"—but he also took a surprising number of fall-away jump shots, and made them. He was a poor foul shooter (like Russell), or his totals would have been even more incredible. And the only possible defense against him, of course, was to try to shove him away or block him out from under the basket.

That meant more roughness, more whistles, and—eventually—no more whistles but no less roughness. The tactical advantages of fouling had been banished forever by the 24-second rule, but the other old pro practice, roughness for the sake of deterrent and for getting away with it, was coming back again in a new cycle.

Chamberlain, as one can imagine, took quite a beating. He gave a lot, too, naturally; but it was not quite the same. Big as he was, anytime he cracked into somebody it was he, Chamberlain, sustaining his part of the collision. His opponents could come at him in relays, and did.

So Wilt climaxed his amazing rookie season by announcing his retirement.

He'd had enough, he said immediately after the last play-off game against Boston was finished. He'd broken the scoring records, he had proved himself. There was no reason to go on. He wanted to be a success in business, like any normal-sized man. He wanted to be appreciated for his brains, not for his genetic accident. The life of a basketball player was simply too unrewarding.

No one took Chamberlain's intention seriously—but it did have a public relations effect. There was nothing original in the cry. Every February, for several years now, Cousy had declared that "he'd had it." The travelling, the tension, the bruising play unchecked by tight refereeing, the overlong schedule—it was more than a man could stand. Until he signed his next lucrative contract, of course, and until a summer's rest revived his competitive juices.

And the travelling really was something. The practice of "farming out" games had grown. A team like the Lakers could take half a dozen or more of its home games to surrounding areas and do better. In the case of the Twin Cities, "surrounding area" meant places like Hibbing, Minnesota, Minot, South Dakota, LaCrosse, Wisconsin. Other teams had more fanciful ideas. Zollner spent part of each winter in Florida—so he had the Pistons play some games at Miami Beach. The 1956–57 schedule, for instance, had listed games in these places as well as Johnstown, Pennsylvania, Buffalo, New York, Louisville, Kentucky, Charlotte, North Carolina, Troy, New York and Moorhead, Minnesota. These were not, by air or rail, on what could be called main routes. Besides that, a schedule of one-night stands meant double travelling, no matter where the games were played. When a team got to the meat of the schedule, there was nothing unusual about having five games—which meant ten plane or train rides (or worse)—in six days.

Others made their complaints more privately, but plenty of newspapers stories appeared expressing dissatisfaction with the roughness and the routine. Now, if the top players in a sport were talking about quitting, even if they didn't go through with it, the impression made on the public was harmful. Baseball and football players complained from time to time, but never to the point of threatening to abandon their craft and their livelihood. There must be something awfully wrong with this pro basketball, many people felt, if these fellows want to quit.

Another cloud was the continuation of petty bickering. Auerbach had always been the number one target, and number one instigator, of trouble with referees. Whether he actually lost his temper, or practiced deliberate intimidation, or both, he was always stamping his feet, shouting at officials, being slapped with technicals, ejected from the games and assessed big fines (usually $200 or so) by Podoloff. On his behalf, the Boston press kept up a vicious drumfire of insult directed at Podoloff (some columnist there called him "Pumpernickel," which succeeded in having a derogatory sound although no one ever figured out the precise connotation).

It was bad enough, for the league's dignity and for Podoloff's power to influence, to have Irish sniping at him in New York and the press raving about him in Boston (thanks to Auerbach's leadership) when the Celtics were just another team. Now that the Celtics were on top, year after year, Auerbach's behavior and the reactions it elicited got much more attention. By any absolute standard, his behavior was mild compared to the earlier days—but the early days happened in relative privacy, with only dedicated fans aware of the sport at all. Now, precisely because it had won big league status, the N.B.A. was making itself look bad even though its manners had improved. And, it went without saying, if the championship coach acted this way, all others kept pace.

In this respect, television had not helped. Its cameras got close-up shots of the most violent, childish exchanges. A few of these were entertaining; after a while, a large number of them seemed disgusting, then boring. Even the television authorities, eventually, didn't like it.

The game-dominating abilities of Russell, Chamberlain and Pettit aggravated the complaints. Gottlieb had declared, after Russell's first few games, that the new center "was playing a one-man zone" and should be stopped. Objectively, Gottlieb was absolutely right: Russell was playing a zone defense, and so were most other teams essentially. But a rule against this type of zone (that is, defensive men simply switching when offensive players crossed, or the big men picking up drivers the little men lost) was as unenforceable as Prohibition, and it certainly didn't do any good for owners to complain, or to back up coaches who did. Once Gottlieb got Chamberlain, he never objected to it again; but until he did, the exchange of insults, charges and countercharges did more to demean the league in the eyes of its expanding public than to stir up excitement among the die-hard supporters of the teams involved.

Kerner, who was coming to understand intellectually the self-defeating nature of these tactics, still hadn't cured himself of acting the old way occasionally. ("Knocking the officiating, as we do," he once said in a moment of lucid self-examination, "is like having the most expensive restaurant in town, and standing out on the sidewalk in front of it yelling, 'My chef stinks!' " It would be some time yet before the league took this observation to heart.)

And something was going subtly wrong with the game itself. The scores were going too high. In 1959–60, while Chamberlain was setting his records, Twyman was averaging 31.6 for runner-up—a figure that would have been a record if not for Wilt. Twyman was not a basketball giant, just a six-foot-six cornerman who had learned to hit with phenomenal accuracy on jump shots. Baylor, in third place, averaged 29.6, also more than the old record. There were thirteen players in an eight-team league who averaged 20 or better, and the team average had soared to 115.3.

The reasons for this were not hard to find. The jump shot, in itself, was unstoppable if properly executed—and by now there was an entire generation of mature jump shooters, who had started to use the shot in childhood. Furthermore, the tactical possibilities of the 24-second rule had been thoroughly worked out (which meant, fast break as much as possible), and the individual players had accepted the implication mentioned before: work on your shooting. They did, and as their accuracy increased, so did the scores.

In short, a note of monotony had crept into the game, so recently saved from chaos by the 24-second rule. It was run and shoot, run and shoot, and not much the defense could do about it. When the Celtics did it, generating their "big innings," they were exciting and adding something new to the concept of the game. Their 17-3, 12-0, 24-6 bursts which would break open a game were not accidents. But when most other teams played, the game settled down to too much basket trading—not out of professional courtesy, as in the old days, but out of defensive helplessness. The "pretty plays" that made basketball so attractive to the older fans, the ball-handling and passing that Cousy epitomized and that Davies, Wanzer, Dick McGuire and Philip had done so well, was disappearing because it was becoming irrelevant. If a rebounder could clear the board and get the ball halfway to midcourt with one pass, and a jump shooter could hit more than half the time from 15 to 20 feet out, only one pass was really needed to connect the two.

All this was heightened by the fact that there were only eight teams, playing each other ten to thirteen times a year with fundamentally the same personnel from year to year. Players knew each other's moves inside out, and so did the more knowledgable fans. Therefore, it became hard to get worked up over anything that happened before the middle of the last quarter. Precisely because the 24-second rule made it impossible to sit on a lead—a highly desirable effect—it also made any large early lead meaningless, and therefore made only the closing portion of the game significant. By then, either one team was far ahead, in which case it wasn't exciting; or the score was close and the issue would be settled in the closing seconds, in which case what had gone before didn't matter.

These were the subsurface, almost subliminal flaws in the game that had grown up around the 24-second clock, and out of the compact league stocked with ever more brilliant stars. As problems, they did not compare to the bigger and tougher ones overcome during the past decade, but they did exist—as a sort of dead weight holding back the full progress of the league, although not as a threat to its fundamental health.

And they continued to exist through the next three years, while the entire nature of the N.B.A. underwent still another groundswell of change.

14 THE NEW STARS

At the end of Wilt Chamberlain's first year, contrary to some alarmist views, the N.B.A. had survived his coming. So had the championship status of the Celtics. But one city and three coaches had not survived.

Minneapolis, so dominant in the previous decade, was through. Short moved his Lakers to Los Angeles, in a two-fold response to changes on the baseball scene, as well as for maximum use of new opportunities of his own.

In 1958, the baseball Dodgers and Giants had left New York and had brought California into the major-league orbit. One consequence of the immediate success of the Dodgers in Los Angeles was that the city administration became very sports-minded, and constructed a modern, 14,000-seat indoor arena adjacent to the University of Southern California's Coliseum, where the Dodgers were playing. A couple of years later, expansion was becoming inevitable for baseball, especially since the American League wanted a piece of the California pie. Minneapolis, then represented in the minor-league American Association, had built a stadium that could be easily expanded to major-league proportions. In fact, before the Giants finally settled on San Francisco, they were ready to go to Minneapolis (which was their farm club). By 1960, it was clear that Minneapolis would have major league baseball before long. (The franchise was actually activated that fall.)

Short could see the general attractions of Southern California's population and growth. He had the new building in Los Angeles as a specific magnet. And he had the example of Kerner's experience in Milwaukee concerning the blotting-out effect on basketball of the first taste of major league baseball.

No further encouragement was needed. Short moved. Irish, not surprisingly, complained of the added expense of travel to the Pacific Coast, but, also not surprisingly, his objections got nowhere. Again, he was hoping that strapped financial circumstances might force Short to sell Baylor to the Knicks—the sort of thinking that renewed the lack of affection his fellow owners felt for him. In another year, they would have a chance to do him a favor, and would refuse. The basketball writers had written a parody on the song "7½ Cents" from the musical "Pajama Game," that went:

Seven votes to one vote,
Every time a ballot's cast
Seven votes to one vote,
That's the score today . . .

and it still applied to most motions brought by Irish.

But Short had even more going for him. He was getting second prize in the college draft, but it was a big prize. Oscar Robertson, of course, was Cincinnati's territorial choice. But the number two man was Jerry West, so highly regarded that there was actually some controversy over which of the two would be the better pro. Although the Knicks had finished last in the East and the Lakers had qualified for the play-offs by finishing third in the West, the Lakers record had been two games worse than New York's, so Short got West and Irish had to settle for the number three man, Darrall Imhoff of California.

Castellani, as Laker coach, had not been able to last even half a season, and Pollard had been brought in as his successor. In Minneapolis, Pollard had meant something, even if the team was losing. In Los Angeles, he would mean nothing at all. So Short hired Fred Schaus, who was West's coach at West Virginia, to take over the Lakers in their new setting. Superficially, this may have seemed like the Baylor-Castellani deal all over again, but it was nothing of the sort. Schaus, it turned out, was thoroughly qualified to be a first-class pro coach, having had extensive N.B.A. experience as a player and having mastered his craft thoroughly at West Virginia.

It was with a pretty shiny package, therefore, that Short set up shop as an absentee owner in Los Angeles: Baylor, the most exciting of the new stars in a way, because he was not so big as Chamberlain; West, the prize rookie; a new, personable coach; Rudy LaRusso, an Ivy Leaguer from Dartmouth, starting his second season as the other cornerman; and such backcourt crowd pleasers as Selvy, Hundley and Bob Leonard.

Castellani had been replaced on January 2. Two others didn't last even that long. In December, Carl Braun became player-coach of the Knicks, replacing Levane, and Dick McGuire, who was playing out his career with Detroit, succeeded Rocha as coach of the Pistons. Both went into 1960–61 as bench coaches.

And before the season could start, three other teams had new coaches too. Cincinnati, with the acquisition of Robertson, was suddenly a valuable property, and its owners had no intention of letting the inexperienced Marshall continue in charge. They settled upon Charley Wolf, a sincere, college-oriented, apparently shy but at times rigid young man who had been coaching at Villa Madonna, a small school in Covington, across the river from Cincinnati.

In St. Louis, Macauley had been coach for nearly two seasons, and had had all the travelling he wanted. Besides, that was about the length of time a coach could see eye to eye with Kerner. Out he went and in came Seymour, for whom frictions had developed at Syracuse even though the team was winning.

And who took charge at Syracuse? Alex Hannum. Since leaving the Hawks, he had coached the Wichita team in the industrial A.A.U. league, and pursued his business interests in California.

That made Johnston, starting his second season, the second oldest coach in the league in point of continuous service. The other, of course, was Auerbach.

To the fans, however, the wholesale reshuffling of generals meant little. Their interest was focused on the troops—and especially on Robertson, Oscar, the Big O.

The 1960 Olympics had been held in Rome, and the United states team there was unquestionably the most exciting ever to appear in international competition: Robertson, West, Jerry Lucas of Ohio State, Terry Dischinger of Purdue, Walt Bellamy of Indiana, Bob Boozer of Kansas State, Adrian Smith of Kentucky—all of whom would be outstanding N.B.A. players later. But Oscar was the one.

He had been marked for greatness from his high school days in Indianapolis. In college, he set scoring records by the bushel, but impressed people just as much with his ability to pass, dribble and rebound. He was six-foot-five, perfectly proportioned, strong, able to jump, both ghostlike and catlike in his movements. His shooting touch was feather-soft and totally reliable. He could move, some writers said, as if through the fourth dimension: now he was in front of his man, now past him putting the ball in the basket.

In college, his full prowess was not quite realized, because he so seldom faced anyone even remotely qualified to push him to his limits. Once he came into the pros, however, it took only a few weeks to show how superb he really was.

He was the complete player. As a passer, mechanically, he was Cousy's equal (but not yet conceptually, although he soon would be). As a shooter, he was unsurpassed by anyone. On defense, he could guard his man and steal the ball, intercept passes with uncanny instinct, rebound with bigger men. Offensively, it seemed he could score any time he really wanted to—on a jump shot, on a drive, going into the pivot.

In his rookie year, Robertson averaged 30.5 points a game. (Only Chamberlain, with 38.4 and Baylor, with 34.8, scored more.) He averaged 9.7 assists per game (leading the league). He made 47.2 per cent of his shots from the floor, and 82.2 per cent of his free throws. He averaged ten rebounds per game, more than any other backcourt man in the league, on a par with most forwards.

And with all that, some of his most valuable contributions came on defense—and he fouled out of only three games out of 71 played.

Consider the above statistics: this was a twenty-two-year-old, first-year pro. Every rebound collared was worth approximately one point, the way pro teams were shooting. Every assist was worth two points, since it meant a teammate had scored. Counting his own points scored, Oscar was contributing directly to 60 points *per game*. In addition, he was providing the intangibles—the soft feeding that made teammates able to score better, the confidence that he could get the clutch baskets and interceptions in the closing moments of a game, and the terrible mental problems he presented to the opposition, which couldn't help overloading its measures against him and leaving other Royals free.

In view of these things, it wasn't surprising that many began to refer to Oscar as the best basketball player the human race had yet produced. The argument: who would you rather have to start building a team, Wilt or Oscar, began to while away many an hour. (The answer, some insisted, was: Russell.)

West did not have as fine a rookie year. It took him more than half the season to overcome a feeling of awe among pros. He felt he should be passing off, was reluctant to shoot, and tense when he did. Once he relaxed, however, it all fell into place. No one could get a jump shot off faster, with greater accuracy. Speed was West's great asset, speed and that absolute concentration on the basket. By the end of the year, he was "Mr. Outside," the perfect complement to "Mr. Inside," Elgin Baylor.

If anyone could match Oscar on the versatility scale (which interested fans more than the special advantages Russell and Chamberlain and Pettit and even Schayes possessed because of height), it was Baylor. He couldn't shoot from quite as far out, but he was deadly from good range. He could hit the boards much better, but wasn't Oscar's equal in ball-handling, feeding or individual defense. Still, Elgin displayed "second effort," the tireless pursuit of the ball in any and all situations, better than anyone else. He held, without doubt, the record (never tallied) for sinking his own rebounds.

In any one game, Baylor had proved that he could be more explosive than anyone. 'Way back in 1949, Fulks had scored 63 points in one game (at Philadelphia against Indianapolis), a total inconceivable to those who didn't see the game, and only a few thousand people did. That remained the league record until November 8, 1959, when Baylor made 64 against Boston at Minneapolis.

Then, on November 15, 1960, at Madison Square Garden, where the publicity media could make the most of it, Baylor scored 71 points in a victory over the Knicks. Now everyone could see, or at least read, how such a thing was done. There was nothing extraordinary about any particular basket (Elgin made 28, and 15 free throws). It was just a matter of steadiness: Baylor kept doing, during every two-minute segment of the game, what any hot shooter does for only a few such segments.

Nevertheless, brilliant as these players were, and as devastating as Chamberlain was, the basic balance of team strength could not be upset. The Celtics were still the Celtics: Russell supreme off the boards, Cousy still himself, Heinsohn nicknamed "Ack-Ack" for the way he fired at the basket from all angles (a "gunner" who justified his "bad" shots by making them go in). If Sharman was slowing up, Sam Jones was taking up the slack, and a rookie from N.Y.U. named Tom (Satch) Sanders was breaking in slowly but usefully. Ramsey was the ultimate in utility men, Conley and Loscutoff the extra men who broke whatever back the opposition still had. These Celtics rolled on serenely, won 57 games in a scheduled increased to 79, and finished 11 games ahead of Philadelphia.

St. Louis was not yet challengeable either. Pettit, Hagan and Lovellette were still operating, and the backcourt had picked up a smooth-functioning rookie in Lenny Wilkens, from Providence. Coach Seymour believed in more running, and got it, and the Hawks posted more victories than ever before, 51. Los Angeles, in second place although seven games below .500, finished fifteen games behind.

Syracuse didn't have the physical resouces to cope with the top three teams over a full schedule, but in the play-offs Hannum's team knocked out Philadelphia. It couldn't give the Celtics much trouble, however, losing four out of five. The Hawks, on the other hand, had a terrible time handling Baylor and West in the semi-finals. The Lakers actually led, three games to two, before the Hawks pulled one out in overtime, 114-113, at Los Angeles, and won the deciding game at home, 105-103.

After that, they had nothing left for the Celtics, who polished them off in five games, the most one-sided final these teams had played.

The Celtics now had won three titles in a row, and four out of five. Their balance made them invulnerable to the individual exploits of star-dependent teams. And their composition had also helped wipe out the last vestige of a quota system for Negroes. Russell, the two Joneses and Sanders comprised half the regularly used champions. Baylor, Chamberlain and Robertson had shattered any lingering notions that Negro players might be "less appealing" at the gate—or that they could be persuaded to work for less money than they deserved. But they, with Russell, were the superstars. Below their level, less gifted Negro players were getting more of a chance, and an opportunity to develop towards stardom through experience: Wilkens, Hal Greer at Syracuse, Guy Rodgers and Al Attles at Philadelphia, Tom Hawkins at Los Angeles, Dick Barnett at Syracuse, Johnny Green in New York, Wayne Embry and Boozer in Cincinnati—these were men who, five years before, might not have been given the same opportunities.

As the 1961 season drew to a close, another fix scandal hit the colleges.

This time, the shock was not the same. The involvements were extensive enough, but did not include players as prominent as the 1951 group had been. These cases centered more on the men doing the fixing (Molinas among them) than on the players they reached. In one sense, the punishments were more stringent, in another the crimes less severe. Players who had been approached, and had rejected dishonest activity, but had failed to report the offers to authorities, were considered "involved," and therefore unacceptable to the N.B.A. Others, who had knowledge that teammates had been approached (or actually "doing business"), and had not reported it, were also barred.

In all these cases the league worked closely with whatever district attorneys were conducting the investigations. Sometimes, proof may have been insufficient for a court of law, but clear enough as to involvement.

The N.B.A. adopted a simple policy: any taint, however slight and indirect, was enough to keep the player out of the N.B.A.

From a legal, civil libertarian, humanitarian and even logical standpoint, this uncompromising position seemed harsh to some people. Undoubtedly, for some of the players (whose moral dilemma in choosing between betraying friends and keeping quiet when no actual crime had been committed, was far more complex, and painful, than their elders had ever faced) banishment from N.B.A. opportunities represented injustice or, at the least, disproportionate punishment.

But psychologically and practically, not to mention morally, the N.B.A. was dead right. Its position, in fact, was not merely correct but inescapable. The existence of the league, the money-making potential of all the honest players as well as of all the people connected with them, depended on the public's belief in the inviolable honesty of the pro game. The susceptibility of basketball to manipulation had been burned into everyone's consciousness; gambling did exist; rumors and suspicions, whether stemming from losing bettors or disinterested cynics, were inevitable from time to time even in the absence of objective evidence. In the final analysis, no one could ever prove conclusively that any given game *wasn't* being manipulated—the most that could ever be done about such a negative proposition was to show that there was nothing to indicate that it had been.

In such a climate, the attitude of bending over backwards, of being the purest of the pure, of being Caesar's wife above reproach, was the only possible one for an established league. It was the old principle of the proper context for rehabilitation. A man who had embezzled money, for instance, was entitled to a job and respectability after he had paid for his crime in some appropriate degree—but one didn't have to put him in charge of a bank vault. Those touched by the new scandals had shown themselves, if not susceptible to the idea of fixing games, at least confused about how to handle such overtures. Rejecting them could be termed overcautious—but extreme caution on this subject was elementary good sense, and responsible action.

This time, however, none of the players affected had college reputations that indicated instant stardom, as Sherman White and Bill Spivey had a decade before. Would the N.B.A. have been more lenient if someone of the caliber of Robertson were involved? It is fair to say, no; its forthright position would have been the same.

This was the situation, however, only in retrospect. At the time the new scandals were breaking, no one could know what might be the next name cited—and no one could be sure that the next day's news wouldn't touch directly on the pros themselves. The chill of fear, the nagging uncertainty, the vague distaste, were felt again; not as intensely as by the more naive (or wilfully blind) world of 1951, but nevertheless felt.

It also contributed to the mood of ill-defined malaise that was sapping, ever so gently, the league's vitality. In 1960–61, the Hawks led the league in home attendance, which was a triumph for Kerner but an indictment of the rest of the league. Why should St. Louis, however successful its team and attractive its promotions, be able to outdraw New York, or Boston with its string of championships, or Philadelphia with Chamberlain and three other first-magnitude home town heroes (Arizin, Gola and Guy Rodgers, the flashy playmaker who had come out of Temple a year before Chamberlain arrived)? Why should Cincinnati, even with Robertson tripling its attendance, still fail to sell out? Detroit, as a business, was being maintained only because Zollner was willing to keep putting money into it. Syracuse was dying, without the population, economic context or seating capacity to exist at the expense levels created by the new salaries and the new travel. Los Angeles, it's true did look promising, but why wouldn't it with so many assets?

But problems or no problems, the basic prosperity dictated expansion, and a ninth team was being added to the league for 1961–62. In stocking it, the Board of Governors was to give Irish a rebuff of major proportions.

15 THE THREAT OF STAGNATION

Chicago was the new team.

Geographically, it was a must. With a team in Los Angeles, another in St. Louis, others in Detroit and Cincinnati and three on the Eastern seaboard, all travel routes led through Chicago anyhow. In population and commerce, it was the third largest metropolis (after New York and Los Angeles). It made no sense for a major league not to have a Chicago franchise.

The problem was where to play, and the new owners settled on the Amphitheater, an attractive building in itself (seating 11,000) but unattractively located in the stockyard neighborhood. From the neighborhood, the new team took its name: the Packers.

Dave Trager was the head of the group of new owners, but associated with him was Max Winter, a member of the old in-group from Minneapolis. To activate the new franchise, and pay for the players that would be taken in a draft from the existing pro teams, the newcomers had to pay the league about $500,000.

It was taken for granted that the "expansion draft" would produce only a background fabric for the new team. None of the existing teams would make any first-line players available, naturally enough. If the new team was going to have a star, he would have to come from the college ranks.

Who was there?

The 1961 crop was nothing like 1960s. Lucas, Dischinger, Chet Walker of Bradley, Billy McGill of Utah, Wayne Hightower of Kansas, Dave DeBusschere of Detroit, Len Chappell of Wake Forest,—the big names in terms of pro potential—were all still juniors. Duke's Art Heyman was only a sophomore.

Of the seniors, one was in a class by himself as far as pro desirability went: Walt Bellamy of Indiana. He was six-foot-eleven, well filled out, and agile. He did not rate, off his college performance, with Baylor, Robertson, Chamberlain or Russell, either in personal statistics or effect on team victory—but he was the only one coming along who had the physical equipment to play men like Chamberlain and Russell on something approaching even terms.

The Knicks, in 1960–61, had finished last in the East again, for the sixth time in seven years—but now, for the first time, they also had clearly the worst won-lost record. After missing out on West and Baylor, they had achieved the right to pick first at last, and with no territorial draft complications.

They would, of course, take Bellamy, and it would put them back on their feet. It would enable them to offer at least respectable opposition in their division, which contained Russell, Chamberlain and the marvellously balanced Syracuse team, and enable them to begin the long process of building up towards a contending team again. Without someone of Bellamy's proportions, they were helpless, and no one exactly like him was on the horizon.

Clearly, it would be in the best interests of the league as a whole to have the New York situation improve. The Garden was still, for publicity purposes, the hub and the showcase. On the road, a New York team, because of its identity, could stir extra interest, and used to—but the satisfaction for home-town fans in "beating New York" evaporated when the Knicks became pitiful. They didn't have to be champions, but they had to be good enough to make beating them meaningful.

A closer race in the East, where Boston was not filling up its Garden despite its string of successes, would be of benefit to everyone, and above all to the television program, which had expanded to include both Saturdays and Sundays but had not increased its rating accordingly.

Besides, on grounds of plain decency and business morality, Irish deserved consideration. He had been in the league from the beginning; he and Walter Brown were the only ones who could say that as owners. His channeling of Madison Square Garden's money and effort had made possible the league's establishment in the early years. He had been thwarted in trying to purchase Macauley, who had been given to Brown because the Celtics were in trouble at that time. When Gottlieb had been in trouble, all sorts of special draft concessions were made to him—including the advance draft of Chamberlain. When Baltimore had folded, Kerner had been given Selvy. The principle that the team on the bottom deserved help, not out of charity but out of the proper collective self-interest of the entire group, had been affirmed again and again.

But not this time.

The other owners decided to give Bellamy to the new Chicago team. It would have first turn in the draft, and the Knicks would be second again.

It was, on the part of the other owners, a vindictive self-destructive, illogical move.

It was, on Irish's side, a measure of his failure as a businessman. That he could not persuade the others to go along with him in a case where right was so clearly on his side was his repayment for years of intransigence and unsympathetic "let them sink or swim" positions with respect to the have-nots. No matter how one looked at it, however, the function of a businessman was to negotiate whatever arrangements were best for his business, and Irish's inability to persuade his colleagues on this point represented a major professional failure.

So the Knicks had to settle for Tom Stith, a six-foot-five forward from St. Bonaventure who, under any circumstances, could never have provided the power at center the Knicks needed so desperately. As it turned out, tragedy struck Stith before he could play: he contracted tuberculosis. He recovered, and did play briefly the following season, but his career was effectively ended before it began.

Stith's coach at St. Bonaventure had been Eddie Donovan, who taught a type of scrambling defense that delighted Garden fans and enabled the Bonnies to excel in tournaments and to lead the country in team scoring (88.5 points per game, in the 40-minute college game with no 24-second rule). Now Irish fired Braun and hired Donovan as coach of the Knicks, the first since Lapchick with college coaching experience.

At the same time, Gottlieb reached even higher into the college coaching ranks for a new coach. He signed Frank McGuire, whose North Carolina team had beaten Chamberlain's Kansas team, and who had enjoyed success at St. John's before that, to take charge of Chamberlain and Co. He was the first non-pure-bred-pro coach the Warriors had ever had.

Chicago's coach was Pollard, who had done relatively well in his half-season with the Lakers before they departed from Minneapolis.

The other six teams started the way they had finished the previous year: Hannum in Syracuse, Seymour in St. Louis, Wolf in Cincinnati, Dick McGuire in Detroit, Schaus in Los Angeles and Auerbach in Boston.

But, suddenly, there were other coaching jobs available, too.

A new league had popped into existence.

It was the personal province of Abe Saperstein, who had made his fortune running the Globetrotters. Its formation reflected three things: the success of the N.B.A., the weakness of the N.B.A., and Saperstein's pique.

In recent years, relations between the Globetrotters and the big arenas had reached breaking point. Economically, the Trotters had ceased to be necessary for a more stabilized N.B.A., especially since few of the current N.B.A. owners actually shared in the profits of the buildings they used. The movement of virtually all new Negro stars into the league proper left the Globetrotters with nothing but comedy to promote, and the routine was wearing thin before N.B.A. audiences who had seen it so often (although it remained as popular as ever all over the rest of the world). There were also undercurrents of emotion connected with the Globetrotter operation that had grown out of step with the times. In one era, the all-Negro team clowning around against an all-white foil suited two sets of unexpressed feelings: Negroes could take pride in the team's competitive superiority (real or imagined) while whites were being presented with a comfortable stereotype of Negroes as comedians. By the 1960s, such internal images were irrelevant, not to say objectionable, to much of society. For excellence, the Negro, if interested, had the real thing—dominant players in top-level serious competition, and to many the Globetrotters now represented a sort of Uncle Tomism if they represented anything at all. (Domestically, that is; in their world tours, the Globetrotters could be accepted more directly as expert humorists and, according to competitive levels in other countries, brilliant players; the whole racial question had different connotations outside the United States proper.)

At any rate, Saperstein was angry at the N.B.A. owners, and specifically angry because he had been denied a Los Angeles franchise before Short moved the Lakers there. To get even, he was going to form his own league.

This decision reflected the success of the N.B.A., because only the visible prospering of the N.B.A. (and its promising future) would interest other businessmen into risking their money on a professional basketball league.

But it also reflected the N.B.A.'s stagnation, to a degree, because only men who felt the N.B.A. was leaving opportunity open would try to compete with it.

Therefore, for the 1961–62 season, Saperstein announced the formation of the American Basketball League. Its teams, and coaches, were:

Chicago Majors	ANDY PHILLIP
Hawaii Chiefs	RED ROCHA
Los Angeles Jets	BILL SHARMAN
Kansas City Steers	JACK MCMAHON
Pittsburgh Rens	NEIL JOHNSTON
San Francisco Saints	PHIL WOOLPERT
Washington Capitols	ELMER RIPLEY
Cleveland Pipers	JOHN MCLENDON

The first five were familiar as N.B.A. players. Woolpert had been Russell's coach at San Francisco. Ripley was well-travelled and a respected college coach, who had coached at Notre Dame, Yale, Columbia and Army. McLendon, a Negro and therefore a pioneer (no baseball or football team had yet seen fit to make a Negro head coach or manager) had been turning out outstanding teams and players at Tennessee State for several years.

A second league meant competition for players—the very thing the merger of 1949 had eliminated.

In 1961, though, it was an unequal battle. The N.B.A. had the history, the arenas, the television exposure, the stars making more than $50,000 a year, prestige, proven stability and, without dispute, the highest caliber of basketball ever played anywhere in the world. The established N.B.A. players were simply not interested in jumping; the college crop was simply not good enough to matter (although the new league did attract Bill Bridges of Kansas, who had been drafted by the St. Louis Hawks); the N.B.A. players who did switch—Ken Sears, Mike Farmer, Dick Barnett (who rejoined his old coach, McLendon), Jim Palmer—weren't too important.

In no way, then, did the new league constitute a threat to the N.B.A.; but it did produce two interesting ideas. On shots taken from more than 25 feet out, a basket was worth three points; and the free-throw lane was widened to 18 feet, to open up the middle still more. All the people with N.B.A. experience expressed satisfaction, subsequently, with the three-point basket, although the N.B.A. never tried it. But the wider foul lane (16 feet) was soon adopted by the N.B.A.

One other aspect of the American League decreased its impact on the N.B.A. The new league accepted the "questionable" players N.B.A. had barred: Spivey, Tony Jackson of St. John's, Connie Hawkins (who had been a freshman at Iowa). Spivey had never been convicted, although he had been accused of being part of a fix, which he staunchly denied; the others had not even been accused of throwing games, only of accepting favors from gamblers and not reporting contacts. Individually, they probably deserved their chance—but, collectively, they added to an atmosphere that made the new league a shade less easy to take seriously. That Saperstein was the Globetrotter man, whose team had always been engaged in prearranged entertainment, didn't help. No one accused, or even hinted, that the new league wasn't completely on the up-and-up in every respect. But there was just enough discomfort in such associations to make some fans cautious about giving full commitment to rooting interest. One could wait and see.

Saperstein had made himself commissioner of the new league, which was a public relations mistake, for the above reasons. Some of the clubs had common ownership, which always hurts the image of competition. The fact that the Globetrotters were used as a lure in double-headers only emphasized the fact that the American League game was the "other" part of the program.

So the league did not survive. It did play through one season, and then gave up halfway through the next, on New Year's Eve 1962. By that time, it was down to six teams: Kansas City, Pittsburgh, Oakland, Philadelphia, Chicago and Long Beach (in the Los Angeles district). Some of the players moved back into the N.B.A.—Barnett, Bridges, Farmer. In a court case, Syracuse won indemnity from Cleveland because Barnett had already signed a Syracuse contract when he jumped, but that didn't really touch upon the controversial reserve clause.

All in all, the effect of the American League on the N.B.A. ranged from miniscule to nil.

Meanwhile, the N.B.A. was having its own troubles.

The 1961–62 N.B.A. season had turned out to be strangely unsatisfying. The schedule now was 80 games, and with a ninth team added, the divisions were uneven again (with Chicago in the West).

Boston spread-eagled the field once more, with a 60-20 record.

Philadelphia, under McGuire, won forty-nine games but still finished ten games behind the Celtics.

Syracuse, with Schayes slowing up and Yardley gone for two years, displayed all the team-play virtues, but got nowhere in the powerhouse Eastern Division.

The Knicks, inadequate in every way, hustled. That's all that could be said for them.

But Bellamy didn't do Chicago that much good, either. He was rookie of the year, all right, and averaging 31.6 points a game finished second only to Chamberlain. Even so, the Packers could win only eighteen games while losing sixty-two—which was a commentary on Bellamy's supporting cast. He didn't draw many people, either, and the Chicago franchise was in trouble, so the decision to deprive the Knicks of Bellamy had helped no one.

In St. Louis, the situation had exploded early in the year. Seymour wanted a running club, Pettit and Lovellette or no Pettit and Lovellette. He and Kerner had a rousing argument, and with the season only fourteen games old, Seymour was gone. Kerner called back Fuzzy Levane, but the old Hawk pattern had been disrupted beyond repair—especially since Wilkens, the new key to the backcourt, was in the Army. The Hawks lost fifty-one games and failed to make the play-offs, although Pettit, with 31.1, scored more than he ever had.

But the end of St. Louis dominance did not provide the Western Division with a race. Los Angeles ran away with it, under remarkable circumstances. West and Baylor, together, proved to be the most explosive combination imaginable—and when Baylor had to go into the Army in mid-season, the Lakers kept right on winning with West producing prodigies of one-man offense. Baylor, able to play on weekends occasionally, took part in forty-eight games and averaged 38.2 a game; West, playing seventy-five of the eighty, averaged 30.8. The Lakers finished first, eleven games ahead of Cincinnati, for whom Robertson surpassed his first-year standards.

It was Chamberlain, though, who had made scoring so ridiculous that all interest in statistical achievement became impossible.

He scored 100 points in one game (against the Knicks at Hershey, Pennsylvania, on March 2, 1962). In others he scored 78, 73, 67 twice, 65 twice, 62 three times in an eight-day stretch.

He averaged 50.4 points a game. *Averaged* it.

Arizin, playing alongside, averaged 21.9—less than half as much.

From that season on, the sensational scoring total of any individual ceased to have the power to excite the public.

It may have been a coincidence, but season attendance actually went down a bit from the previous year, after several years of steady (and practically inevitable) increase. The level reached, including play-offs, was just about 2,000,000.

Then again, it may not have been a coincidence. The league's scoring average was up to 118.8 points per game per team, an all-time high, and more than 40 per cent of the shots being taken from the floor were going in. Scoring was too easy, too abundant, too uninteresting.

And then came, from Podoloff's viewpoint, the crowning blow: N.B.C. decided to drop the N.B.A., after eight years. There would be no national television in 1962–63. The growing monotony of the game, the absence of close pennant races, and the constant complaining to officials had killed the show.

And this had happened despite some spectacular play-off games (which, perhaps, served only to emphasize the contrast with regular-season games). This time, the Warriors did not permit Syracuse to sidetrack them, although it was a hard-fought, full-length five-game series. (Philadelphia took the first two, Syracuse the next two, and the Warriors the fifth game, 121-104.) The semifinal with Boston that followed was a clash of giants: the home team won each of the first six games. In the seventh, at Boston, a goal-tending call against Chamberlain in the closing seconds gave Boston the victory, 109-107. The Warriors were able to try a long pass towards the basket at the buzzer—much like the one Hannum had tried for the Hawks back in the double-overtime game in 1957—but it didn't work.

Now the Celtics had to face a fresher Laker team, which had breezed past Detroit in its semifinals. The first two games, at Boston, were split (the Lakers taking the second). The next two, at Los Angeles, were also split (Boston winning the second). Then the Lakers stunned everyone by winning the fifth game, at Boston 126-121; one more victory which could now be pursued at home, would give the Lakers the title. But the Celtics struck back as champions should, and won there, 119-105.

So it came down to a seventh game, in Boston. As the final seconds of regulation time ticked away, the score was tied. As the buzzer sounded, Frank Selvy got off a little jump shot, to the left of the basket, from no more than eight feet away. It hit the near rim, bounced across, hit the far rim, and fell off. Reprieved, the Celtics won in the overtime period, 110-107.

The Celtics had done it again—but by what a narrow margin! A goaltending call in one series, and then Selvy's shot. While that ball was bouncing, with time already run out, the matter had been entirely out of Boston's hands. If that shot had dropped in, their string of championships would have been over, then and there.

But it hadn't gone in. The Celtic streak was intact, and the details were quickly forgotten. Four straight championships. Not even Mikan's Lakers had done that, and a curious split developed in the mental image the Celtics had created. To most fans, and certainly to most of those whose main contact with the sport was through reading or television, the key man was Cousy, now idolized as the most distinguished name in basketball. His identifiability, and status as a universally admired star, were of the same sort (if not on the same scale) as Mickey Mantle in baseball, or Arnold Palmer in golf. People who didn't know or care much about basketball, knew that Cousy was a great player. That he was "small" and "smart" made him that much more appealing. But those who took the game more seriously (and, no doubt, more narrowly), and who saw more games, insisted that Russell was more important. Cousy had been there before Russell, and no championships had been won; whenever Russell had been physically able to play there had been no failure to win a championship.

The two theories would soon be tested.

As for Chamberlain, a still stranger reaction was crystalizing around him. For scoring 100 points in a game, and averaging 50, one would think a man could only be admired. After all, even if one wanted to sneer about the game itself, others were playing it and not scoring anything like that. At worst, one would suppose,

Chamberlain's achievements could be minimized or rationalized away, because of his size. But what they really generated was resentment and criticism—an irrational response that wasn't softened by Wilt's independent and at times arrogant behavior. Now he was castigated for "shooting too much," for "being selfish"—and, paradoxically, for "not making more use of his size by going to the basket instead of trying that fall-away shot." He was blamed for playing 48 minutes a game, and blamed for loafing while he did it. (If he was scoring too much, and still loafing, which result did his detractors want? More effort for more points?)

Some of this criticism, from rival players and coaches, had self-serving and insincere elements. Wilt was so tough a man to cope with, that it was worth trying to put him off psychologically. If he could be persuaded that the way he was playing wasn't worthy of respect, it might worry him a bit, or even con him into scoring less. By and large, though, Wilt handled himself well. By playing 48 minutes, and scoring as much as possible, he was doing exactly what his employer expected of him; and if he really had a better chance to score than his teammates on a team that had generally poor shooters except for Arizin, why shouldn't he do most of the shooting?

Beyond all that, however, there was a serious point to be made. The fact remained that Boston was winning the championships, and that other players respected Russell more than Chamberlain. There had to be a real reason.

There was. It was called defense.

Russell was the master of goal-guarding (in a figurative sense, since actual goal-tending was illegal). He had revolutionized basketball by his ability to block shots and to time his leaps to the defensive board. He had made possible the most devastating of all fast breaks by not merely getting rebounds, but by freeing his teammates for breaking down court at all times, secure in the knowledge that he could pick up any man who got by. Since his arrival, all big men—and some not so big, but with great spring in their legs, like Johnny Green—had become shot-blockers on occasion. Even the awkward Ray Felix (finishing his career with the Lakers) did it. Only Russell did it more often, more effectively. Against him, the driving lay-up was actually a bad shot. A pull-up jump-shot from ten feet had a better chance, although even for this shot, shooters had to alter the normal trajectory.

This, in turn, created mental hazards and mechanical inaccuracies for the shooters.

Chamberlain, concentrating on offense, could not and did not play this kind of defense. Russell, for his part, neglected offense, sometimes not even following his teammates down the floor. He could afford to, since all the other Celtics were terrific scorers.

But then, to Russell's individual skills—which were based on timing, study of opponents, and quick court sense—Auerbach added some concepts of team defense as a whole.

If Russell could be so effective a rear guard when drivers slipped by accidentally, why couldn't more accidents be risked? Auerbach developed, therefore, more and more pressing defenses. In Sam and K. C. Jones, he had two first-class backcourt men who had to share time as it was. Now the Celtics could put on a full-court press, picking up the other team for close guarding almost as soon as it put the ball into play. More and more steals, interceptions and forced errors—turnovers—could be obtained this way, and more fast breaks and easy baskets. The two traditional prices that pressing defenses always had to pay, fatigue and openings, were escaped by the Celtics. Depth of quality players took care of the fatigue, Russell plugged up the holes.

As always, in all sports, persistent winners set trends. As the Celtics piled up titles, rivals tried to use Celtic methods, and some significant changes in style started to come about. Emphasis on defense was always the cornerstone of basketball thinking for most coaches; now it became respectable, even glamorous, in the eyes of fans and players, because the Celtics were making the importance of defense more evident.

Thus, in 1962–63, league scoring went down, for the first time since the 24-second rule had been adopted. From a high of 118.8 per team the previous year, it dropped to 115.3, and the reason was more attention to more and more aggressive defense.

During the summer of 1962, two important losses occurred. Philadelphia lost the Warriors, and Cincinnati lost Lucas, the six-foot-eight All-American coming out of Ohio State.

Gottlieb, with the chance of a lifetime to make a large capital gains profit, sold the Warriors to a group in San Francisco headed by Matty Simmons and Tom Gray. The team would keep its name, Warriors, and Gottlieb would go along to run it for the first year. It would play in the Cow Palace (another 14,000-seat building), and have a natural rivalry with Los Angeles. Since Frank McGuire was unwilling to move that far from the Atlantic Seaboard (for family reasons), Gottlieb chose as coach a top-drawer basketball personality in the Bay area—Bob Feerick.

And Philadelphia, one of the charter members of the B.A.A. and a city with the richest pro basketball tradition of all, was simply out of the N.B.A., just like that.

To balance the divisions, Cincinnati now became an Eastern team. It had been waiting three years for Lucas, who would give the Royals, with Oscar, a one-two punch comparable to West and Baylor. But Saperstein's American League was still functioning, and a group in Cleveland was seeking a franchise in the N.B.A. Competition, for Lucas was keen, and he finally signed with the Cleveland group, which, it developed, had no team at all but did keep him from playing for Cincinnati.

In Chicago, the Packers had failed, and had their next move planned—but they had to stay in Chicago another year until a big new arena in Baltimore would be ready. The team changed its name to the Zephyrs, put Frank Lane (of baseball fame) in charge, moved to a smaller building (the Chicago Coliseum, seating 7,100), and named Jack McMahon coach.

Kerner, in St. Louis, also had a new coach (since Levane had been an acknowledged temporary appointment). The newcomer was Harry Gallatin, who had finished his N.B.A. career with 682 consecutive games played, and had then done an impressive college coaching job at Central Illinois. Harry was dedicated to conditioning, discipline and the controlled fast break when pattern play was not possible.

The other six teams kept their coaches for the 1962–63 season, and substantially the same teams, although the draft was more productive in some way. The Hawks got a new center in Zelmo Beaty, who was to become surprisingly good. Detroit took Dave DeBusschere, Syracuse took Len Chappell, San Francisco took Hightower, Chicago (picking first) took Billy McGill, and the Knicks—making a terrible mistake—took Paul Hogue.

But the Celtics, picking last, did best: they got John Havlicek, of Ohio State, who turned out to be a bigger Frank Ramsey, an all-court player of invaluable versatility. And Auerbach also picked up Lovellette, as relief man for Russell. The Celtics were stronger than ever.

As the 1962–63 season started, Cousy made it known that it would be his last. His visit to each city, therefore, became a farewell tour to rival Sarah Bernhardt's. Honors were heaped upon him, and gifts; there was a "night" for him in every arena; and he had earned it all.

It was a triumphal procession in every respect. The Celtics finished far ahead, again, in their realigned division. With 58-22, they beat Syracuse by ten games and Cincinnati by sixteen. In the play-offs, they were pushed to the seven-game limit by the Royals, who had eliminated Syracuse, on the strength of Robertson's prodigies. But the Celtics got by (142-131 in the last game) and went on to face the Lakers again. This time it took six games, with Cousy playing a key role in checking a Laker rally and turning the tide in the final minutes of the sixth game.

So now the Celtics had five straight titles (and six of the last seven). Only the 1949–53 Yankees in baseball and the Montreal Canadians in hockey had done that at major league levels. The N.B.A. finally had something unquestionably exceptional to talk about on the general sports scene. The Celtics were providing the sort of competitive respectability that builds major-league images.

And the N.B.A. had reached a point, once again, where its image needed all the polishing it could get.

16 ENTER MR. KENNEDY

Cousy's departure from the N.B.A. (to coaching at Boston College) coincided with an accelerating change in cast throughout the league.

Podoloff, now 73 years old, had finally reached the point of retirement.

Gottlieb was becoming less prominent in the San Francisco picture, as young Franklin Mieuli became chairman of the board and Feerick was made general manager.

Syracuse, the last small-city vestige of earlier days, finally gave up the ghost. The team was sold to a group headed by Irv Kosloff and Ike Richman, who moved the franchise to Philadelphia and named the team the 76ers. (Richman had been attorney for the Warriors when they were in Philadelphia, and was Chamberlain's personal lawyer; Kosloff was a paper manufacturer.) Biasone was still listed as a consultant, but he too was no longer in the foreground once Syracuse was out of the league.

The Chicago owners, having failed in their two-year experiment, moved the team to Baltimore, where the new building was ready, and made Paul Hoffman the general manager.

These changes made Kerner, Brown (with Auerbach more and more at his side since he had been made a vice-president as well as coach back in 1958), Irish and Short the effective powers in league affairs, with Gottlieb in the position of elder statesman and maker of the schedule patterns.

A successor to Podoloff was the first order of business, and the search was a short one. There was a man available who seemed ideally suited: Walter Kennedy, who had been the B.A.A.'s first publicity man.

Since leaving the N.B.A., Kennedy had travelled much further afield. He had gone into politics and had been the mayor of Stamford, Connecticut. He was totally at home in the world of television, advertising, promotional marketing and publicity. He had experience and skill in administration, negotiation and public relations. He even had a pretty fair grasp of basketball, for a layman. Considering the league's history, it was lucky to get a man with such qualifications.

But Podoloff's retirement was not without traces of bitterness. Through all the years of struggle, he had been vilified with gusto but seldom, in compensation, given any credit for his achievements. Acting as a lightning rod for any criticism anyone ever wanted to heap on the league, he was always to blame, while actually his biggest flaw was that the owners who hired him restricted his powers. (In this, he was more victim than culprit; of course, if he had been stronger and wiser, he might have found ways to assert his latent powers; and, if they had been more sensible and united, they would have given him coherent policies to carry out; but they, too, preferred too often baiting him to helping themselves.) Yet, as he stepped down, the league was seventeen years old and had just broken its season attendance record.

Loss of the television, however, had been a big thing—no overlooking that, especially since Podoloff had worried so about this very thing, and had scrambled around so much trying to maintain it. During the 1962–63 season, he had managed to put together a free-lance network to carry the All-Star Game from Los Angeles and the final of the play-offs, and it had worked well enough to insure a more extensive program of the same sort for 1963–64. But unless one of the Big Three networks was involved, exposure was too limited.

In one other area, Podoloff had left an unsolved problem. The players, who had been pressing for a pension plan for five years, still didn't have one, and in his dealings with the player representatives Podoloff had made predictable mistakes. His standard procedures—put off, delay, compromise, get everyone to give in a little, avoid commitment, keep talking, find technicalities—had real value when dealing with individualistic owners in league affairs. The owners, no matter how ornery in a particular instance, always had the underlying understanding that they were all in business together, and that whatever couldn't be settled at this meeting would be taken care of at the next, or the next, or the next. It might be annoying, but it was workable, because, as owners, they weren't going anywhere: they'd still be partners next year and the year after (or intended to be). To players, however, such tactics amounted to a runaround, which they recognized for what it was. They had no guarantee, as one owner did from another, that sooner or later their interests would be satisfied.

So the pension plan was unfinished business when Podoloff retired, and it was soon to cause Kennedy's first crisis.

As Kennedy took over, though, he found a going proposition, and for this Podoloff certainly deserved recognition.

The new Baltimore team, named the Bullets again, remained in the Western Division, because there were strong pressures keeping Cincinnati in the East. The Royals had finally landed Lucas, and felt capable of challenging the Celtics.

Coaches had played musical chairs. When Syracuse moved to Philadelphia, Hannum moved to San Francisco and Schayes, finished as a player except for emergencies, was made coach of the 76ers.

Wolf, dropped by Cincinnati, was hired by Detroit, which dropped Dick McGuire. The Cincinnati job went to Jack McMahon, who had been fired in mid-season in Chicago, where Bob Leonard replaced him. And Leonard was still the coach as the ex-Zephyrs began their career in Baltimore. Auerbach and Schaus were fixtures, of course, and Gallatin was back in St. Louis (having won coach-of-the-year honors for bringing the Hawks home in second place). Donovan still had the Knicks, since it was impossible to blame him for anything in view of the talent that had been given him.

The rules had been refined a little further in the 1962–63 season. Now a team was permitted only one team foul in the last two minutes of each period, even if its allotment for the whole quarter (which was cut to five) wasn't used up.

But the problem of officiating remained. The chief of officials was Sid Borgia, who had refereed from the very first season of the B.A.A. until now. He had succeeded Jocko Collins as chief in 1961–62, and he was unable to solve three basic difficulties. The first was that all referees, including the best, were paid on a per-game-and-expenses basis, instead of being full-time, fully-controllable employees of the league; therefore, not every referee could be sent anywhere at any time, in the best interests of the league. The second was that referees were fundamentally underpaid, and certainly under-respected, so that no substantial influx of younger men with talent was either encouraged or provided for. These two weaknesses, it goes without saying, were beyond Borgia's power to control. But the third was his own doing, because he was its chief advocate: the loosely called game. In his own refereeing, Borgia (who was an outstanding official, fearless, perceptive and decisive) believed in calling the "justice" of the play as he saw it, rather than the rules as written. ("You walked —you made him—Blue ball!" was one of his classic decisions when two players collided near midcourt.) Such an attitude promoted rough play, since it stressed to the utmost the "no harm, no foul" philosophy which quickly became, in the pro context, "no blood, no foul." Now Borgia, as an individual referee, had the judgment and knack to call this kind of game and still keep it within bounds, but most other men did not. As a supervisor, therefore, he was neither setting a good example nor providing proper supervision. On the other hand, while permitting rough play, Borgia's leadership did promote the trend towards lessening home-court advantage. Home teams, which won 75 per cent of the games in 1951 and 71 per cent as late as 1957, were now down to about 60 per cent.

The college draft, in the spring of 1963, was relatively unproductive again, not so much because there was any absence of quality among the college seniors, but because the gap between college and pro was constantly widening. By any standard, players like Robertson and Russell and Chamberlain could be expected to come along only rarely. But once they did, they remained on the pro scene for many years, and improved still further. For outstanding players below this superman level, the process was even more true: a player of a certain ability turned pro, grew, developed, became tougher and was still at a physical peak five years later at the age of twenty-seven. A player who came out of college two years later, even with the same original ability, could never beat the first man out for a job. By now, the N.B.A. was saturated with still young experienced pros, and many a college star who would have made the league a few years before hardly got a chance now. (Slater Martin, for instance, would never even be drafted high under present conditions.) This was, in some cases, unfair and harmful to the league, since it stacked the deck against those who might develop, more slowly, into real stars if given the chance.

Because of this, pressure for expansion (which really came

from the hope of cashing in on the league's assets in new areas) had an underpinning of validity. In this sport, at least, there could be as many stars as there was room to develop them.

The Knicks, choosing first, took Art Heyman, a unanimous All-American but a back courtman. They passed up Nate Thurmond, a six-foot-eleven center from Bowling Green who had little offense to recommend him, but defensive potential along the lines of Russell.

In the case of the Knicks, this was the same old mistake: choosing reputation and immediate publicity value over on-court reality. The Chicago team, knowing it was moving to Baltimore, chose Rod Thorn of West Virginia, hailed there as the third wizard in the Hundley-West lineage.

But San Francisco, choosing third, didn't let Thurmond get away—even though Chamberlain's presence would relegate Thurmond to relief duty or an unfamiliar position in the corner. Hannum and Gottlieb had too much basketball experience to miss the significance of such a property. Detroit then took Eddie Miles of Seattle, who turned out to be an outstanding shooter, and Chicago-Baltimore got its real prize on the second round, Gus Johnson of Idaho, a six-foot-six cornerman of exceptional strength.

Chamberlain's scoring in 1962–63 had "dropped" to 44.8 points a game, while criticism of his "selfishness" increased. The plain fact was, however, that Wilt was making 52.8 per cent of his shots while all his teammates put together were making 40.8 per cent. On a poor shooting team, other things being equal, it was only sensible for him to be doing most of the shooting.

But Hannum, taking over, had some ideas about not accepting "other things being equal" as an inevitability. Wilt had to be his principal scorer—but if shooting accuracy was the team's weakness, the porportions could be shifted in favor of defense by playing the most deliberate game possible under the 24-second rule. In this case—with Wilt and Thurmond to sweep the boards—the fewer shots taken in a game, the better for the Warriors.

Chamberlain, as always, did what his boss primarily wanted him to do. He started to work harder at the defensive end, at the sacrifice of some offensive power—although still did most of his team's reduced amount of shooting. With Tom Meschery back from service (he had been a fine rookie in 1961–62), Rodgers and Attles buzzing around in backcourt, and Hightower working well from the corner, Hannum put together a team that startled everyone by winning the Western Division title by posting the best defensive record in the league.

For most of the sports world, however, what happened in San Francisco was of secondary interest. The real question was: would the Celtics keep rolling without Cousy? Had it been his quarterbacking, or Russell's dominance, that accounted for the string of championships?

Russell answered the question rather decisively. The Celtics did win again, although the Robertson-Lucas combination at Cincinnati gave them a good chase, winning fifty-five games and finishing only four behind Boston. For the third straight season, Russell was named player of the year. The Joneses, in back court, were not as fancy as the Cousy-Sharman combination had been, but faster and stronger Sam could score even faster than Sharman had, and K.C. was the defensive whirlwind that could make the press so devastating a weapon. Heinsohn, Havlicek, Ramsey, Sanders—and Willie Naulls, the annual outstanding "pick-up"—meant imposing depth and versatility. The Celtics were still the Celtics.

In the play-offs, the Celtics were at their peak. They brushed aside Cincinnati, four games to one, and San Francisco by the same margin. The final series was really no contest, but it did contain a hint of future developments. Chamberlain, man to man, had become too much for Russell to handle. Russell didn't have to, of course, but that was the point: if you took both Russell and Chamberlain away, the remainder of the Celtics would have been even more superior to the remainder of the Warriors. It made one wonder what would happen if the two giants had approximately equal supporting casts.

By the play-offs, however, Commissioner Walter Kennedy was about five years older than he had been in September, thanks to the night of January 14, 1964, in Boston.

That was the night of the All-Star Game, back in its first home and built up as something special. Since only the free-lance network was carrying N.B.A. games that year, a wider hook-up for the All-Star game became the key to landing a major network contract for the future. This was to be the showcase—and some showcase it was, too, with West, Baylor and Chamberlain on one team and Russell, Robertson and Lucas on the other. An "old-timers game" of former stars was arranged as a preliminary, and the Original Celtics were brought together for the first time in years for a pregame ceremony. It was to be pro basketball's most glamorous, and most widely displayed, hour.

A couple of hours before game time, the all-star players threatened to strike.

For five years, they had been put off, one way or another, on their pension requests (and, equally important, on full recognition of their right to bargain). Time and again, Podoloff had promised them that owners would "do something," but nothing had happened.

Now they had an ultimatum: a pension agreement, on the spot, or no game.

No game meant no television, at the last moment. No game meant a blow to pro basketball's prestige that might never be overcome. If the television people couldn't be guaranteed a production, if the public couldn't rely on their sports entertainers staying in their appointed niche—seventeen years of growth might be undone.

That, at least, was the dramatic confrontation as it looked then. All the owners were supposed to be on hand; Kennedy could communicate with them. But they wouldn't, and he couldn't make them, give in "at the point of a gun." The players, on the other hand, obviously had no intention of being put off with another delay: this was their one opportunity to exert muscle in a labor-management negotiation, and they wouldn't have another.

All this was happening during a blizzard that had delayed the arrival of many people in Boston, and had added to an atmosphere of incipient hysteria. Actually, not all the owners were present, although the players thought they were.

At 8:30 P.M., half an hour before game time, with the old-timers on the floor and pregame ceremonies in progress, with newspapermen running around trying to find out what was really happening, and with television officials breeding new ulcers, Kennedy met with the players of both teams in the dressing room.

In essence, he staked everything on his personal persuasiveness and integrity. He didn't say it in so many words, but he made it clear that he wasn't going to follow the Podoloff route. He would guarantee them only his own maximum efforts to make the owners come through. They had to believe in his sincerity, as a person.

Really, they had no choice. Their accumulated grievance against Podoloff couldn't really be transferred to this man, whom they were confronting for the first time. They had to give him a chance to make good, at least once—and they had, after all, forced a promise.

At 8:55 the teams came out on the court. The game was played, and the East won, 111-107.

Disaster had been averted, but not all harm had been escaped. The game seemed perfunctory, and all the stories for weeks afterward concerned labor troubles, not basketball. Once again the N.B.A. had shown a remarkable capacity for fouling its own nest, for spoiling its best moments, for wasting its best opportunities. Short-sightedness by the owners had permitted an obviously bad situation to deteriorate to breaking point.

Perhaps, this time, they learned a lesson. At any rate, when the season was over, Kennedy made good, and a modest pension plan was signed and put into effect.

During the 1964 season, as Chamberlain won the scoring title again at 36.9—a drop of almost 14 points from his level of two years before—there were discernible changes in pattern. Defense, in response to the long-range example of the Celtics and the recent one of the Warriors, was capturing the attention of the fans and writers, as well as of players and coaches. It was not only effective, but fashionable. And it had a strange effect: it speeded up the game.

The defense being used now, as perfected by Boston, involved constant harassment of the man with the ball. The pressing principle, made safe with a Russell or Chamberlain planted under the defensive board, was to force bad passes, keep shooters off balance, and not give the offense any opportunity to make the play the way it would like.

On the surface, this made games "sloppier"—more fumbles, interceptions, wild passes—and many observers condemned this. More realistically, however, what was happening was an increase in tempo: everything was happening faster, under more pressure, and the more frequent errors were the result of the necessity to try to make plays against these hazards. The careful pass, deliberate movement, simply wouldn't work any more, so the more dangerous plays had to be attempted.

It could be summed up this way: the idea became, "attack the ball," wherever it is, in the shooter's hand or being dribbled or passed, rather than "guard the man." Going after the ball, traditionally, was considered bad technique, an invitation to be passed by. But giant goal-tenders and more aggressive guards had reversed that value—in the context of the 24-second clock.

More and more, defenses concentrated on the side of the court the ball went to, switching men and helping out. At bottom, this was zone defense—but extremely active zone defense, without the drawbacks that had prompted outlawing it in the first place. For that matter, forbidding zone defense was an anachronism; once the 24-second rule came in, there was no longer any need to ban it, since it couldn't slow up the game anyhow. Even though a new rule had been put in that forbade the defensive man, as well as the offense, to be stationary for more than three seconds in the free throw lane, it was not observed in practice, any more than the zone defense prohibition—or the ban on the spitball in baseball.

The new tempo was crowd-pleasing. In 1963–64, attendance went up more than twenty per cent, to about 2,500,000, a new high. For 1964–65, Kennedy succeeded in getting a television contract, a three-year deal for $650,000 a year for Sunday afternoon telecasts on A.B.C. This was raised, within a couple of years, to about $1,000,000 a year.

All the coaches who started the 1963–64 season finished it, and all but Leonard were still in place to open the 1964–65 campaign—a miracle of stability. The new Baltimore coach was Buddy Jeannette, who linked up with the city's old basketball tradition, since he had been player-coach of the 1948 Bullets who had won the B.A.A. championship in their first year.

Kennedy, unlike Podoloff, was low-key in personality and so direct a speaker as to be totally uninteresting (though sound). His posit on was strengthened, as the owners replaced his original three-year contract with a five-year pact. Going into the 1964–65 season, his regime was projecting an air of calm, middle-class (and perhaps middle-age) respectability for what would certainly be the league's most prosperous season.

17 • EXIT MR. AUERBACH

On September 7, 1964, Walter Brown died.

The originator, most loyal believer, most human personality and most experienced hand, was gone. He had fallen to the bottom, and had then enjoyed six straight championships. His passing symbolized the disappearance of the old guard.

Pieri and Brown's heirs took over, putting all active direction in Auerbach's hands, but soon they had to sell. A group headed by Marvin Kratter, a New York real estate man, and Jack Waldron bought the club for about $3,000,000 after the 1965 season.

By that time, however, an even bigger purchase had taken place. Short had sold the Lakers, in the spring of 1965, to Jack Kent Cooke, a Canadian industrialist with a wide variety of business interests. (He had tried to start a Toronto team in the projected Continental League which had forced baseball to expand, and he was soon to buy a team in the expanding National Hockey League.) The price for the Lakers was $5,000,000.

When Gottlieb had sold the Philadelphia Warriors to San Francisco, the price had been $850,000. Thus, from the Warriors to the Lakers, the worth of an N.B.A. franchise had quintupled in less than three years.

Even Irish was playing a less prominent role. Madison Square Garden had begun planning a new building, to be constructed over Penn Station on 33d Street. The Corporation itself had expanded, diversified, become more aggressive. Irish had taken on more and more generalized responsibilities, and had less time for strictly Knick business. Halfway through the 1964–65 season, he promoted Donovan to general manager and hired Gallatin as coach.

Gallatin had been fired by Kerner only a few weeks before that, having set a record by coaching the Hawks for two and a half years. Holzman had coached longer for Kerner, but fewer games. Taking his place was Richie Guerin, who had spent most of his career playing for the Knicks and had been traded to St. Louis early in the 1963–64 season. Guerin would be player-coach.

In San Francisco, Mieuli had taken full command, although Feerick was still general manager. Gottlieb was now listed as "Eastern Representative."

Richman was now the active head of the Philadelphia 76ers. Trager, Hoffman and Jeannette were running Baltimore, but getting ready to sell.

Only Irish, Kerner and Zollner, therefore, remained from the "old days," and only Kerner was going full blast in league affairs. Zollner took part in various committees, but he wasn't promotion minded and basketball was a small part of his responsibilities. Subjects like television, expansion and systematic promotion were Kerner's province.

None of the 1964 college seniors promised to be as exciting as the younger stars already playing in the N.B.A. During preseason exhibition games, Chamberlain had been ill (with pancreatitis). Baylor was having trouble with his knees. Robertson and Lucas had failed to upset Boston, which had proved it could win without Cousy. Baltimore had been successful at the gate and its expansion team, in its third year, moved out of the cellar with a respectable nucleus in Bellamy, Dischinger, Johnson and Thorn. The Knicks were still hopeless.

In other words, looking ahead to the 1964–65 season, there was little reason for eagerness. The N.B.A. was established, stolid, staid; it was a welcome change in a way—but dull, and the pendulum was swinging again towards college interest. There were some spectacular newcomers on the college scene—Bill Bradley of Princeton, Cazzie Russell of Michigan, Jimmy Walker of Providence, and a whole fast-breaking U.C.L.A. team. In general, there seemed to be a shortage of big men and a wealth of small-forward or big-guard in-between men of great all-around ability. But at least one new giant was on the way, a seven-foot one-inch high school boy in New York named Lew Alcindor, for whom one hundred colleges were bidding.

And the 1964–65 season started as quietly as one would expect. The Celtics got off by winning their first 11 games—so that was that. The Lakers were themselves again, apparently, and won 15 of their first 21. Chamberlain was obviously not himself (although his detractors scoffed at the idea of his illness) and the Warriors immediately fell out of any sort of contention, by losing 16 of their first 21. Philadelphia, with Schayes finished and Kerr old, was just another team. Cincinnati simply couldn't match Boston's pace. As for St. Louis, anything that happened was saddened by the knowledge that Pettit was playing his final year. (Early in the season, he scored his 20,000th point, the first player to reach such a milestone.)

The All-Star Game, on January 13, 1965, was held in St. Louis. It had a hectic ending because the East, with a 16-point lead going into the last quarter, saw it melt to one before coming out with a 124-123 victory.

What was really hectic, however, was the two-hour period immediately after the game.

Chamberlain was traded.

Back to Philadelphia.

For Paul Neumann, a back court reserve; Connie Dierking, a journeyman center; Lee Shaffer, a forward who was holding out—and $150,000.

In that moment, the competitive balance of the league, and its power to stir the public's imagination, were drastically altered.

Chamberlain and Russell were back in the same division. But this time, Chamberlain was going to a team that had a history of the closest possible type of teamwork, a team whose hallmark had been balanced scoring, aggressive defense, a running game. It had shooters and passers. It had always lacked size. Now it had Chamberlain. The possibilities were intriguing.

And this was the division that had Cincinnati. All of a sudden, anticipatory excitement—the sort sports live by—was alive again. And Chamberlain's departure from the Western Division opened up the competition there.

Was it a senseless deal for San Francisco? No. In that city, the public had never taken to Wilt. The acquisition of Thurmond had made possible the replacement of Wilt defensively. Dropping his high salary, and using Philadelphia's money, the Warriors might rebuild a weak franchise, which had not drawn well even when Chamberlain had led it to a divisional title.

Most of all, in the large view, it was the most important trade in pro basketball history, a news event that transcended narrow N.B.A. affairs in its impact.

The shift of Chamberlain was too late to have much effect on the pennant races. Boston and Los Angeles were too firmly established, and anyhow, it would take Chamberlain and his new teammates some time to get accustomed to one another. All thoughts leaped ahead, immediately, to the play-offs. It no longer mattered what the standings would be at the end: the 76ers would have their chance, and by then Chamberlain would be integrated into their patterns. The champion Celtics might be knocked off, after all, and this was something worth waiting to see—whether the attempt succeeded or not.

The anticipations were correct. It was something to see.

Boston wound up with a 62-18 record, its best ever. Cincinnati had 48-32. Philadelphia, 22-23 when Chamberlain joined it, finished at 40-40. Now the 76ers had to get past Cincinnati, and they did: the first two games were squeakers, won by the visiting team, but then Philadelphia won two in a row to end it.

The Chamberlain-Russell confrontation was on.

For support, Chamberlain had Hal Greer and Larry Costello in back court, an expert pair: Greer was the scorer, Costello was the feeder (and the last two-handed set shooter in the league, now thirty-four years old and underrated most of his career). Flanking him were Chet Walker and Lucious Jackson, a veteran and a rookie, both powerful, both fine shooters. Kerr and Dave Gambee were the important reserves.

Boston, of course, had its usual alignment: lots of everything.

Boston drew first blood, at Boston. The 76ers also won at home. Boston took the third game handily, 112-94, and it began to seem that the threat wasn't so great after all.

In the fourth game, at Philadelphia, the Celtics had a two-point lead with one second to play. But the 76ers had the ball out of bounds. They threw in to Greer, who made a long jump shot that sent the game into overtime—and in the extra period, the 76ers won it, 134-131.

Back in Boston, the Celtics took the fifth game, but back in Philadelphia the 76ers won the sixth.

Now it was down to a seventh game, just as it had been three years before for a totally different Philadelphia team but for the same center, Mr. Chamberlain.

The seventh game was a bitter battle. Twice, Boston seemed to have complete control. Its lead was six points into the closing moments. But Chamberlain, as the fourth quarter wore on, took more and more of the game into his own hands, and finally brought the 76ers to within a point on a driving three-pointer.

With the score 110-109, Boston's favor, the 76ers tried to work the ball to Chamberlain for a shot—but lost it. Now it was Boston's ball, out of bounds, with two seconds to play. Russell had it beyond the end line. All he had to do was throw it in and the Celtics would kill the two seconds.

Russell held the ball over his head, threw it—and it hit the guide wire connecting the edge of the backboard to a support in the stands.

Philadelphia's ball.

Time out.

Bedlam.

The 76ers set up their play. Most likely, they would try to give Chamberlain the last shot, but Greer was also a possibility. At any rate, Greer took it out of bounds, to start the play. He threw in to Walker, who would return it to Greer or to Chamberlain.

But just before Walker could catch the ball, Havlicek raced, leaped, and deflected the pass-in away from him. Sam Jones grabbed the ball, the buzzer went, the game was over and Philadelphia had never managed to take the last shot.

Again, the Celtics had survived. For the second time in three years, they had reached a point where survival was out of their own hands. If Selvy's shot had dropped in, in that final game in 1962, they would have been beaten; and while Greer held the ball out of bounds, they were at the mercy of an accurate shot by any 76er who took one.

By such margins the Celtic streak continued. The Lakers, in the final, were not fit to compete with Boston. Baylor was out of action, needing knee surgery. West was fantastic—he averaged 40 points a game for the play-offs that year, a record—but he was alone. Boston wrapped it up in five games.

Seven straight titles. Would they ever stop?

Soon.

The near miss in the semifinals revived the interest of the more fickle portion of the sports public. As always, nothing succeeds like a spectacular game with a championship at stake; that's the foundation on which all the promotional and business decisions must rest.

Looking back, the owners—most of them newcomers, now—and Kennedy had reason to be content with the 1964–65 season. Attendance had passed the 2,750,000 mark.

The Celtics, the Lakers and 76ers seemed firmly established as strong teams with strong followings, and the Royals were still only one player shy (to add to Robertson and Lucas) of equality with the best.

Baltimore had improved steadily, had finished third and had knocked off St. Louis in the play-offs before being eliminated by Los Angeles in six games.

San Francisco had hit bottom, Detroit was going nowhere. In St. Louis, an era was ending with Pettit's retirement, which also took some of the heart out of Kerner, since their personal bond had been strong. And the Knicks, as helpless as ever, were showing just the tiniest little glimmer of hope.

The draft rule that had victimized them in the past had been changed in 1961. Since then, the two last-place finishers, regardless of won-lost record, were entitled to first pick in the draft, the order between the two to be determined by flip of coin.

Now, in the spring of 1965, an additional concession was being made for the tailenders. The last-place teams were given, for one year only, two choices each before the rest of the league would draft. The Knicks, winning the toss, were entitled to pick numbers one and four. The San Francisco Warriors would get numbers two and three.

In the 1964 draft, the Knicks had done well: Willis Reed, chosen on the second round, had been rookie of the year, a six-foot-nine center who could shoot; three other players were good enough to be regulars.

But this time, the Knicks faced one of those dilemmas so often reserved for them in the past. They had first choice, and there was no question who the best college player was: Bill Bradley of Princeton. He was six-foot-five, a phenomenal shooter with "all the moves" and leadership qualities that made pro scouts drool. He had the temperament and the intelligence—and that was the trouble: he was also a Rhodes Scholar, and was going to Oxford for two years.

If the Knicks passed him up, and he changed his mind—or even if he only came back to play pro ball two years later—they could never justify it to their remaining fans. They had to pick him, knowing he wouldn't be available, for at least two years.

So San Francisco, picking second, chose Rick Barry, a six-foot-seven sharpshooter from the University of Miami, who was to be nothing less than the man to dethrone Wilt Chamberlain as scoring champion.

At that time, Barry's reputation was not so high. His college statistics had been amazing, but he was "too skinny" for the pros, many scouts felt.

They were wrong.

Meanwhile, the coaching sweepstakes were on again. Early in the 1964–65 season, Detroit dropped Wolf and made DeBusschere —only twenty-four years old and the team's best player—playing coach. He stayed on, giving up his baseball pitching career to do so. Jeannette, his appetite for coaching whetted, moved into the front office (under new ownership) at the end of the season and hired Paul Seymour for 1965–66. (The new Baltimore owners were people from Washington: Abe Pollin, Earl Foreman and Arnie Heft, who had been an N.B.A. referee for many years. Eckman, who was from the Baltimore area and had dabbled in local politics, now emerged as a broadcaster for the Bullets. Evidently, refereeing prepared a man for all sorts of basketball chores, from coaching to owning.)

Gallatin was starting again in New York, and Guerin was to coach and play again for St. Louis. Schayes, Schaus, McMahon seemed secure, and so did Hannum in San Francisco.

And Auerbach, starting his twentieth year as an N.B.A. coach —a veritable Connie Mack among basketball coaches—announced that this would be his last year. Once more around, and he would become a front-office executive exclusively.

There was one overriding question in peoples' minds—fans' and professionals'—as the 1965–66 season opened: what would the 76ers do with Chamberlain on hand for a full season, and with the first stages of accommodation worked out the previous year?

They'd soon see.

Early in the season, the Knicks made an important trade: they acquired Bellamy from Baltimore (for Barnes, Johnny Green and Johnny Egan, a flashy backcourt man). At long last, they had the kind of center who could compete with Chamberlain and Russell, although not match them. This meant a problem for

Reed, who had to switch to forward, but it formed a basis, at least, for future improvement.

If there would be any, however, Gallatin wouldn't enjoy it. In another couple of weeks, he was dismissed and replaced by Dick McGuire, who hadn't coached since leaving Detroit.

The league now had two playing coaches (Guerin, DeBusschere), six coaches who were former N.B.A. players (McGuire, Seymour, McMahon, Schaus, Hannum and Schayes), and Auerbach. It had certainly produced its own talent, and the identity of the coaches drove home the realization of how new a generation was playing.

These new players, under these lifelong N.B.A.-oriented coaches, were producing an ever-increasing tempo of play. Shooting was unbelievable: off balance, pressed or not pressed, from thirty feet out or dunking the ball, with tap-ins restrained by a "no offensive goal-tending" rule, more than forty-two per cent of all the shots taken by the whole league were going in. If a big center didn't hit more than fifty per cent, there was something wrong. "A .400 hitter," considered a superb marksman a decade before, was below average now.

More and more, however, a player's individual status depended on his ability to contribute something to the defense. That he could score was taken for granted. He had to be able to do something more.

The television program was being handled better, too. The games selected, each week, were now the ones that shaped up as the most attractive at the time, according to standings, match-ups, or any recent newsworthy event.

Early in the season, Johnny Kerr, who had moved on to Baltimore (making the trade of Bellamy to the Knicks possible), missed a game. It was the first one he'd missed since 1954, and ended his streak at 917 consecutive regular-season and play-off games. Gallatin's original iron-man streak had reached 746. Schayes had stopped at 799, the day after Christmas, 1961. Now Kerr, angular and good-humored (he had always threatened to write a book called "Twelve Years in the Pivot Without the Ball") had taken over the durability title. Now thirty-three, he was still able to help the Bullets continue their improvement.

The Celtics were now playing without Heinsohn, and the 76ers without Costello. Baylor, because of his knees, was a poor facsimile of his old self. But the Celtics, using Havlicek more at forward because they had acquired Larry Siegfried for backcourt, didn't appear weaker, and the 76ers had come up with a prize corner rookie in Billy Cunningham. The Lakers, bolstered by the two little backcourt men who had led U.C.L.A. to its N.C.A.A. titles, Walt Hazzard and Gail Goodrich, also maintained their power despite Baylor's difficulties.

On an entirely different front, there had been a radical change. For the 1965–66 season, Chamberlain would be receiving $100,000 from the 76ers. Not to be outdone, Russell asked for, and got, $100,001 a year from the Celtics. Both contracts were for three years.

Such figures meant much more than increased wealth for the men involved. To the public, they established that basketball stars were getting six-figure salaries comparable to those the biggest men in baseball and football got. The prestige involved, for the league as a whole, was considerable; the fact that other salaries moved upward accordingly was a benefit to all players; and the fact that clubs felt they could pay this kind of money proved better than anything else how prosperous, and therefore stable, the league had become.

The play-off pool prize money had become worthwhile too. In the first year of the B.A.A., it had totalled something under $50,000 and members of the championship team cleared about $1,500 apiece. Now the pool was $180,000, and winning players could count on about $4,000—again, more comparable to other major sports.

All this provided the framework for the season-long battle between Boston and Philadelphia.

The Celtics, as usual, started well. They were 14-5 at the end of November, to Philadelphia's 12-8. By New Year's, the Celtics had a slightly larger margin, 25-9 to 21-13. And on February 12, when the Celtics won a bitter 85-83 struggle from the 76ers at Syracuse, Boston made its record 42-19 to Philadelphia's 37-22.

Then the Celtics stumbled. As if worn out by that effort, they lost the next three games, yielding 384 points to Los Angeles, Cincinnati and San Francisco. At the same time, the 76ers won three straight and pulled even in the loss column, although they were still in second place with two fewer victories.

And that was exactly the situation on March 5, when the

teams started a home-and-home series in Philadelphia. The 76ers won big, 102-85—and won again in Boston, 113-110. That gave Philadelphia the season series with Boston, six games to four, and possession of first place. The 76ers made sure they would keep it by not losing another game. Neither did the Celtics, sweeping their last six, but it was too late.

After nine straight years as Eastern Division champions, the Celtics had been dethroned, even though they had won fifty-four games.

For Chamberlain, there was considerable vindication in the result. All through his career, the absence of a championship had been thrown in his face, regardless of individual achievements. Now, at last, his team had finished ahead of Russell's. He had led the league in scoring again, for the seventh year in a row—but with only 33.5 points a game, the lowest average of his career. There was no mystery about that aspect of it: he was shooting less because he had teammates who could shoot well, and to whom it made sense to give the ball. He took less than twenty-five per cent of his team's shots, and almost doubled his assists—back to the level of 1964, when he had enabled San Francisco to win in the West.

But the job wasn't done yet. There were still the play-offs. A divisional championship, in the N.B.A. scheme of things and in the eyes of the public, was a very minor matter, even though it took a whole season's work to achieve. The real champion emerged only from the play-offs.

Having finished second, the Celtics simply got more grim and bore down. Forced into a preliminary play-off round for the first time in a decade, they had their hands full with Cincinnati. The Royals won the first game in Boston, and the third, after the Celtics had evened the score in Cincinnati. Now Boston had to win again on the road to avoid elimination—and it did. The fifth game was the only one won by the home team; the Celtics took it despite thirty-seven points by Oscar, and were entitled to their crack at Philadelphia.

All this time, the 76ers had been idle, competitively speaking. They had finished their regular season with tremendous momentum: they had won the last 11 straight, 18 of their last 21. Their pennant-clinching game, in which they made up a 16-point deficit in Baltimore, had been played on March 20. The first play-off game against Boston was on April 3, exactly two weeks later.

Sometimes a rest helps; in this case, it simply cooled the 76ers off—and the Celtics, weary as they were, had found their groove. They simply played Chamberlain & Co. right off the court. It took only five games. The first two were slaughters, 115-96 and 114-93. Then the 76ers won, at home. The fourth game was crucial and Boston won it in overtime, then closed out the rout at Philadelphia.

Chamberlain's vindication had turned to ashes.

And Auerbach's final triumph was in the making.

The Lakers, with Baylor regaining strength through the season, had finished first in the West again, seven games ahead of Baltimore. But Richie Guerin's Hawks upset Baltimore in three straight, and the Lakers needed the full seven games to get by the Hawks.

For the Celtics, of course, the Lakers would be no competition, not after the way the Celtics had handled the 76ers.

Of course.

So the first game of the final, in Boston, went into overtime and ended Los Angeles, 133; Boston, 129.

To steal the headlines, and to try to hypo his own team, Auerbach announced the next day a decision that had been taken about a week earlier:

Russell would be his successor as coach of the Celtics. Playing coach.

It was a major news story. "The first Negro to coach a major league team in any sport," everyone wrote—partly out of ignorance or willingness to ignore McLendon, partly with justification since, in this sense, Saperstein's league had never won accepted status as "major." In any case, even though Auerbach had not intended it that way, it was a major sociological breakthrough.

Russell, always militant for Negro rights and outspoken about it (with considerable damage to his "popularity") also minimized this aspect of his new position. In this, as in everything else, he wanted to be judged as an individual man, not as a symbol of any kind.

Whether or not the announcement was responsible (as Auerbach believed), the tide of the series promptly turned. The Celtics won the next three games handily. All they needed was one more, at home, to nail down their eighth straight championship and retire Auerbach at the top.

But the Lakers weren't yielding so easily. They won the fifth game in Boston, and the sixth back home. Once again, for the fourth time in their experience but for the first time since 1962, the Celtics were down to one 48-minute basketball game for their prized title.

This one reproduced, in miniature, the whole series. The Celtics took command, by nineteen points, but still the Lakers fought back. Leading by eight with 15 seconds to go, the Celtics were finally safe—only to see the Lakers score six points before the final buzzer left the Celtics with a 95-93 victory.

The dynasty had been preserved. But not forever.

18 • END OF AN ERA

The 1966–67 season would be the N.B.A.'s 21st, and the league had come of age in every way.

Attendance had crossed the 3,000,000 mark. A tenth team was being added—another Chicago enterprise—and others were clamoring for admission. Russell, as player-coach, was getting $125,000 a year (or $125,001), and Chamberlain had been given a raise too. Others, like Robertson, if not in the six-figure class were on its edge. The television program was thriving, and the weakest franchises had gained strength.

In San Francisco, Barry had become rookie of the year and averaged 25.7 points a game, surpassed only by Chamberlain, Robertson and West. Thurmond had been handicapped by a bad back, but that seemed correctible with special shoes. Mieuli, who had put the whole operation on its feet, dropped Hannum at the end of the season and hired Sharman in his place.

The Knicks, who hadn't done any better with Bellamy but still had prospects, won the toss with Detroit for first choice in the draft. They chose Cazzie Russell, by far the most publicized college star, but in the opinion of most scouts not clearly more desirable than Dave Bing of Syracuse, a smoother backcourt man. Detroit promptly took Bing, and signed him. The Knicks had a tougher time, however. Negotiating for Russell was Arthur Morse, the lawyer who had been in charge of the Chicago Stags back at the beginning of the B.A.A., and he did his job well. When Russell finally signed with the Knicks, on the eve of preseason training, he received a three-year package worth $250,000.

This staggering amount again pushed the N.B.A. into more rarefied major-league heights in the public's mind. No bonus of such proportions had ever been offered in basketball; it would soon be exceeded. In New York, Russell's arrival generated more interest in the Knicks than anything in the last ten years, and that was good for the whole league too.

The addition of a Chicago team, called the Bulls, meant shifting Baltimore into the Eastern Division, where it should have been all along. With five teams in each division, for the first time since 1953, the old play-off pattern was revived, with the first four teams in each division qualifying and no first-round bye for the divisional champion.

Russell and Sharman weren't the only new coaches. Displeased with his team's play-off showing, Kosloff fired Schayes—and hired Hannum, who had been so successful with Chamberlain in San Francisco, and with some of the present 76ers in Syracuse. He was, everyone agreed, as good a coach as pro basketball had ever produced.

In Baltimore, Seymour was gone and the team had been entrusted to Mike Farmer, whose playing career had just ended. Chicago chose Johnny Kerr as its first coach, with Al Bianchi—Kerr's longtime roommate while a backcourt man for Syracuse—as an exceptionally important assistant coach.

The Bullets, unaccountably, had weakened themselves and strengthened Boston by trading Bailey Howell, an all-star veteran forward, for Mel Counts, a young seven-footer who had been strictly a reserve at Boston.

Getting Howell was considered a coup, and the roles Risen, Phillip, Lovellette and Naulls had played in helping Boston win were now recalled. There was, however, a difference. In the past, these veterans had contributed to a substantially young team. Now the front-liners themselves were no longer young: Russell would be thirty-three by the end of the season, Sam Jones thirty-four, K. C. Jones thirty-five. (K. C., in fact, had intended to retire and had a coaching job waiting for him at Brandeis, but when Russell, his closest friend, became coach, K. C. had to give it one more year.) Howell would be thirty in January, and another major "pick-up"—Wayne Embry—would be thirty in March. (Embry had been the bulky center spoon-fed by Robertson for several years in Cincinnati; he was disenchanted with the situation there and decided not to play any more; Auerbach then got permission to sign him.) Now, thirty was by no means old, but for corner men who had to rebound under N.B.A. conditions, it was right on the borderline of full effectiveness. Backcourt men of that age were still in their prime, but forwards might not be—not, at any rate, night after night.

With these additions, then, and Don Nelson, who had blossomed forth the previous year in Heinsohn's place after three undistinguished seasons in Chicago and Los Angeles, Boston would be able to finish on top again, many felt. The 76ers, after all, had finished the previous season with a rush not likely to be duplicated. If Boston didn't win, it would be because of Russell's failure—either failure as a coach, or because coaching decreased his unique effectiveness as a player.

It was good reasoning—except that it turned out to be all wrong.

Almost as soon as play began—within two months—certain things became clear.

Russell was doing perfectly fine as a coach, and perfectly fine as a player—but Boston wasn't going to win it.

The difference was not Russell; it was Hannum.

Hannum had persuaded Costello to return from retirement. More help for the backcourt came from Wally Jones, two years out of Villanova, who always had exciting potential and was now finding himself. Along with Greer, they formed a backcourt that gave nothing away to Boston's.

And with such a backcourt, and three such powerful forwards as Walker, Jackson and Cunningham, Hannum could have Chamberlain do what he had never been able to do without reservation before: not worry at all about scoring.

To a degree, Wilt and Hannum had won a pennant playing this way in San Francisco, but only to a degree. There, it was still true that unless Chamberlain scored, the team didn't, and low scoring had to be the key. Here the 76ers had plenty of offense, and tremendous physical power: they had, without doubt, the strongest (in the physical sense) front line any team had ever had. Consider: Wilt was about four inches taller, a trifle heavier, and incomparably more agile than Mikan had been; Jackson was about Vern Mikkelsen's size, and a better shooter; Walker was taller, broader and stronger than Pollard (although he didn't have all of Pollard's skills).

With such partners, Chamberlain could finally become what people had feared originally: unbeatable. He could concentrate on the defensive board, and play Russell-style defense, blocking shots and triggering fast breaks—since he was no longer essential at the scoring end. When the fast break didn't score, and Wilt did join the offense, he became the perfect post man, handing off and passing out, scoring only when absolutely necessary and turning to the offensive board after getting rid of the ball.

No one could handle that.

Well, almost no one. Boston could. The Celtics were still the "better" basketball team—smarter, smoother, more cohesive, better balanced, with a better bench. The first time the teams met, on October 29 at Philadelphia, the 76ers smashed Boston in unprecedented fashion, 138-96—but a week later in Boston, the Celtics turned tables, and went on to win the season series, five games to four.

But nobody else could cope with the 76ers and, night after night, Hannum had them going all out. They won 45 of their first 49 games, a pace unmatched for that length of time in any professional sport, ever. Their power gave lesser teams no chance; Boston's finesse could be off on a particular night, and the Celtics could have a brief slump. The 76ers, with Chamberlain rising to every key period, could not.

So they ran away with the title, smashing all records. They won 68 games, lost only 13, an .840 pace. The Celtics, under Russell, won 60 games—five more than they had under Auerbach the year before—but finished second by an eight-game margin. The 76ers were eastern champions, and no mistake.

Chamberlain's statistics told the story. He averaged only 24.1 points a game, placing behind Barry and Robertson in total points and fifth in average. But he was third in the league in assists, behind only Rodgers (now with Chicago) and Robertson, with a 150 more than Russell, who was fourth. He led the league in rebounding, and since he was only shooting when a shot couldn't be passed up, he had the incredible average of .683 from the floor. The one flaw in him was his foul shooting, which, unaccountably, got worse than ever. He hit only .441 on free throws, and the strategy of fouling him deliberately wherever he was on the court led to a mid-season change of rules: fouling a man out of the play was henceforth treated as a technical foul, with the fouled team keeping possession after the shot.

When Wilt had averaged 50.4 points, in his last previous full year in Philadelphia, he had taken 3,159 shots—more than one-third of all his team's shots. Now he took only 1,150—less than one-seventh.

Countless stories blossomed about "the New Wilt"—naturally.

But they were unfair in their implication, as well as inaccurate historically. Yes, Wilt was playing the best basketball of his career, by far—but not because of any innate deficiency in the past; it was only because he had the right team situation at last—the kind of situation Russell had stepped into from the first when he joined a team that had Cousy, Sharman and Heinsohn and Auerbach to coach it.

Before mid-season, therefore, it was obvious that once again the race wouldn't count: the 76ers would win that. What would really matter would be the reconfrontation in the play-offs. Did Boston really have Philadelphia's number, or did last year's two-week layoff really hurt the 76ers? The Celtics were sure that was an alibi; the 76ers were sure it wasn't, but they couldn't prove it. Everything became only an elaborate preliminary to the play-offs.

Meanwhile, other things were happening.

Schayes was still on the scene in an unexpected capacity: he was the new supervisor of officials. His basic job, since he had no refereeing experience himself, was more to recruit and reorganize than to supervise the more experienced officials. At last the recognition that refereeing talent had to be found and developed was getting lip service.

Barry had taken over as the new scoring leader, and with Thurmond sweeping in rebounds at a greater rate than anyone but Wilt, Sharman had produced a winning team at San Francisco. Barry's scoring—he finished with 35.6 a game—excited the fans there as Chamberlain never had. At six-foot-seven, he wasn't so blatantly a giant, and his remarkable touch was mostly from outside (and he played a good all-court game too). And it would have been naive, at best, to deny the fact that he wasn't a Negro was part of his attractiveness at that particular time and place. So the Warriors prospered at last.

Kerr's group of castoffs at Chicago, built around Rodgers and Boozer, got off to a fine start and made an immediate hit with the local fans. The Bulls hung on well enough to make the play-offs in their first year, beating out Detroit for fourth.

Interest in Cazzie, who proved less than sensational, and an improved team built around the Bellamy-Reed axis, stirred up the New York fans, who set an attendance record by the time the season was over—more than 400,000 for what was to be the last full season in the "old" Garden.

Detroit had drawn a real prize in Bing, who became rookie of the year. Lou Hudson of Minnesota, a forward who turned out to be the leading scorer of the Hawks, was the other top-drawer newcomer. Late in the season, in a last-ditch try for the play-offs, Detroit let DeBusschere turn the coaching over to Donnis Butcher, so that he could concentrate on playing, but it didn't help.

The Lakers, although Baylor was better physically, were a disappointment, and finished nine games under .500. West was injured repeatedly, missing a total of fifteen games and playing below par in others, and aside from West and Baylor they just didn't have much.

Cincinnati, too, was disappointing, although it finished strong to take third place from the Knicks. Like the Lakers, the Royals had a gaping hole where it counted, at center. Two great players, no matter how great, could not cope with teams that had Chamberlain, or Russell, or Thurmond.

Baltimore was a complete bust. Farmer lasted only a few games as coach. Jeannette had to come back to the bench for a while, and then Gene Shue was hired to finish out the season. The Bullets wound up with the worst record in the league, 20-61.

On-court affairs, however, were taking a back seat to off-court developments as the wait for the play-offs went on.

Another new league was in the works.

This one, to be called the American Basketball Association, was the brainchild of a Madison Avenue group, attracted by the money-making potential of extra-curricular marketing in sports—television, endorsements, products with emblems, civic promotions. A dozen cities had groups interested, and many cities not in the N.B.A. had suitable arenas. The prospects for such a league were considerably brighter than for the one Saperstein had started—if it would really be run on a major-league basis.

Reports about the new league, and its formal announcement in February, brought to a head three problems.

It forced the N.B.A. to move faster on its own expansion. A plan had been drawn up, and now Kennedy announced that San Diego and Seattle would be added to the league in 1967–68 (over Irish's objections—just to prove that not everything had changed). Two more teams would be taken in the following year, and two more the year after that, so that by 1970 the N.B.A. would be an 18-team circuit. The entry fee, which included purchase of surplus players (to be put into an expansion pool, the same way Chicago had been stocked) came to $1,750,000 for each newcomer—$3,500,000 to be divided among the ten existing clubs.

The promise of a new league—and the announcement of the money coming into the N.B.A. from expansion—greatly increased the bargaining power and the militancy of the N.B.A. players. They had formed their own association, with Robertson as president, and had acquired as chief advisor a young New York lawyer named Larry Fleischer. Since the previous summer, they had been pressing for a greatly enlarged pension plan, review of certain contract provisions, schedule limitations and so forth—and getting nowhere.

Encouraged by the worrisome (to owners) possibility that there would be a new league to compete for their services, the players decided to press harder.

They threatened to strike the play-offs. Unless a new pension plan were worked out by the time they were to start, in mid-March, they would not play. When the owners said money wasn't available, the players promptly pointed to the expansion windfall.

This wasn't quite as desperate as the All-Star Game revolt of 1964, because it wasn't as immediate. But the positions were roughly the same. The owners weren't going to "give in to intimidation"; the players weren't going to scatter for the off-season without using the one weapon they had. And Fleischer threatened to file for formal certification as a union—a point no sport had reached.

For a couple of weeks, the fate of the play-offs was in doubt. The owners set a deadline—one week before the first play-off game—for full commitment to play, or they would cancel the play-offs themselves. The players kept silent. At the last moment, Kennedy and Fleischer worked out an agreement—essentially the same sort of guarantee that Kennedy had given in 1964: that he would use his own maximum efforts to get the owners to agree to what the players sought. As in 1964, his word was accepted, and, as in 1964, when the season was over he delivered. In June, the pension went up to a level of about $500 a month for a man with ten years of N.B.A. service, and a review of the contract was agreed upon.

The contract itself was the third problem that the proposed A.B.A. brought into focus. The new league was going after N.B.A.

players, expressing confidence that the "reserve clause" (which bound a player to his team from one year to the next, as in baseball) would not stand up in court. The players, of course, welcomed the bidding for their services. And even if not too many N.B.A. players jumped, the competition for stars coming out of college was the very thing the original merger with the National League had been designed to eliminate. The two major football leagues had just merged for the very same reason. If anything had been proved repeatedly in the history of American sports, it was that competing leagues involved in "player wars" could only threaten bankruptcy for all concerned if allowed to go on very long. Yet, everyone did believe that the reserve clause was questionable, if brought to court. Even those who believed it necessary couldn't be sure it would be held legal.

The new league had named Mikan as commissioner, and had among its coaches other old N.B.A. names—Zaslofsky in New York, Hagan in Dallas, Pollard in Minneapolis, Slater Martin in Houston. In this, it was like Saperstein's American League—and also in the fact that it signed up Connie Hawkins, Tony Jackson and the other "gray area" figures from the 1961 scandals. But the financing seemed sounder, and certainly the publicity was better. Whether this would be a real threat to the N.B.A., or a harmless rival, could not be foretold at this point—but it certainly was something to worry about.

Worry wasn't unbearable, however, and once the threatened strike was settled, there was too glamorous a set of play-offs coming up for anyone to waste time worrying.

Philadelphia vs. Boston.

If the Celtics could not be dethroned this time, then they might never be. No team had ever had a season like the 76ers; if, one more time, they proved incapable of beating the Celtics hand to hand, they could never expect a better chance. On the other hand, if the Celtics could do it again now, they would be showing themselves to be even more superb than ever.

Of course, they couldn't play each other immediately. In the ten-team league, each had to go through a first-round series.

The 76ers had to play Cincinnati—and promptly revived memories of last year's failure by losing the first game, 120-116, on their own court. But there was no nonsense after that. The 76ers won the next three games by margins of 21, 15 and 18 points.

The Celtics began in the opposite fashion: they blasted the Knicks in the first game, 140-110, putting on as close to perfect a performance as one could imagine.

But then, strangely enough, the Celtics began to reveal a weakness. Before the play-offs began, the feeling was that the Celtic-76er meeting would be a toss-up. The way they finally defeated the Knicks, however, raised doubts. The Knicks, decimated by late-season injuries, simply threw the pressing defense in Boston's face—and the Celtics started to show their age. They still had enough savvy, skill, shot-making ability, experience and determination to fight off the Knicks in two of the next three games, to win the series; but they had shown themselves vulnerable to fatigue and to physical pressure.

And that's what the 76ers had to apply: physical pressure.

All the games followed the same pattern. Boston would be in command most of the time in the first and third quarters, but Philadelphia would pull away (or pull even) as play continued, and dominated the second and fourth quarters. Boston would make a counterdrive late in the game, but it would fall short and the 76ers would wrap it up.

Chamberlain was all. He made the Boston shooters hurried and distracted, as Russell had done for them against everyone else all those years. Offensively, Wilt took charge as much as necessary, and when he did, he brushed aside all resistance, more impressively than Mikan used to do in a simpler, slower age.

It was the 76ers, now, who were producing "big innings."

In the middle of the first half of the first game, they outscored Boston 36-14 and led by 17 at intermission. Boston never came closer than 11, and the 76ers won by 127-113. Wilt had outrebounded Russell, 32-15, had made 13 assists and had scored 24 points.

In the second game, at Boston, the Celtics led by 11 with 65 seconds to go in the first half, but left the floor leading only 58-55. By the opening minutes of the fourth quarter, Philadelphia was 14 ahead, 89-75—but the Celtics fought back and closed to within one point before yielding, 107-102. Cunningham's driving and Chamberlain's rebounding were decisive down the stretch.

Game number three made the final result inevitable. The Celtics, using Siegfried and Havlicek as starters, roared to a 24-15 lead in the first nine minutes. But the 76ers, with Wilt going to the offensive board, moved ahead with a 21-7 burst over the next six minutes. By halftime, Chamberlain had 25 rebounds. Again, Boston fought back, inched ahead late in the third quarter, and was behind by only 91-90 with eight and a half minutes to play. The 76ers pulled away, the Celtics came back, and it was 100-99 with four minutes left.

Then Wally Jones hit three fantastic long jump shots, each matching a score by Boston, and with Greer sinking clutch free throws, the 76ers closed out a 115-104 victory. Chamberlain finished with 41 rebounds, a play-off record; Greer, who had scored 39 in the first game and 17 in the second, made 30 in this one.

The fourth game, in Boston on Sunday afternoon, April 9, was televised nationally. Down 3-0, the Celtics realized as well as anyone that their reign had reached its end. But they weren't going to admit it, or give in. This one was close all the way and Sam Jones (32 points) and Havlicek (31) were hitting. Boston won it, 121-117, surviving some tremendous corner shooting and rebounding by Jackson, and Greer's 28 points. For one more performance, to a maximum audience, they were still the supreme Celtics.

And so, the fifth game came up at Philadelphia—with just a grain of doubt possible. The 76ers, for all their power, were essentially a seven-man team. (Costello had been injured halfway through the season, and was not playing). They were human, too. Fatigue could tell. And suppose something happened, an injury, to Chamberlain or Greer or Wally Jones or Jackson; wouldn't Boston still be able to take advantage of it? If the Celtics could win the fifth game, they would be favored in the sixth, at home. Then a seventh game would be needed, and that was like playing roulette—as both teams had experienced so vividly in recent years. Although this was only the fifth game, then, it had as much tension as a deciding game.

The Celtics gave it their best shot, with Russell starting at his best. They ran the 76ers silly, and started off with an 8-0 lead. They made it 17-6, absorbed a counterpunch, then put it back to 37-26 by the end of the quarter. They had shot .552 from the floor and had outrebounded Philadelphia, 20-14 (10-5 for Russell against Wilt). By the middle of the second period, they had a 59-43 lead.

And at that point, Chamberlain just took the ball game in his two huge hands and turned it around. He rebounded, drove, blocked shots, fed—even hit his old fadeaway jumper. Aided by Walker's hot hand, he triggered a 22-9 rally. At intermission, the 76ers were back in business, trailing 70-65.

That really turned the tide. In the third quarter, Wally Jones hit from all sides, making eight out of nine, while the Celtics fought to stay even. They fell behind, then inched ahead for the last time, 91-90, with four and a half minutes to go in the third quarter.

But they were being beaten off the boards now, and they were spent, and their shots weren't hitting—which meant that Chamberlain was gathering in the misses. As the period neared its end, the 76ers had a 10-3 burst and the final quarter started with Philadelphia leading, 100-94.

And finally—after ten years, really—the Celtics had nothing left. The 76ers, and their partisan, record crowd of 13,007, went crazy. They ran the score up to 131-104. It ended 140-116. In the last 16 minutes of play, they had outscored Boston 50 to 25.

In his book, *Go Up for Glory,* Bill Russell had written, a year and a half before, about Boston's last-quarter blast against Los Angeles in the fifth and final game of 1965.

> Then it became frightening, [he described.] We were not just beating this team. We were destroying it. The people were screaming. They were yelling for blood. It was like the Colosseum of Rome. They were yelling for all their frustrations, all their pent-up feelings about the world. They were egging us on to destroy, to kill, to reduce an opponent to nothing. And we were responding. We were, in a basketball sense, killing them, leaving them shattered among the ashes of their pride. We were running over them like a man might run over a floundering cripple with his car. Compelled. Unable to stop. Meshing together all the years and running like a precise, perfect machine. It was my worst moment in sports. There was the horror of destruction, not the joy of winning.

And that was the way it ended for the Celtics—on the receiving end.

Whether Chamberlain and the other 76ers felt anything like Russell had, or not, the fact was that they did not gloat when it was over. Hannum almost expressed it in words: they seemed to feel a certain humility at their own power, and awed by what the

Celtics had stood for—the excellence, after all, that gave such meaning to Philadelphia's triumph.

But it wasn't a full triumph yet. Only a year ago, the 76ers had apparently achieved it in the regular season, only to be bumped back to earth by the play-offs. There was still another series to play.

"We haven't done anything at all," said Chamberlain, "until we win the final."

That the final was against San Francisco naturally added to the emotional overtones for Chamberlain and Hannum. And they knew all too well the danger—perhaps the inevitability—of being "flat" after the victory over Boston. The rest of the world took for granted that Boston was the real hurdle, that the championship was already Philadelphia's. But the 76ers themselves couldn't feel that—and didn't.

Their apprehensions were sound. The Warriors, who had reached the final by sweeping L.A. in three games and disposing of St. Louis in six, had their own aspirations. They put up a tremendous battle in the first game and the 76ers had to pull it out in overtime, 141-135. (Actually, Thurmond was now a more even match for Chamberlain than Russell was.)

Philadelphia's sluggishness lasted only the one game, however. If they had lost it, the final might have been interesting. This way, they had an easy time in the second game, 126-95. They lost the first game at San Francisco, 130-124, but won the next, 122-108, but they ended it in San Francisco on April 24, by a 125-122 score that was not as dramatic at the finish as it sounded.

Now it was official.

The most devastating basketball player in the world was Wilt Chamberlain. The "best," artistically, might still be Oscar Robertson, but the toughest was Wilt. In the process, he had proved several things, but most among them was basketball's oldest lesson: one man can't do it alone, no matter how big or how good; but, given adequate teammates, one dominant figure means championship—as Mikan used to, and as Russell did for so long. Now it was Wilt.

In all sorts of ways, then, the end of Boston's string of championships marked the end of an era for the N.B.A. In the course of their decade of dominance, the Celtics had seen—and had done more than anyone to make possible—growth from a struggling enterprise to a circuit that had "major league" status unquestioningly accorded to it. The longevity of Boston's reign had brought a sort of prestige that no sequence of different annual champions could have provided.

But now that phase was over, and it had done its work. It was unlikely that any team would ever be so dominant so long again. But all the teams that would follow, through decades to come, would be compared again and again to the Celtics. They had established the yardstick and—like the Yankees of an earlier era in baseball—had combined attractiveness of style and personality with victory and efficiency.

Almost all the figures of the building years were gone, one way or another, from the front line of activity—Podoloff, Brown, Biasone, Gottlieb, Bob Short, Max Winter, Lester Harrison. Irish was less involved, and even Kerner was losing interest since the departure of Pettit and his own suffering through a series of illnesses. In the middle of the 1966–67 season, he had announced that he was ready to sell the Hawks, for about $3,000,000, but the deal was not consummated. He remained in the market, and his departure would not be far off.

Only Zollner continued his serene way, unchanged, with limited involvement, running his team his own way—the Phil Wrigley of basketball.

The new owners were a different breed. The ones who had built the league, whatever their shortcomings, had been basketball men to the core. Now—as in most other sports—owners were money men, business executives with extensive interests who had invested in a going proposition for the economic and publicity advantages it offered; they might be fans, too, but they hadn't gone through the struggle and had no intention, or possibility, of giving their newly acquired enterprise their exclusive attention.

Whether this would prove good or bad, no one could say, but it certainly seemed inevitable. And Kennedy was clearly the right kind of man to be president of this kind of group.

For the fan, an era had ended also, not only because Boston lost. The emphasis was swinging back to team achievement. In their day, Cousy, Schayes, Pettit, Mikan, Stokes, Arizin and their like had the power to excite by individual exploit. When Russell,

Robertson, Baylor, West and Chamberlain came along, this was still possible. But Chamberlain had made statistics meaningless, and Robertson, Baylor and West had made incredible moves commonplace. More and more, the public was starting to respond to how well the team did, and to recognize the values and techniques of team defense, balanced offense and blending. The dedicated fans had always appreciated these things, but they had been (and must always be) few. The large arenas and television had brought the game to new fans, who responded to the individual star. But now, in the third decade of the league, a sufficiently educated large body of fans existed to make the new attitude widespread.

In 1958–59, the all-league team consisted of Pettit, Baylor, Russell, Cousy and Sharman. One might put Schayes on it instead of Sharman, and assert that that was the best five-man unit imaginable in the history of the game to that point.

A mere seven years later, one could name another all-time all-star team which any of the above would have trouble making. Robertson and West would certainly usurp the backcourt positions, and Chamberlain would be the center. And who knew what levels Barry and Lucas, still early in their careers, might reach as forwards, pushing Schayes and Pettit into an honored but perhaps outdated category with Mikan? Baylor would be the hardest man to displace on this imaginary team.

New stars were on the way. Bradley, back from Oxford, signed a four-year contract with the Knicks worth $500,000. He would be the focus of anticipation for the fans in the next couple of years. Jimmy Walker, of Providence, clearly the number one draft pick of 1967, got $275,000 from Detroit for a three-year agreement. These were players, one six-foot-five and the other six-foot-three, whose pro success was by no means absolutely assured—let's say, to the extent Russell's, Chamberlain's, Baylor's and Robertson's had been. Yet they were getting this kind of money before they had played a game. How new could an era get?

But the most ironic, and gratifying, feature of the whole story was that the N.B.A., after two decades, had evolved into exactly what the originators of the B.A.A. had dreamt about. It was stable, prosperous, based in huge arenas, using college stars as a matter of course, playing (thanks to its improved rules) a "clean" game that provided college-type action from beginning to end, only better. The men who had committed themselves to that idea had lived through every obstacle and every apparent reversal of direction—and had emerged by evolution at precisely the goal they had failed to achieve by purposeful action.

In that, there must lie some sort of moral.

Podoloff, if he were still in office, would find, no doubt, some complex way to articulate it.

Irish, with considerable justice but little psychological insight, might, say, "If they'd listened to me they would have got there sooner and lost less money along the way."

Gottlieb, proud of his schedule patterns and his firm grasp of every aspect of the business which occupied him for more than twenty years, would scoff at morals to stories and at theories. "You do the best you can with what you've got," he'd say.

Biasone had never been part of the original concept anyhow. All he wanted was good basketball, and to be part of its scene; and when the scene was on the verge of suicide, it was the rule he advocated that saved everyone. He would shrug at proverb-building.

Kerner could see it clearly. "You concentrate on creating a good product, and then you really work at it—then the public will buy it. But you've got to have a good product."

And yet, perhaps it all boiled down to something Lapchick used to say, in a variety of ways, in varying circumstances. "I'm a pro at heart," he'd say, "and I'm proud to be a pro." Perhaps the ultimate success of the N.B.A. was not, as the founders had dreamed, that it would achieve "college-type" respectability, but that it would give to the word "pro" in basketball the respect and admiration it deserved, and had long since earned in other sports.

To bring honor and distinction to what once had been in ill-repute—and to prosper in the process; that was no mean achievement. That was what the N.B.A. really accomplished in its first twenty-one years.

The moral was, therefore—or, at least, the guideline on the basis of the N.B.A.'s experience was—

Aim high.

Keep shooting.

Within, of course, 24 seconds.

19 • THE NEW STATUS

Stories don't end neatly in real life, for the simple reason that life always goes on. The completion of twenty-one years and the end of Boston's string of championships made a natural ending for the story of the National Basketball Association's development. In one real sense, the story was complete: the league and the whole concept of professional basketball on a major-league level were permanently established beyond any possibility of extinction. Whatever changes lay ahead, the basic format had been stabilized, and the most important element of any mass-interest sport created: a continuing tradition.

And yet the 1967–68 season, on and off the floor, was perhaps more eventful than any one season that went before.

First of all, there was the new rival, the American Basketball Association. Those who failed to keep in mind that the sincerest form of flattery is imitation misinterpreted much of the significance of the new league's first season.

Some people talked of the A.B.A. as a "threat" and a "competitor" to the N.B.A. Throughout the spring and summer, speculation about the extent of the conflict and its consequences often found its way into print. And for a while it did seem that a player war might be in the making.

But the basic forces at work were quite different. There wasn't much the A.B.A. could do to hurt the N.B.A. in tangible terms, although it could—and did—hurt a particular club. That was in Oakland, the only place where head-to-head competition for customers existed between the new league and the San Francisco Warriors. Anywhere else, success of one league at the gate could have no direct effect on the other.

By bidding for college players and giving marginal N.B.A. pros an alternative, the new league did, by its mere existence, push salary expenses higher. But there was a built-in limit here, too. The new teams knew they would have to pour hundreds of thousands, if not millions, of dollars into building up their situations over a period of years during which the inflow of money would be minimal. The N.B.A. clubs were already established and, on the whole, turning a good profit. If it came to serious competition in the form of bonuses, the N.B.A. could certainly afford extravagance better than the new people could.

And that's the way it turned out. Jimmy Walker, the big prize in the college draft, chose the N.B.A., signing with Detroit. Of all the other first-round draft choices, only one—Mel Daniels of New Mexico—went into the A.B.A., with Minnesota.

Far more exciting, and potentially dangerous, would be a concerted move by the new league to woo the established superstars away from the N.B.A. Rumors started immediately: Chamberlain was going to jump, Robertson had an offer that "couldn't be turned down," Havlicek was interested, and so forth.

But here, too, beneath the headline-grabbing, there was a modifying factor. One way or another, getting N.B.A. players to switch meant breaking the reserve clause, either by a favorable court ruling or by making the N.B.A. surrender meekly. However, the very same reserve clause (in whatever form and by whatever name) was essential to the new league for control of its players. Conceivably, a strong enough "anti-slavery" case could put everybody out of business, old and new league alike; but people who were just starting to invest large sums of money in the A.B.A. were unlikely to pursue their own destruction that far. After all, if the revolutionary did happen, and the existing system had to be junked, most N.B.A. teams could dissolve with their ledgers in the black; the A.B.A. people, who hadn't made any money yet, would be left only with permanent losses. In the crunch, therefore, a vigorous attack on the reserve clause by the A.B.A. was unlikely.

The A.B.A. did file an anti-trust suit in 1968, but it seemed more like a weapon to force acceptance than something to be pursued bitterly through the courts.

The players, meanwhile, played the two leagues off against each other as much as they could, naturally enough. So what fans saw as a doubtful or unresolved situation (concerning Robertson's or Chamberlain's eventual affiliation) was really nothing more than a form of bargaining with old employers.

Nevertheless, some players did jump, and one N.B.A. superstar was lost to it, although not gained by the A.B.A. He was Rick Barry, the new scoring champion, who found himself in a peculiar situation and whose case put an end to any warlike ideas the A.B.A. may have had.

The Oakland club in the new league had Pat Boone, the singer and Hollywood star, as its principal owner. He hired Bruce Hale as coach. Hale had been Barry's college coach at Miami. And Hale was also Barry's father-in-law.

Franklin Mieuli, the young owner for whom the Warriors had blossomed into such a success, knew that both Barry and Thurmond would be approached and that he faced the only truly competitive situation between the two leagues. The A.B.A. did have a New York franchise, but it had nowhere to play and would have no effect on the Knicks and the new Madison Square Garden; the Anaheim team, in the A.B.A., was trying to tap a quite different area than the established Lakers were in Los Angeles; but the Warriors played many of their home games in the new Oakland Arena, and the San Francisco Bay area was not nearly so populous as New York or Los Angeles. Every other A.B.A. team was in a city that had no N.B.A. basketball nearby, but the Warriors and Oakland Oaks would meet head on.

Mieuli thought of Thurmond and Barry as two pieces of one machine, which they certainly were in a basketball sense, and had reason to believe that they had agreed between them to stay together. So, after signing Thurmond, Mieuli took his family to Europe, confident that Barry could be signed when he returned.

It was a mistake.

Barry, who certainly faced understandable pressures, signed with Oakland, amid much publicity. Not only did he have family ties, but in Boone he had an owner who offered an entry into the glamorous world of entertainment and promotion, a field in which Barry had ambitions.

But this was a mistake, too, because Barry's existing contract with the Warriors gave them an option on his services for the following season, at least until September.

When Mieuli returned from Europe, he promptly sought an injunction to prevent Barry from playing with Oakland (or with anyone other than the Warriors).

It was granted.

Now a whole new set of complications arose. The judge ruled that Barry had violated the option provision he had freely and knowingly signed—the provision that is, in effect, the reserve clause. But he also ruled, apparently (the legal tangle got very thick here), that Barry had a perfect right to sit out one year and then play for Oakland.

That would mean a "playing-out-one's-option" possibility which pro football had but baseball and basketball did not. No one had been looking for that solution, and while Barry acted on it (by deciding not to play in 1967–68 but to work for the Oakland team as a broadcaster), it didn't really clarify much for anyone else.

The option in the player's contract is only one half of the reserve-clause pincers; the other half is a league rule that forbids a team to use a player unless he has signed a contract for the current year—with a brand-new option for the following year in it. There was no way, therefore, a man could ever "play out" his option, because the league wouldn't let him play; all he could do would be to sit it out.

Only Barry, however, proved willing to do this. Other players jumped—and jumped back. LeRoy Ellis of Baltimore, Joe Strawder of Detroit and Jim Barnes of Los Angeles declared for A.B.A. clubs, only to wind up back with the N.B.A. teams by the time the season began.

The second most prominent jumper, after Barry, was Lou Hudson, who had been the outstanding rookie cornerman of the St. Louis Hawks in 1967. Hudson was a University of Minnesota alumnus and found the idea of playing for the new Minnesota team attractive—for a couple of days. Kerner quickly got him back into the Hawk fold, but then a third league—the United States Army—stepped in and pre-empted Hudson's services, so he played only part of the season for St. Louis.

Throughout all this, fabulous sums were being mentioned. The $100,000 contract was commonplace (in conversation). Part ownerships were being offered to players ("but part of nothing is still nothing," Chamberlain observed). The suits that were instituted were for millions of dollars (whether they were followed up or not was another story), and legal fees alone could make the difference between profit and loss for the season.

It was in this context that Kerner's mother, his most loyal fan, became incensed when she heard that Hudson was deserting the Hawks.

"Imagine, that nice boy doing a thing like that to you," she declared. "Ben, I think you should fight him all the way, take it to court as far as it has to go—even if it costs $500!"

At heart, though, neither side wanted to fight.

The A.B.A. people had two possibilities in mind, with the football merger as their model. One was getting into business long enough to attract a national television contract and, thus subsidized, force the N.B.A. to recognize it and come to terms (eventually) on some sort of supra-organization encompassing the two leagues. The other was that if their league couldn't make it as a league, the stronger individual members would be absorbed into the N.B.A. one way or another, at some time or other.

The N.B.A.'s attitude was still simpler: ignore the A.B.A. as much as possible. It might simply fail and go away; but if it didn't, there would be plenty of time to deal with it once it had proved its ability to survive.

So the A.B.A. set up shop in eleven cities—New York, Pittsburgh, Kentucky (Louisville), Indiana (Indianapolis) and Minnesota (Minneapolis-St. Paul) in an Eastern Division, New Orleans, Anaheim, Oakland, Dallas, Houston and Denver in the West. But even before the season began, New York became New Jersey. The team, owned by Arthur Brown, intended to play at the 69th Regiment Armory, which the Knicks had used originally, but couldn't get dates. So it changed its name to the New Jersey Americans and moved into an armory in Teaneck, New Jersey, not far from the George Washington Bridge. Brown vowed he would build a new arena eventually, but the change in name was deflating, if not to Brown, to the rest of the league.

The television contract sought by Mikan—a key factor in the new league's economics—never materialized. Still, all the teams that started the season finished it, and competition was keen although crowds were small. Pittsburgh won the championship, and two of its outstanding players were Connie Hawkins, one of those borderline "unacceptables" to the N.B.A., and Art Heyman, who had sat on the benches of three other N.B.A. clubs after being discarded by the Knicks.

The A.B.A. game rules were substantially the same as the N.B.A.'s, with one exception: the three-point field goal from beyond twenty-five feet, which had proved popular with the experienced basketball players who had seen it in Saperstein's ill-fated American League, was used. The arenas, travel conditions, pay scales and other details, modeled on N.B.A. practices, were certainly "big league"—more so than they had been in the N.B.A. years after it began.

But the real battle lay ahead, and it was named Lew Alcindor. The hot collegian coming out of college in 1968 was Elvin Hayes of Houston. The A.B.A. had a team in Houston. Yet Hayes chose to sign (for about $350,000 for four years) with San Diego, the N.B.A. team that drafted him. But Hayes did not have the stature of Alcindor, who had made U.C.L.A. virtually invincible, and Alcindor would come out in 1969. It was widely believed that the A.B.A.'s power to command merger or absorption into a larger unit with the N.B.A. would rest on its ability to land him.

In a sense, the N.B.A. had now proved its maturity in the most conclusive fashion of all: at the age of twenty-two, it had an offspring. It had succeeded, in two decades, to such a point that it was able to lure responsible business people, all over the country, into investing large sums of money in trying to duplicate the N.B.A.'s success. It had made pro basketball so respected and attractive that it made others want to share the gravy—and these others, willing to stretch their imaginations to the limit and unconfined by traditions, still could find few changes to make in the patterns the N.B.A. had developed.

More to the point, the N.B.A. was able to attract investors directly. San Diego and Seattle, with fine new arenas, had come into the league in 1967. They were stocked by an "expansion draft" and had losing teams, but their attendances were respectable and they were thoroughly integrated into the league setup. For 1968, two new teams were added: Milwaukee and Phoenix. In Milwaukee, the fine arena Kerner had once used was still available, and there was no competition from baseball since the Braves had moved to Atlanta. In Phoenix, the league was tapping an entirely new area, where no major-league sport had yet been established.

For the second straight year, then, the existing N.B.A. owners would be cutting the $4,000,000 or so that represented the entry fees (in the form of "purchasing" expansion-pool players) of the new teams.

By far the most exciting features of 1967–68, however, turned out to be the competitive events. The playing season, now eighty-two games long, produced surprise after surprise.

The 76ers would win again, of course, and Boston was too old. The Knicks were stronger and might challenge them, and Cincinnati still had Robertson and Lucas. The Western Division, with Barry gone and three expansion clubs (including the Chicago Bulls, now in their second year), was wide open.

But the Knicks floundered. In December, Bradley finished his Air Force tour of duty and joined them—obviously unready to jump into such intensive competition after two years away from topflight basketball and without the benefit of preseason training. The Knicks floundered worse, and Dick McGuire was replaced as coach by Red Holzman, who had been acting as the team's chief scout for eight years, ever since he had left the Hawks on the threshold of their championships. A couple of days later, Bradley was shaken up when struck by a car while crossing a street and was put out of action for a couple of weeks. At the same time, under Holzman, the Knicks suddenly started to play the way people had expected and finished the season with a rush.

Philadelphia had finished first again, as expected, and Boston a strong second. In the West, St. Louis emerged as the divisional champion, making Richie Guerin coach of the year, but in the closing weeks Los Angeles looked stronger because Baylor was entirely himself again, and West was still West. The Lakers had a new coach, Bill Van Breda Kolff, who had coached Bradley at Princeton and who had once played for the Knicks in the league's earliest years. In the East, Detroit had started well, thanks to Dave Bing, and had saved a playoff berth at the end from Cincinnati, for whom Robertson lost too much time because of injuries.

There was great anticipation building up for the 1968 playoffs. Even the settings were changing. In mid-season, the Lakers moved into their own brand-new building, the Forum. Cooke had built this for his basketball and hockey teams after squabbling with Los Angeles County officials about rental arrangements in the

Arena. The new Madison Square Garden, behind schedule, finally opened in February, with a basketball capacity of more than 19,000. The 76ers were playing in the Spectrum, a new 15,000-seat arena adjacent to Municipal Stadium (where the Army-Navy football games are played) with two problems: its owner, Jerry Wolman, who owned the football Eagles, was in the process of going bankrupt, and the roof of the building had holes blown in it by storms in February and March.

It was the games, though, and not the settings, that counted. The Knicks, having beaten Philadelphia three times in their last four meetings during the regular season, believed they could upset them. When Billy Cunningham broke his wrist during Philadelphia's overtime victory in the third game of the four-of-seven series, the upset became more possible. But as the Knicks were winning the fourth game, evening the set at 2-2, they lost their own prize rookie, Walt Frazier, through a leg injury. With half their own team crippled and with Chamberlain rising to the occasion, the 76ers won the next two games and were ready to dispose of Boston.

The Celtics had been having their own troubles. They had trailed Detroit, two games to one, before winning the next three to wrap up that series, and everyone knew they were too old. The semifinal against the 76ers began the night after Dr. Martin Luther King's assassination, and although it was decided to play (after consultation with both Russell and Chamberlain), it was a strangely subdued game, which Boston won. But Philadelphia won the next three, and things seemed normal enough. A tremendous upset had taken place in the Western playoffs when San Francisco knocked out St. Louis, four games to two, even though the Warriors hadn't had Nate Thurmond since mid-season (because of injury) and were suffering from other injuries; but by now, the Lakers had polished off San Francisco in four straight and were waiting for their crack at Chamberlain and the 76ers.

But Mr. Russell and his friends, particularly one John Havlicek, one Bailey Howell, one Larry Siegfried, one Don Nelson and one Sam Jones, had plans of their own.

They won three in a row from the 76ers, including a seventh game at the Spectrum in which Mr. Chamberlain hardly took a shot in the second half. There were no recriminations, no alibis, only universal respect and wonder at Boston's achievement. For Russell, as a coach and as a player both, it was a tremendous vindication; for Kratter, the hard-rooting owner, it was sheer ecstasy (which he expressed, a few weeks later, by taking the whole club and their families to Hawaii for a vacation).

But all this was really the start of a new story, not the end of the old one. Hannum, the coach who was always ambitious and never content to stay in one niche, resigned—not because the 76ers lost but because the general managership and part ownership he craved were never offered him. Then he made a stunning move by signing a long-term contract with Pat Boone's Oakland team in the A.B.A.—although the long-term future of that league was by no means yet assured and the legal position of Rick Barry was still in doubt. (Mieuli claimed that even if the court ruling was that Barry could "play out" his option, he hadn't played but sat, and that the Warriors were still entitled to a season of his services.)

At the same time Bill Sharman, whose Warriors had upset St. Louis, also resigned and went to the new league, with the Los Angeles team, which abandoned Anaheim and moved into the downtown arena the Lakers had left open by moving into their Forum.

And soon after the season ended, Kerner suddenly announced that he had sold his Hawks to a group in Atlanta. The Hawks, despite their competitive success in St. Louis year after year, were stuck in an antiquated building (Kiel Auditorium) and squeezed by larger rivals in a limited market—the World Champion St. Louis Cardinals and the football Cardinals, both installed in a brand-new downtown stadium, and a major-league hockey team. So Kerner, another of the builders, was gone from the scene.

When the 1968–69 season began, the N.B.A. had two seven-team divisions: New York, Boston, Philadelphia, Baltimore, Detroit, Cincinnati and Milwaukee in the East; Los Angeles, San Francisco, Seattle, San Diego, Phoenix, Chicago and Atlanta in the West. It had won the rookie war again, with Hayes in San Diego, Wes Unseld of Louisville in Baltimore, and most of the other top draft choices safely in hand. But the A.B.A., for all its difficulties, was ready to operate too. Brown's New Jersey Americans had acquired a New York name again, but they were isolated far out on Long Island as the New York Nets; the champion Pittsburgh Pipers had moved to Minneapolis, and the old Minneapolis team had become Miami; still, together with Indianapolis, Louisville, New Orleans, the two California teams, the two Texas teams and Denver, the clubs formed a viable eleven-team league that upheld major-league standards of operation even if it could not compare to the N.B.A. in basic playing talent.

But whatever the geography, the topography of the N.B.A. had changed in a fundamental way because of another sensational deal involving Chamberlain.

The 76ers, disappointed by the loss to the Celtics and unsettled by Hannum's departure, faced up to making drastic changes. Ramsay, while continuing as general manager, would take over the coaching—and Chamberlain, whose close personal relationship had been to Ike Richman (who had died in 1965), would be allowed to move on. The offer for him came from the Lakers: Cooke, who always thought big, decided that he would provide Baylor and West with the one thing they lacked, an overwhelming center. The Lakers gave up Archie Clark, their other backcourt starter; Darrall Imhoff, now a veteran center; and Jerry Chambers, a forward.

The experts, and most fans, promptly awarded the Lakers the championship, without waiting for a game to be played. Chamberlain, West and Baylor on the same team! It boggled the imagination. Why, they should be good for 85–90 points a game just by themselves. This would be the greatest team ever assembled—which was exactly what Cooke intended. He promptly signed Wilt to what was reported as a four-year million-dollar contract: $250,000 a year. No one really knew whether those figures were real or not, but no one doubted that Wilt had the best deal any established player had yet received.

If an owner's willingness to spend money could produce a dynasty, Cooke had just done it.

But could it?

20 • TO BE CONTINUED

Turmoil along the knife-edge of survival.

That had been the life of the N.B.A. in its early years.

Turmoil amid affluence, with no doubt about survival but increasing doubt about the exact shape of the future.

That was the N.B.A. experience as the league headed into its second quarter-century.

In midsummer 1968, no one was prepared to forecast the degree of affluence and the degree of uncertainty that would exist in midsummer 1970.

In the intervening two seasons, the legal tangles (and expenses) grew into a full-fledged jungle. The A.B.A. did not wither away, but it did not fully blossom either, and the issue of amalgamation was finally faced—only to provoke serious resistance from the N.B.A. Players Association, whose members took their case to court.

At the same time, attendances and public interest soared to unprecedented levels, and by the start of the new decade, pro basketball—which meant, really, N.B.A. basketball—was the hot item in the volatile world of Madison Avenue.

Only a new generation, accustomed to watching split-screen techniques on their television sets and in the latest movies, could hope to follow the intricate, accelerating events that unfolded now.

On the floor, the 1968–69 season was, without quibbling, spectacular. The Lakers, obviously, were too strong for the other western clubs and ran up a 26–10 record by late December. But there were difficulties. Van Breda Kolff and Chamberlain did not pull in the same direction. The coach was dedicated to a flowing, moving, balanced game; Wilt was convinced his best contribution would be to play close to the basket. There were words, magazine stories, tumult. After all, the owner of the club had made the decision to get and pay Wilt, and that automatically placed some limit on the coach's options of how to utilize or not utilize the big man. Van

Breda Kolff, a pretty explosive personality in his own right, never resolved the situation, and by the time the regular season ended, the Laker record of 55–27 was good enough to beat Atlanta by a seven-game margin, but not good enough to be the best in the league.

That distinction went to Baltimore, and the race in the East was the good one. Unseld, by his rebounding (despite the fact that he was a "small" NBA center at six-foot-eight), transformed the Bullets into a first-place team. Earl Monroe came into his own, Gus Johnson was better than ever before until he was hurt midway through the season, and the Bullets under Coach Gene Shue broke in front and stayed there. The 76ers, despite the loss of Luke Jackson by injury, played the type of mobile game, with aggressive pressing defenses, that Ramsey and the other coaches of this era favored, and they stayed right on Baltimore's heels.

The Knicks, off to another terrible start, began winning in November, and in mid-December the team made a trade that altered the balance of power: they sent Walt Bellamy and Howie Komives to Detroit for Dave DeBusschere, and in one stroke all the pieces fell into place for New York. Willis Reed, forced to play the corner while Bellamy was there, moved back into his natural position at center. DeBusschere played the corner better than Reed had. Walt Frazier, in his second season now, started to produce consistently as the all-around backcourt man, and Dick Barnett continued along his apparently ageless path. When Cazzie Russell got hurt, Bradley got a chance to play forward, and he started to fit in admirably.

By the time the race ended, Baltimore was still first, two games ahead of Philadelphia, but the Knicks, a game further back, were recognized as the hot club. The Celtics, with Russell often hampered by injury, with K. C. Jones gone (to coach Brandeis), and with their reserve strength again stripped by expansion, came in fourth—six games behind the Knicks but not in any danger of failing to make the playoffs.

Thereupon the Knicks wowed their supporters by blasting Baltimore right out of the playoffs in four straight. The Celtics "upset" Philadelphia—and then upset the Knicks in six games. The Lakers, meanwhile, lumbered past San Francisco in six games, and picking up momentum, Atlanta in five.

And there—for a change—was another final between Boston and Los Angeles, but this time with a big difference. West and Baylor had Chamberlain on their side now, and for the first time a weapon to cope with Russell. Here would be, at last, vindication after all those years of final-round frustration.

But Mr. Russell didn't see it that way.

The series went seven games, in true big-league surroundings—the new Forum with 17,500 seats in Los Angeles, an enlarged Boston Garden seating more than 15,000. Some games, including the final one on a Monday night in early May, were televised nationally, in prime time. It was a fierce game, in which the Celtics took a big lead in the third quarter as the Laker offense died; then, as the aging Celtics started to tire, the Lakers began closing in. Chamberlain, going for a rebound, injured his leg and had to leave the game; the Lakers kept closing anyway, and came to within a point with a couple of minutes to play. But a shot by Don Nelson that hit the back rim, bounced straight up and fell through, was the one that made the difference, and the Celtics were champions again.

For Russell, this was literally the ultimate triumph. He retired from basketball. For the Lakers, this was the worst frustration yet, and the friction between Chamberlain and Von Breda Kolff quickly led to the coach's departure. But as an event that fired the imagination of the sports public, this latest Celtic victory was the biggest thing yet to happen to the N.B.A. Evidently the Boston dynasty, supposedly ended in 1967, wasn't quite dead yet. Eleven championships in thirteen years was an indelible record.

Nevertheless, it *was* over. There was a difference between victory, however well earned, and dominance, which the Celtics no longer held. What the 1969 season had really demonstrated was a balance of strength among the better teams in the league so well distributed that even a West–Baylor–Chamberlain combination could not dominate.

That was on the floor. In the offices other things were stirring.

In the battle for Alcindor, the N.B.A. won. A flip of coin gave the rights to Milwaukee instead of to Phoenix, and Wes Pavalon, the owner of the Bucks, produced a $1.4 million multiyear package that Alcindor and his advisors accepted. Evidently, the personal impression made by Pavalon on the rather strong-willed young giant was a major factor in Alcindor's decision. At any rate, Milwaukee had the big prize, and it was promptly assumed the A.B.A. would evaporate.

It did not. It had completed its second season with Barry playing for Oakland, and the Oaks, under Hannum, won the league championship. The fourteen-team N.B.A. had drawn about 4,400,000, its best showing ever; but even the A.B.A. pulled in 1,400,000 (at admittedly lower prices). Obviously, there was a market for pro basketball that was nowhere near saturation point. The A.B.A. did not succeed in getting a regular television contract, but each new success of the N.B.A. was helping to make sponsors and network executives pro-basketball-conscious. Unable to get a real share of the new stars, and unable to win away for immediate use any of the established N.B.A. stars, the A.B.A. continued to grow at a modest rate anyway, and even to strengthen its position.

One way was to sign up N.B.A. stars for future delivery. For 1970, the A.B.A. shifted two franchises: Houston to Charlotte (where the team would represent all of North Carolina), and Oakland to Washington, D.C. (where the new owner was Earl Foreman, recently a part-owner of the Baltimore Bullets).

The Carolina Cougars, led aggressively by Jim Gardner, signed Billy Cunningham, who had been a star at Chapel Hill in his college days, to join the team whenever he finished a current multi-year contract in Philadelphia. Foreman did the same with Dave Bing, a native of Washington. But when the Los Angeles Stars signed up Zelmo Beaty, who was having his differences with the Atlanta management, Beaty decided to sit out the 1969–70 season (following the Barry precedent), so the N.B.A. lost him without the A.B.A. gaining him.

But the most important player of all went the other way.

Connie Hawkins was generally regarded as the best player in the A.B.A. The N.B.A. had kept him out after the 1960–61 round of college scandals on what now appeared to be hazy grounds. Hawkins sued the N.B.A. and made a strong enough case for the N.B.A. to settle with him for an amount reported to be $1 million or more, spread out over many years. Thus made eligible, Hawkins joined the Phoenix Suns, giving that expansion team a potential superstar to compensate at least partly for the loss to Milwaukee of Alcindor. At six-foot-eight, Hawkins would probably be a cornerman in the N.B.A., and everyone expected him to be an outstanding one.

These developments underlined a fact of life: the immediate interests of players and owners do not always coincide. There was ample proof now, over a two-year period, how much bargaining power every player gained by having two leagues to choose from—and the same proof showed how much potential club profit was being diverted. The pressures for some sort of amalgamation began to build. If the A.B.A. was not going to fold up quietly, there seemed no point in protracted conflict. If there was any lesson at all in sports history, that was it.

What began to happen now could only be called kaleidoscopic.

The 1969–70 season began with Cousy back on the scene, as coach of the Cincinnati Royals; with Van Breda Kolff coaching Detroit and Joe Mullaney, a graduate of the early years of the league, and then spectacularly successful as coach at Providence College, as the new coach of the Lakers; with the Celtics, still under the direction of Auerbach, now owned by Trans-National Communications, with Jack Waldron as president, and with Heinsohn as Russell's successor as coach; and with Pat Williams, a young live-wire promoter, breathing new vim into the Chicago situation as general manager; and with Len Wilkens as player-coach in Seattle.

By the time the season was half over, headlines had been made in the following ways:

The Knicks, with a record eighteen-game winning streak that gave them a 23-1 start, ran away from the rest.

Chamberlain and Thurmond were hospitalized for knee operations.

Kerr was dropped as coach of Phoenix, to be replaced by Jerry Colangelo, who was also general manager; McMahon was out as San Diego's coach, replaced by, of all people, Hannum; and George Lee of the San Francisco Warriors was replaced by Al Attles.

Hannum had quit, and Barry had tried to jump back to the N.B.A. when the A.B.A. Oakland team went to Washington, but a court ruling kept Barry in the A.B.A.

Merger talks were begun.

Expansion of the N.B.A. into four more cities was planned.

By the time the regular schedule ended, in mid-March, 1970, the Knicks and the Atlanta Hawks were divisional champs; Chamberlain was back in action, making a remarkable recovery from surgery; Alcindor was everything his opponents had feared, and Milwaukee had jumped from last place to second; Hawkins was an all-star forward; West was, for the first time, league scoring champion; merger talks had been broken off and resumed; and three new teams—Cleveland, Buffalo and Portland, Oregon—had been accepted for the 1970–71 season, at an entry fee of $3.5 million each. A Houston franchise, voted in with the others, didn't produce the necessary money in time and never got started, leaving the league with seventeen teams, which were grouped into four divisions.

Attendance and television ratings were soaring like moon rockets. The Knicks, selling out the new Garden for almost every game, wound up (after the playoffs) with almost a million paid admissions, an incredible total for basketball. The Lakers drew 700,000, the Milwaukee Bucks, nearly 500,000 and so forth. Alcindor was a tremendous road attraction, and league attendance passed 5,100,000 (while the A.B.A. got up to 1,900,000, aided greatly by an improved situation with the New York Nets, who had been purchased by Roy Boe and now awaited a new arena being built in Hempstead, Long Island). In short, pro basketball was selling about six times as many tickets (at much higher prices) than it had the year before the 24-second rule was adopted.

But there were frictions, too.

In Cincinnati, Cousy was determined to rebuild from the ground up. Lucas, he felt, was "too slow" for the style Cousy wanted to install, so he was allowed to make what was in effect his own trade with San Francisco. Robertson would have to go too—not because he didn't "fit," but because the Royals could not afford the kind of money Oscar would seek when his current multiyear contract ran so. So the Royals traded him to Baltimore, only to run into a stone wall when Oscar exercised the special right his contract contained to veto any trade. He finished the year with the Royals and finally was traded, with his own approval, to Milwaukee when the season was over. That created an Alcindor–

Robertson combination for the 1970–71 season, and true basketball fans found it hard to stay calm all summer as they waited to see it in action.

The merger talks didn't go smoothly, either. The N.B.A. didn't like the idea that some A.B.A. club owners kept making advances to N.B.A. players, even while supposedly discussing a peace treaty, and they didn't like Denver's signing Spencer Heywood of Detroit University before he became a senior. Heywood had been America's Olympic star in Mexico City in 1968 and an All-American collegian in 1969, but with million-dollar packages floating around Heywood could not turn his back on a legitimate offer. The N.B.A. had a rule, of course, against signing anyone until his college class had graduated, and had kept Chamberlain out for a year when Wilt quit Kansas. Still, the overriding necessity for some arrangement to reduce the competition for players kept breathing new life into merger discussions.

The N.B.A. had been through it before, of course. In fact, that was the reason the organization *was* the N.B.A. instead of still the B.A.A. But only Irish, Zollner, Gottlieb (who was the schedule-maker) and Kennedy (who had been a publicity man) were still around from those day. Most of the men making decisions now were arriving at their conclusions from present experience.

As the merger rumors mounted, the N.B.A. Players Association members crystalized their ideas. They had excellent leadership from Larry Fleischer, a New York attorney who also represented some of the top stars individually, and they decided that the proper course would be to file an anti-trust suit as individuals, seeking an injunction against merger.

They got it, too, as all but one player (Hawkins, who had promised not to sue the league when he had made his own settlement) joined in the suit. By this time, the two leagues had worked out the general outlines of a merger agreement. They asked the court for permission to present a merger plan to Congress, which could of course approve it by passing a special law and thereby sidestepping the anti-trust question. The court allowed this, and on June 18 both leagues announced that full agreement had been reached on merger terms. The players, who had anticipated this, prepared to shift their battleground to Washington, where they could lobby effectively, with Bill Bradley and Oscar taking the lead.

It seemed possible, then, in mid-1970, that merger would eventually be accomplished, perhaps at the price of a major modification in the reserve clause—which was, at that point, under full-scale attack in baseball in Curt Flood's anti-trust case, whose trial had just been completed.

These events naturally complicated life for the behind-the-scenes people who had always worked so hard at keeping things on an even keel. In Podoloff's day, when the office was in the Empire State Building (and still included, for a while, the American Hockey League), the "staff" was Connie Maroselli, a young lady who quickly developed encyclopedic knowledge, fierce loyalty to referees (who were assigned out of that office) and the ability to take over the entire statistical operation for many years. Now, after nineteen years with the league, Connie was in a larger office in 2 Penn Plaza, adjacent to the new Garden, surrounded by a real staff. In 1968 Kennedy had hired Carl Scheer as an administrative assistant—and when Scheer moved on to become president of the new Buffalo club, two administrative assistants grew in the spots he vacated, Mike Burns and Simon Gourdine. When Haskell Cohen finally severed his connection with the league (under pressure of outside business), Nick Curran moved in from Detroit as the league's publicity man. Mendy Rudolph was now in charge of referees, while still working games himself, and Schayes, who had been supervisor of referees, moved on to coach Buffalo (whose general manager, Eddie Donovan, had decided to leave the Knicks at their height for family reasons). The new supervisor was John Nucatola, for years a college refereeing administrator.

The hectic air created by new merger possibilities, lawsuits, expansion and ever-increasing publicity demands put a burden on everyone.

Fortunately for all concerned, these bewildering legal questions were pushed into the background by the most spectacular set of playsoffs the N.B.A. ever had, and the best publicized.

The Knicks captured the country. They had a remarkable collection of strong, clear, attractive personalities: Reed, now Most Valuable Player in the league; Frazier, "the next Oscar"; Barnett, now an elder statesman; DeBusschere and Bradley, the "squares" of the squad as far as mod dress was concerned, but the epitomes of "unselfishness" on the basketball floor; Cazzie Russell, the explosive scorer; Dave Stallworth, forced out of action three years before by a heart attack but now able to play again; and a super-sub named Mike Riordan, whose aggressiveness and drive made him a valuable contributor.

This team, built by Donovan and brought to a high polish by Holzman, played a kind of basketball often described as "perfect." Its greatest strength lay in a harassing, pressing defense: a sort used by the Celtics when they had Bill Russell behind them to correct their mistakes, but with the Knicks it was a five-man operation. Their scoring was perfectly distributed, their passing sure, their movement constant, and as much as any team ever did, they played as "five fingers of one hand." They weren't as physically powerful as the 76ers had been with Chamberlain, and they didn't have the spectacular shooting of some of the Celtic teams, but they put things together so well that they were sometimes referred to as "a textbook come to life."

Nevertheless, they were no cinch. Baltimore, after all, had been beaten in 1969 without Johnson; now Johnson was healthy and in top form. In the first round, the Knicks were lucky to win the first game in double-overtime at home, and they won the second at Baltimore. The Bullets, however, with Unseld outplaying Reed, won the next two, and it took a superperformance by Reed (36 point, 36 rebounds) to lead the Knicks to victory in the fifth game, at New York. But the Bullets evened the series again, and in the seventh game it took one of the best efforts of the entire season to get the Knicks through.

Milwaukee, meanwhile, had won more games than New York since December, and had annihilated Philadelphia in the first round, four games to one. How would the Knicks cope with Alcindor? Beautifully, by shutting out the rest of the Bucks, although the four-of-five series with Milwaukee was tougher than that final tally suggested.

In the West, the Lakers, still struggling to get acclimated to Chamberlain's return, lost three of their first four games to Phoenix —but they won the next three and advanced. Atlanta, considered by some experts potentially the toughest team of all, had brushed Chicago aside in five games, but in the first game against the

Lakers they blew a big lead at home and lost Walt Hazzard with a broken wrist. So the Lakers, rolling now, closed out that series in four straight, and reached the final again.

This time there were no Celtics in their way.

But the Knicks proved just as frustrating.

To the highest degree yet, this was a World Series setting for basketball: New York and Los Angeles, the two biggest cities, with the two biggest brand-new arenas, and two superteams.

It was a seven-game series full of melodrama. The first two games, played in New York, were split, the next two, in Los Angeles, both went into overtime and were split.

In the fifth, at New York, the Lakers got off to a big lead and, late in the first quarter, Reed crashed to the floor with a severe muscle tear in his thigh. This seemed to be the one bad break the Knicks had feared, and the one good break the Lakers had awaited all these years—but the Knicks, with a wild second-half rally, pulled the game out. Without Reed in the sixth game, they were crushed as Chamberlain took complete charge. But when the seventh game began, back in New York, a heavily medicated Reed limped out and took his place in the starting line-up, and the inspired Knicks won the championship by playing their greatest game of all. Reed scored only four points—two baskets right at the start—but he did keep Chamberlain under control; and Frazier hit his peak with 36 points and 19 assists. The Knicks had a 27-point lead at halftime, and the final score was 113–99.

So it had happened again to the Lakers, and in the most depressing fashion of all: because they had only themselves to blame for the lost opportunity in the fifth game. Baylor, the oldest player in the series, had played magnificently, and so had West, as usual. But the full utilization of the blend of their talents with Chamberlain's had escaped Mullaney, as it had Van Breda Kolff.

In a sense, the triumphs of the Knicks brought into focus all the original hopes of the B.A.A., and pointed more than ever to a prosperous future.

Here was, indeed, "college-style" basketball raised to the highest professional level and played in a big-league setting. Because most of the communications industry, and the fields of advertising and promotion, have leaders who live and work in New York, the success of any New York sports club has a disproportionate effect on their thinking. The sustained success of the Knicks, starting with the winning streak in November and running through the playoff dramatics of April and May, lifted pro basketball to a level of prestige and marketability that all the Celtic victories couldn't reach. This was not fair to the Celtics: artistically speaking, eleven titles in thirteen years was a feat unique in American sports, and without the long-term greatness of the Celtics there might not have been a firm base for what the Knicks did. But in the realities of the marketplace, in commanding television interest and dollar volume, the Knicks and their new Garden brought basketball a status the sport had never had before.

As the league's twenty-fifth birthday approached, therefore, the future was rosy—and indistinct. That the league, in whatever form (and the merger plan called for thirty teams in an integrated schedule by 1974), would thrive, was beyond question. That major turmoil, restructuring and unforeseeable changes were on the horizon as just as certain.

But one retrospective observation was undeniable: none of the other major leagues, in their first twenty-four years, had come so far or gone so high.

BIBLIOGRAPHY

The following books provide valuable insight and information concerning the N.B.A.:

Red Auerbach, by Arnold (Red) Auerbach and Paul Sann. Little, Brown and Company, Boston, 1967.

Go Up for Glory, by Bill Russell, as told to William McSweeny. Coward-McCann, Inc., New York, 1966.

Bob Pettit: The Drive Within Me, by Bob Pettit with Bob Wolff. Prentice-Hall, New York, 1966.

All statistical and record material about the N.B.A. is available in the league's guides and record books, published annually by *The Sporting News,* St. Louis, Missouri. Bill Mokray, of Boston, pioneered this work and established most of the basic figures. Individual clubs also have annual yearbooks that can be ordered from them.

APPENDIX: RECORDS

LEAGUE

LIST OF CHAMPIONS

Year	East	West	Play-Offs
1947	Washington	Chicago	Philadelphia
1948	Philadelphia	St. Louis	Baltimore
1949	Washington	Rochester	Minneapolis
1950	Syracuse	Indianapolis (Central—Minneapolis)	Minneapolis
1951	Philadelphia	Minneapolis	Rochester
1952	Syracuse	Rochester	Minneapolis
1953	New York	Minneapolis	Minneapolis
1954	New York	Minneapolis	Minneapolis
1955	Syracuse	Fort Wayne	Syracuse
1956	Philadelphia	Fort Wayne	Philadelphia
1957	Boston	St. Louis	Boston
1958	Boston	St. Louis	St. Louis
1959	Boston	St. Louis	Boston
1960	Boston	St. Louis	Boston
1961	Boston	St. Louis	Boston
1962	Boston	Los Angeles	Boston
1963	Boston	Los Angeles	Boston
1964	Boston	San Francisco	Boston
1965	Boston	Los Angeles	Boston
1966	Philadelphia	Los Angeles	Boston
1967	Philadelphia	San Francisco	Philadelphia
1968	Philadelphia	St. Louis	Boston
1969	Baltimore	Los Angeles	Boston
1970	New York	Atlanta	New York

YEAR-BY-YEAR FINAL LEAGUE STANDINGS

1946-47 Season

EASTERN DIVISION

	Won	Lost	Pct.	Games Behind
Washington	49	11	.817	
Philadelphia	35	25	.583	14
New York	33	27	.550	16
Providence	28	32	.467	21
Toronto	22	38	.367	27
Boston	22	38	.367	27

WESTERN DIVISION

	Won	Lost	Pct.	Games Behind
Chicago	39	22	.639	
St. Louis	38	23	.623	1
Cleveland	30	30	.500	8½
Detroit	20	40	.333	18½
Pittsburgh	15	45	.250	23½

1947-48 Season

Philadelphia	27	21	.563	
New York	26	22	.542	1
Boston	20	28	.417	7
Providence	6	42	.125	21

St. Louis	29	19	.604	
*Baltimore	28	20	.583	1
*Chicago	28	20	.583	1
*Washington	28	20	.583	1

* In a special playoff for second place Chicago beat Washington and Baltimore beat Chicago. Thus Baltimore was awarded second, Chicago third and Washington fourth.

1948-49 Season

Washington	38	22	.633	
New York	32	28	.533	6
Baltimore	29	31	.483	9
Philadelphia	28	32	.467	10
Boston	25	35	.417	13
Providence	12	48	.200	26

Rochester	45	15	.750	
Minneapolis	44	16	.733	1
Chicago	38	22	.633	7
St. Louis	29	31	.483	16
Fort Wayne	22	38	.367	23
Indianapolis	18	42	.300	27

1949-50 Season

Syracuse	51	13	.797	
New York	40	28	.588	13
Washington	32	36	.471	21
Philadelphia	26	42	.382	27
Baltimore	25	43	.368	28
Boston	22	46	.324	31

Indianapolis	39	25	.609	
Anderson	37	27	.578	2
Tri-Cities	29	35	.453	10
Sheboygan	22	40	.355	16
Waterloo	19	43	.306	19
Denver	11	51	.177	27

Central Division

*Minneapolis	51	17	.750	
Rochester	51	17	.750	
*Fort Wayne	40	28	.588	11
Chicago	40	28	.588	11
St. Louis	26	42	.382	25

* Minneapolis beat Rochester in a playoff for first place, and Fort Wayne beat Chicago for third place.

1950-51 Season

Philadelphia	40	26	.606	
Boston	39	30	.565	2½
New York	36	30	.545	4
Syracuse	32	34	.485	8
Baltimore	24	42	.364	16
*Washington	10	25	.286	..

Minneapolis	44	24	.647	
Rochester	41	27	.603	3
Fort Wayne	32	36	.471	12
Indianapolis	31	37	.456	13
Tri-Cities	25	43	.368	19

* Disbanded.

1951-52 Season

Syracuse	40	26	.606	
Boston	39	27	.591	1
New York	37	29	.561	3
Philadelphia	33	33	.500	7
Baltimore	20	46	.303	20

Rochester	41	25	.621	
Minneapolis	40	26	.606	1
Indianapolis	34	32	.515	7
Fort Wayne	29	37	.439	12
Milwaukee	17	49	.258	24

1952-53 Season

New York	47	23	.671	
Syracuse	47	24	.662	½
Boston	46	25	.648	1½
Baltimore	16	54	.229	31
Philadelphia	12	57	.174	34½

Minneapolis	48	22	.686	
Rochester	44	26	.629	4
Fort Wayne	36	33	.522	11½
Indianapolis	28	43	.395	20½
Milwaukee	27	44	.380	21½

1953-54 Season

New York	44	28	.611	
Boston	42	30	.583	2
Syracuse	42	30	.583	2
Philadelphia	29	43	.403	15
Baltimore	16	56	.222	28

Minneapolis	46	26	.639	
Rochester	44	28	.611	2
Fort Wayne	40	32	.556	6
Milwaukee	21	51	.292	25

1954-55 Season

Syracuse	43	29	.597	
New York	38	34	.528	5
Boston	36	36	.500	7
Philadelphia	33	39	.458	10

Fort Wayne	43	29	.597	
Minneapolis	40	32	.556	3
Rochester	29	43	.403	14
Milwaukee	26	46	.361	17

1955-56 Season

Philadelphia	45	27	.625	
Boston	39	33	.542	6
*New York	35	37	.486	10
*Syracuse	35	37	.486	10

Fort Wayne	37	35	.514	
†Minneapolis	33	39	.458	4
†St. Louis	33	39	.458	4
Rochester	31	41	.431	6

* Syracuse beat New York in playoff for third place.
† Minneapolis beat St. Louis in playoff for second place.

1956-57 Season

Boston	44	28	.611	
Syracuse	38	34	.528	6
Philadelphia	37	35	.514	7
New York	36	36	.500	8

*St. Louis	34	38	.472	
*Minneapolis	34	38	.472	
*Fort Wayne	34	38	.472	
Rochester	31	41	.431	3

* In playoff for first place St. Louis won; Minneapolis placed second and Fort Wayne third.

1957-58 Season

Boston	49	23	.681	
Syracuse	41	31	.569	8
Philadelphia	37	35	.514	12
New York	35	37	.486	14

St. Louis	41	31	.569	
*Detroit	33	39	.458	8
*Cincinnati	33	39	.458	8
Minneapolis	19	53	.264	22

* Tied for second. Detroit won coin flip for home court advantage in playoffs.

1958-59 Season

Boston	52	20	.722	
New York	40	32	.556	12
Syracuse	35	37	.486	17
Philadelphia	32	40	.444	20

St. Louis	49	23	.681	
Minneapolis	33	39	.458	16
Detroit	28	44	.389	22
Cincinnati	19	53	.264	30

1959-60 Season

Boston	59	16	.786		St. Louis	46	29	.613	
Philadelphia	49	26	.653	10	Detroit	30	45	.400	16
Syracuse	45	30	.600	14	Minneapolis	29	50	.333	22
New York	27	48	.360	32	Cincinnati	19	56	.253	27

1960-61 Season

Boston	57	22	.721		St. Louis	51	28	.645	
Philadelphia	46	33	.582	11	Los Angeles	36	43	.456	15
Syracuse	38	41	.481	19	Detroit	34	45	.430	17
New York	21	58	.266	36	Cincinnati	33	46	.418	18

1961-62 Season

Boston	60	20	.750		Los Angeles	54	26	.657	
Philadelphia	49	31	.612	11	Cincinnati	43	37	.537	11
Syracuse	41	39	.512	19	Detroit	37	43	.462	17
New York	29	51	.362	31	St. Louis	29	51	.362	25
					Chicago	18	62	.225	36

1962-63 Season

Boston	58	22	.725		Los Angeles	53	27	.663	
Syracuse	48	32	.600	10	St. Louis	48	32	.600	5
Cincinnati	42	38	.525	16	Detroit	34	46	.425	19
New York	21	59	.263	37	San Francisco	31	49	.388	22
					Chicago	25	55	.313	28

1963-64 Season

Boston	59	21	.738		San Francisco	48	32	.600	
Cincinnati	55	25	.688	4	St. Louis	46	34	.575	2
Philadelphia	34	46	.425	25	Los Angeles	42	38	.525	6
New York	22	58	.275	37	Baltimore	31	49	.388	17
					Detroit	23	57	.288	25

1964-65 Season

Boston	62	18	.775		Los Angeles	49	31	.613	
Cincinnati	48	32	.600	14	St. Louis	45	35	.563	4
Philadelphia	40	40	.500	22	Baltimore	37	43	.463	12
New York	31	49	.388	31	Detroit	31	49	.388	18
					San Francisco	17	63	.213	32

1965-66 Season

Philadelphia	55	25	.688		Los Angeles	45	35	.563	
Boston	54	26	.675	1	Baltimore	38	42	.475	7
Cincinnati	45	35	.563	10	St. Louis	36	44	.450	9
New York	30	50	.375	25	San Francisco	35	45	.438	10
					Detroit	22	58	.275	23

1966-67 Season

Philadelphia	68	13	.840		San Francisco	44	37	.543	
Boston	60	21	.741	8	St. Louis	39	42	.481	5
Cincinnati	39	42	.481	29	Los Angeles	36	45	.444	8
New York	36	45	.444	32	Chicago	33	48	.407	11
Baltimore	20	61	.247	48	Detroit	30	51	.370	14

1967-68 Season

Philadelphia	62	20	.756		St. Louis	56	26	.683	
Boston	54	28	.659	8	Los Angeles	52	30	.634	4
New York	43	39	.524	19	San Francisco	43	39	.524	13
Detroit	40	42	.488	22	Chicago	29	53	.354	27
Cincinnati	39	43	.476	23	Seattle	23	59	.280	33
Baltimore	36	46	.439	26	San Diego	15	67	.183	41

1968-69 Season

Baltimore	57	25	.695		Los Angeles	55	27	.671	
Philadelphia	55	27	.671	2	Atlanta	48	34	.585	7
New York	54	28	.659	3	San Francisco	41	41	.500	14
Boston	48	34	.585	9	San Diego	37	45	.451	18
Cincinnati	41	41	.500	16	Chicago	33	49	.402	22
Detroit	32	50	.390	25	Seattle	30	52	.366	25
Milwaukee	27	55	.329	30	Phoenix	16	66	.195	39

1969-70 Season

New York	60	22	.732		Atlanta	48	34	.585	
Milwaukee	56	26	.683	4	Los Angeles	46	36	.561	2
Baltimore	50	32	.610	10	Chicago	39	43	.476	9
Philadelphia	42	40	.512	18	Phoenix	39	43	.476	9
Cincinnati	36	46	.439	24	Seattle	36	46	.439	12
Boston	34	48	.415	26	San Francisco	30	52	.366	18
Detroit	31	51	.378	29	San Diego	27	55	.329	21

PLAYOFF WINNERS

1946-47	Philadelphia, beat Chicago 4 games to 1
1947-48	Baltimore, beat Philadelphia 4 games to 2
1948-49	Minneapolis, beat Washington 4 games to 2
1949-50	Minneapolis, beat Syracuse 4 games to 2
1950-51	Rochester, beat New York 4 games to 3
1951-52	Minneapolis beat New York 4 games to 3
1952-53	Minneapolis, beat New York 4 games to 1
1953-54	Minneapolis, beat Syracuse 4 games to 3
1954-55	Syracuse, beat Fort Wayne 4 games to 3
1955-56	Philadelphia, beat Fort Wayne 4 games to 1
1956-57	Boston, beat St. Louis 4 games to 3
1957-58	St. Louis, beat Boston 4 games to 2
1958-59	Boston, beat Minneapolis 4 games to 0
1959-60	Boston, beat St. Louis 4 games to 3
1960-61	Boston, beat St. Louis 4 games to 1
1961-62	Boston, beat Los Angeles 4 games to 3
1962-63	Boston, beat Los Angeles 4 games to 2
1963-64	Boston, beat San Francisco 4 games to 1
1964-65	Boston, beat Los Angeles 4 games to 1
1965-66	Boston, beat Los Angeles 4 games to 3
1966-67	Philadelphia, beat San Francisco 4 games to 2
1967-68	Boston, beat Los Angeles 4 games to 2
1968-69	Boston, beat Los Angeles 4 games to 3
1969-70	New York, beat Los Angeles 4 games to 3

YEAR-BY-YEAR COMPLETE PLAYOFF RESULTS

1946-47

SEMIFINALS

Apr. 2—Chicago 81 at Washington 65
Apr. 3—Chicago 69 at Washington 53
Apr. 8—Washington 55 at Chicago 67
Apr. 10—Chicago 69 at Washington 76
Apr. 12—Washington 67 at Chicago 55
Apr. 13—Washington 61 at Chicago 66

Apr. 2—St. Louis 68 at Philadelphia 73
Apr. 5—Philadelphia 51 at St. Louis 73
Apr. 6—Philadelphia 75 at St. Louis 59

Apr. 2—New York 51 at Cleveland 77
Apr. 5—Cleveland 74 at New York 86
Apr. 9—Cleveland 71 at New York 93

Apr. 12—New York 70 at Philadelphia 82
Apr. 14—Philadelphia 72 at New York 53

FOR CHAMPIONSHIP

Apr. 16—Chicago 71 at Philadelphia 84
Apr. 17—Chicago 74 at Philadelphia 85
Apr. 19—Philadelphia 75 at Chicago 72
Apr. 20—Philadelphia 73 at Chicago 74
Apr. 22—Chicago 80 at Philadephia 83

1947-48

SEMIFINALS

Mar. 23—Philadelphia 58 at St. Louis 60
Mar. 25—Philadelphia 65 at St. Louis 64
Mar. 27—St. Louis 56 at Philadelphia 84
Mar. 30—St. Louis 56 at Philadelphia 51
Apr. 1—Philadelphia 62 at St. Louis 69
Apr. 3—St. Louis 61 at Philadelphia 84
Apr. 6—Philadelphia 85 at St. Louis 46

Mar. 27—New York 81 at Baltimore 85
Mar. 28—Baltimore 69 at New York 79
Apr. 1—New York 77 at Baltimore 84

Mar. 28—Chicago 79 at Boston 72
Mar. 31—Chicago 77 at Boston 81
Apr. 2—Chicago 81 at Boston 74

Apr. 7—Baltimore 73 at Chicago 67
Apr. 8—Chicago 72 at Baltimore 89

FOR CHAMPIONSHIP

Apr. 10—Baltimore 60 at Philadelphia 71
Apr. 13—Baltimore 66 at Philadelphia 63
Apr. 15—Philadelphia 70 at Baltimore 72
Apr. 17—Philadelphia 75 at Baltimore 78
Apr. 20—Baltimore 82 at Philadelphia 91
Apr. 21—Philadelphia 73 at Baltimore 88

1948-49

SEMIFINALS

Mar. 23—Washington 92 at Philadelphia 70
Mar. 24—Philadelphia 78 at Washington 80

Mar. 23—New York 81 at Baltimore 82
Mar. 24—Baltimore 74 at New York 84
Mar. 26—Baltimore 99 at New York *103

Mar. 22—St. Louis 64 at Rochester 93
Mar. 23—Rochester 66 at St. Louis 64

Mar. 23—Chicago 77 at Minneapolis 84
Mar. 24—Minneapolis 101 at Chicago 85

Mar. 29—New York 71 at Washington 77
Mar. 31—Washington 84 at New York *86
Apr. 2—New York 76 at Washington 84

Mar. 27—Minneapolis 80 at Rochester 79
Mar. 29—Rochester 55, Minn. at St. Paul 67

FOR CHAMPIONSHIP

Apr. 4—Washington 84 at Minneapolis 88
Apr. 6—Washington 62 at Minneapolis 76
Apr. 8—Minneapolis 94 at Washington 74
Apr. 9—Minneapolis 71 at Washington 83
Apr. 11—Minneapolis 66 at Washington 74
Apr. 13—Washington 56, Minn. at St. Paul 77

*—Denotes overtime period.

1949-50

Central Division 1st place tie
Mar. 21—Minneapolis 78 at Rochester 76
Central Division 3rd place tie
Mar. 20—Chicago 69 at Ft. Wayne 86

SEMIFINALS

Mar. 22—Philadelphia 76 at Syracuse 93
Mar. 23—Syracuse 59 at Philadelphia 53
Mar. 21—New York 90 at Washington 87
Mar. 22—Washington 83 at New York 103

Mar. 26—New York 83 at Syracuse *91
Mar. 30—Syracuse 76 at New York 80
Apr. 2—New York 80 at Syracuse 91
Mar. 22—Chicago 75 at Minneapolis 85
Mar. 25—Minneapolis 75 at Chicago 67

Mar. 23—Fort Wayne 90 at Rochester 84
Mar. 25—Rochester 78 at Fort Wayne *79

Mar. 27—Fort Wayne 79 at Minneapolis 93
Mar. 28—Minneapolis 89 at Fort Wayne 82

Mar. 21—Sheboygan 85 at Indianapolis 86
Mar. 23—Indianapolis 85 at Sheboygan 95
Mar. 25—Sheboygan 84 at Indianapolis 91

Mar. 21—Tri-Cities 77 at Anderson 89
Mar. 23—Anderson 75 at Tri-Cities 76
Mar. 24—Tri-Cities 71 at Anderson 94

Mar. 28—Anderson 74 at Indianapolis 77
Mar. 30—Indianapolis 67 at Anderson 84
Apr. 1—Anderson 67 at Indianapolis 65

Apr. 5—Anderson 50 at Minneapolis 75
Apr. 6—Minneapolis 90 at Anderson 71

FOR CHAMPIONSHIP

Apr. 8—Minneapolis 68 at Syracuse 66
Apr. 9—Minneapolis 85 at Syracuse 91
Apr. 14—Syracuse 77, Minn. at St. Paul 91
Apr. 16—Syracuse 69, Minn. at St. Paul 77
Apr. 20—Minneapolis 76 at Syracuse 83
Apr. 23—Syracuse 95 at Minneapolis 110

*—Denotes overtime period.

1950-51

SEMIFINALS

Mar. 20—New York 83 at Boston 69
Mar. 22—Boston 78 at New York 92

Mar. 20—Syracuse 91 at Philadelphia *89
Mar. 22—Philadelphia 78 at Syracuse 90

Mar. 28—Syracuse 92 at New York 103
Mar. 29—New York 80 at Syracuse 102
Mar. 31—Syracuse 75 at New York 97
Apr. 1—New York 83 at Syracuse 90
Apr. 4—Syracuse 81 at New York 83

Mar. 20—Fort Wayne 81 at Rochester 110
Mar. 22—Rochester 78 at Fort Wayne 83
Mar. 24—Fort Wayne 78 at Rochester 97

Mar. 21—Indianapolis 81 at Minneapolis 95
Mar. 23—Minneapolis 88 at Indianapolis 108
Mar. 25—Indianapolis 80 at Minneapolis 85

Mar. 29—Rochester 73 at Minneapolis 76
Mar. 31—Rochester 70 at Minneapolis 66
Apr. 1—Minneapolis 70 at Rochester 83
Apr. 3—Minneapolis 75 at Rochester 80

FOR CHAMPIONSHIP

Apr. 7—New York 65 at Rochester 92
Apr. 8—New York 84 at Rochester 99
Apr. 11—Rochester 78 at New York 77
Apr. 13—Rochester 73 at New York 79
Apr. 15—New York 92 at Rochester 89
Apr. 18—Rochester 73 at New York 80
Apr. 21—New York 75 at Rochester 79

*—Denotes overtime period.

1951-52

SEMIFINALS

Mar. 20—Philadelphia 83 at Syracuse 102
Mar. 22—Syracuse 95 at Philadelphia 100
Mar. 23—Philadelphia 73 at Syracuse 84

Mar. 19—New York 94 at Boston 105
Mar. 23—Boston 97 at New York 101
Mar. 26—New York 88 at Boston **87

Apr. 2—New York 87 at Syracuse 85
Apr. 3—New York 92 at Syracuse 102
Apr. 4—Syracuse 92 at New York 99
Apr. 8—Syracuse 93 at New York 100

Mar. 23—Indianapolis 70 at Minneapolis 78
Mar. 25—Minneapolis 94 at Indianapolis 87

Mar. 18—Fort Wayne 78 at Rochester 95
Mar. 20—Rochester 92 at Fort Wayne 86

Mar. 29—Minneapolis 78 at Rochester 88
Mar. 30—Minneapolis 83 at Rochester 78

Apr. 5—Rochester 67 at Minneapolis 77
Apr. 6—Rochester 80 at Minneapolis 82

FOR CHAMPIONSHIP

Apr. 12—New York 79, Minn. at St. Paul *83
Apr. 13—New York 80, Minn. at St. Paul 72
Apr. 16—Minneapolis 82 at New York 77
Apr. 18—Minneapolis 89 at New York *90
Apr. 20—New York 89, Minn. at St. Paul 102
Apr. 23—Minneapolis 68 at New York 76
Apr. 25—New York 65 at Minneapolis 82

*—Denotes overtime period.

1952-53

SEMIFINALS

Mar. 17—Baltimore 62 at New York 80
Mar. 20—New York 90 at Baltimore 81

Mar. 19—Boston 87 at Syracuse 81
Mar. 21—Syracuse 105 at Boston ****111

Mar. 25—Boston 91 at New York 95
Mar. 26—New York 70 at Boston 86
Mar. 28—Boston 82 at New York 101
Mar. 29—New York 82 at Boston 75

Mar. 20—Fort Wayne 84 at Rochester 77
Mar. 22—Rochester 83 at Fort Wayne 71
Mar. 24—Fort Wayne 67 at Rochester 65

Mar. 22—Indianapolis 69 at Minneapolis 85
Mar. 23—Minneapolis 81 at Indianapolis 79

Mar. 26—Fort Wayne 73 at Minneapolis 83
Mar. 28—Fort Wayne 75 at Minneapolis 82
Mar. 30—Minneapolis 95 at Fort Wayne 98
Apr. 1—Minneapolis 82 at Fort Wayne 85
Apr. 2—Fort Wayne 58 at Minneapolis 74

FOR CHAMPIONSHIP

Apr. 4—New York 96 at Minneapolis 88
Apr. 5—New York 71 at Minneapolis 73
Apr. 7—Minneapolis 90 at New York 75
Apr. 8—Minneapolis 71 at New York 69
Apr. 10—Minneapolis 91 at New York 84

*—Denotes overtime period.

1953-54

SEMIFINALS

Mar. 16—Boston 93 at New York 71

Mar. 17—Syracuse 96 at Boston *95
Mar. 18—New York 68 at Syracuse 75

Mar. 20—New York 78 at Boston 79
Mar. 21—Syracuse 103 at New York 99
Mar. 22—Boston 85 at Syracuse 98

Mar. 25—Boston 94 at Syracuse 109
Mar. 27—Syracuse 83 at Boston 76

Mar. 16—Fort Wayne 75 at Rochester 82
Mar. 17—Rochester 88 at Minneapolis 109
Mar. 18—Minneapolis 90 at Fort Wayne 85
Mar. 20—Fort Wayne 73 at Minneapolis 78
Mar. 21—Rochester 89 at Ft. Wayne 71
Mar. 23—Minneapolis at Rochester (cancelled)

Mar. 24—Rochester 76 at Minneapolis 89
Mar. 27—Minneapolis 73 at Rochester 74
Mar. 28—Rochester 72 at Minneapolis 82

FOR CHAMPIONSHIP

Mar. 31—Syracuse 68 at Minneapolis 79
Apr. 3—Syracuse 62 at Minneapolis 60
Apr. 4—Minneapolis 81 at Syracuse 67
Apr. 8—Minneapolis 69 at Syracuse 80
Apr. 10—Minneapolis 84 at Syracuse 73
Apr. 11—Syracuse 65 at Minneapolis 63
Apr. 12—Syracuse 80 at Minneapolis 87

*—Denotes overtime period.

1954-55

SEMIFINALS

Mar. 15—New York 101 at Boston 122
Mar. 16—Boston 95 at New York 102
Mar. 19—Boston 116 at New York 109

Mar. 22—Boston 100 at Syracuse 110
Mar. 24—Boston 110 at Syracuse 116
Mar. 26—Syracuse 97 at Boston *100
Mar. 27—Syracuse 110 at Boston 94

Mar. 16—Rochester 78, Minn. at St. Paul 82
Mar. 18—Minneapolis 92 at Rochester 94
Mar. 19—Rochester 110, Minn. at St. Paul 119

Mar. 20—Minn. 79, Fort Wayne at Elk'rt, Ind. 96
Mar. 22—Minn. 97, Fort Wayne at Indianapolis *98
Mar. 23—Fort Wayne 91 at Minneapolis *99
Mar. 27—Fort Wayne 105 at Minneapolis 96

FOR CHAMPIONSHIP

Mar. 31—Fort Wayne 82 at Syracuse 86
Apr. 2—Fort Wayne 84 at Syracuse 87
Apr. 3—Syracuse 89, Fort Wayne at Indpls. 98
Apr. 5—Syracuse 102, Fort Wayne at Indpls. 109
Apr. 7—Syracuse 71, Fort Wayne at Indpls. 74
Apr. 9—Fort Wayne 104 at Syracuse 109
Apr. 10—Fort Wayne 91 at Syracuse 92

*—Denotes overtime period.

1955-56

SPECIAL PLAY-OFFS TO BREAK TIES

Mar. 15—New York 77 at Syracuse 82
Mar. 16—Minneapolis 103 at St. Louis 97

SEMIFINALS

Mar. 17—Syracuse 92 at Boston 110
Mar. 19—Boston 98 at Syracuse 101

Mar. 21—Syracuse 102 at Boston 97

Mar. 23—Syracuse 87 at Philadelphia 109
Mar. 25—Philadelphia 118 at Syracuse 122
Mar. 27—Syracuse 96 at Philadelphia 119
Mar. 28—Philadelphia 104 at Syracuse 108
Mar. 29—Syracuse 104 at Philadelphia 109

Mar. 17—Minneapolis 115 at St. Louis 116
Mar. 19—St. Louis 75 at Minneapolis 133
Mar. 21—St. Louis 116 at Minneapolis 115

Mar. 22—St. Louis 86 at Fort Wayne 85
Mar. 24—Fort Wayne 74 at St. Louis 84
Mar. 25—St. Louis 84 at Fort Wayne 107
Mar. 27—Fort Wayne 93 at St. Louis 84
Mar. 29—St. Louis 97 at Fort Wayne 102

FOR CHAMPIONSHIP

Mar. 31—Fort Wayne 94 at Philadelphia 98
Apr. 1—Philade'phia 83 at Fort Wayne 84
Apr. 3—Fort Wayne 96 at Philadelphia 100
Apr. 5—Philadelphia 107 at Fort Wayne 105
Apr. 7—Fort Wayne 88 at Philadelphia 99

1956-57

SEMIFINALS

Mar. 16—Syracuse 103 at Philadelphia 96
Mar. 18—Philadelphia 80 at Syracuse 91

Mar. 21—Syracuse 90 at Boston 108
Mar. 23—Boston 120 at Syracuse 105
Mar. 24—Syracuse 80 at Boston 83

Mar. 14—Fort Wayne 103 at St. Louis 115
Mar. 16—Minneapolis 111 at St. Louis 114

Mar. 17—Fort Wayne 127 at Minneapolis 131
Mar. 19—Minneapolis 110 at Fort Wayne 108

Mar. 21—Minneapolis 109 at St. Louis 118
Mar. 24—Minneapolis 104 at St. Louis 106
Mar. 25—St. Louis 143 at Minneapolis **135

FOR CHAMPIONSHIP

Mar. 30—St. Louis 125 at Boston *123
Mar. 31—St. Louis 99 at Boston 119
Apr. 6—Boston 98 at St. Louis 106
Apr. 7—Boston 123 at St. Louis 118
Apr. 9—St. Louis 109 at Boston 124
Apr. 11—Boston 94 at St. Louis 96
Apr. 13—St. Louis 123 at Boston **125

*—Denotes overtime period.

1957-58

SEMIFINALS

Mar. 15—Philadelphia 82 at Syracuse 86
Mar. 16—Syracuse 93 at Philadelphia 95
Mar. 18—Philadelphia 101 at Syracuse 88

Mar. 19—Philadelphia 98 at Boston 107
Mar. 22—Boston 109 at Philadelphia 87
Mar. 23—Philadelphia 92 at Boston 106
Mar. 26—Boston 98 at Philadelphia 111

Mar. 27—Philadelphia at Boston 93

Mar. 15—Cincinnati 93 at Detroit 100
Mar. 16—Detroit 124 at Cincinnati 104

Mar. 19—Detroit 111 at St. Louis 114
Mar. 22—St. Louis 99 at Detroit 96
Mar. 23—Detroit 109 at St. Louis 89
Mar. 25—St. Louis 145 at Detroit 101

Mar. 27—Detroit 96 at St. Louis 120

FOR CHAMPIONSHIP

Mar. 29—St. Louis 104 at Boston 102
Mar. 30—St. Louis 112 at Boston 136
Apr. 2—Boston 107 at St. Louis 111
Apr. 5—Boston 109 at St. Louis 98
Apr. 9—St. Louis 102 at Boston 100
Apr. 12—Boston 109 at St. Louis 110

1958-59

SEMIFINALS

Mar. 13—Syracuse 129 at New York 123
Mar. 15—New York 115 at Syracuse 131

Mar. 18—Syracuse 109 at Boston 131
Mar. 21—Boston 118 at Syracuse 120
Mar. 22—Syracuse 111 at Boston 133
Mar. 25—Boston 107 at Syracuse 119
Mar. 28—Syracuse 108 at Boston 129
Mar. 29—Boston 121 at Syracuse 133
Apr. 1—Syracuse 125 at Boston 130

Mar. 14—Detroit 89 at Minneapolis 92
Mar. 15—Minneapolis 103 at Detroit 117
Mar. 18—Detroit 102 at Minneapolis 129

Mar. 21—Minneapolis 90 at St. Louis 124
Mar. 22—St. Louis 98 at Minneapolis 106
Mar. 24—Minneapolis 97 at St. Louis 127
Mar. 26—St. Louis 98 at Minneapolis 108
Mar. 28—Minneapolis 98 at St. Louis *97
Mar. 29—St. Louis 104 at Minneapolis 106

FOR CHAMPIONSHIP

Apr. 4—Minneapolis 115 at Boston 118
Apr. 5—Minneapolis 108 at Boston 128
Apr. 7—Boston 123, Mpls. at St. Paul 120
Apr. 9—Boston 118 at Minneapolis 113

*—Denotes overtime period.

1959-60

SEMIFINALS

Mar. 11—Syracuse 92 at Philadelphia 115
Mar. 13—Philadelphia 119 at Syracuse 125
Mar. 14—Syracuse 112 at Philadelphia 132

Mar. 16—Philadelphia 105 at Boston 111
Mar. 18—Boston 110 at Philadelphia 115
Mar. 19—Philadelphia 90 at Boston 120
Mar. 20—Boston 112 at Philadelphia 104

Mar. 22—Philadelphia 128 at Boston 107
Mar. 24—Boston 119 at Philadelphia 117

———

Mar. 12—Minneapolis 113 at Detroit 112
Mar. 13—Detroit 99 at Minneapolis 114

———

Mar. 16—Minneapolis 99 at St. Louis 112
Mar. 17—Minneapolis 120 at St. Louis 113
Mar. 19—St. Louis 93 at Minneapolis 89
Mar. 20—St. Louis 101 at Minneapolis 103
Mar. 22—Minneapolis 117 at St. Louis *110

Mar. 24—St. Louis 117 at Minneapolis 96
Mar. 26—Minneapolis 86 at St. Louis 97

FOR CHAMPIONSHIP

Mar. 27—St. Louis 122 at Boston 140
Mar. 29—St. Louis 113 at Boston 103
Apr. 2—Boston 102 at St. Louis 86
Apr. 3—Boston 96 at St. Louis 104
Apr. 5—St. Louis 102 at Boston 127
Apr. 7—Boston 102 at St. Louis 105
Apr. 9—St. Louis 103 at Boston 122

*—Denotes overtime period.

1960-61

SEMIFINALS

Mar. 14—Syracuse 115 at Philadelphia 107
Mar. 16—Philadelphia 114 at Syracuse 115
Mar. 18—Syracuse 106 at Philadelphia 103

———

Mar. 19—Syracuse 115 at Boston 128
Mar. 21—Boston 98 at Syracuse 115
Mar. 23—Syracuse 110 at Boston 133
Mar. 25—Boston 120 at Syracuse 107
Mar. 26—Syracuse 101 at Boston 123

———

Mar. 14—Detroit 102 at Los Angeles 120
Mar. 15—Detroit 118 at Los Angeles 120
Mar. 17—Los Angeles 113 at Detroit 124
Mar. 18—Los Angeles 114 at Detroit 123

Mar. 19—Detroit 120 at Los Angeles 137
Mar. 21—Los Angeles 122 at St. Louis 118
Mar. 22—Los Angeles 106 at St. Louis 121
Mar. 24—St. Louis 112 at Los Angeles 118
Mar. 25—St. Louis 118 at Los Angeles 117
Mar. 27—Los Angeles 121 at St. Louis 112
Mar. 29—St. Louis 114 at Los Angeles *113
Apr. 1—Los Angeles 103 at St. Louis 105

FOR CHAMPIONSHIP

Apr. 2—St. Louis 95 at Boston 129
Apr. 5—St. Louis 108 at Boston 116
Apr. 8—Boston 120 at St. Louis 124
Apr. 9—Boston 119 at St. Louis 104
Apr. 11—St. Louis 112 at Boston 121

*—Denotes overtime period.

1961-62

SEMIFINALS

Mar. 16—Syracuse 103 at Philadelphia 110
Mar. 18—Philadelphia 97 at Syracuse 82
Mar. 19—Syracuse 101 at Philadelphia 100
Mar. 20—Philadelphia 99 at Syracuse 106
Mar. 22—Syracuse 104 at Philadelphia 121

Mar. 24—Philadelphia 89 at Boston 117
Mar. 27—Boston 106 at Philadelphia 113
Mar. 28—Philadelphia 114 at Boston 129
Mar. 31—Boston 106 at Philadelphia 110
Apr. 1—Philadelphia 104 at Boston 119
Apr. 3—Boston 99 at Philadelphia 109
Apr. 5—Philadelphia 107 at Boston 109

Mar. 16—Cincinnati 122 at Detroit 123
Mar. 17—Detroit 107 at Cincinnati 129
Mar. 18—Cincinnati 107 at Detroit 118
Mar. 20—Detroit 112 at Cincinnati 111

Mar. 24—Detroit 108 at Los Angeles 132
Mar. 25—Detroit 112 at Los Angeles 127
Mar. 27—Los Angeles 111 at Detroit 106
Mar. 29—Los Angeles 117 at Detroit 118
Mar. 31—Detroit 132 at Los Angeles 125
Apr. 3—Los Angeles 123 at Detroit 117

FOR CHAMPIONSHIP

Apr. 7—Los Angeles 108 at Boston 122
Apr. 8—Los Angeles 129 at Boston 122
Apr. 10—Boston 115 at Los Angeles 117
Apr. 11—Boston 115 at Los Angeles 103
Apr. 14—Los Angeles 126 at Boston 121
Apr. 16—Boston 119 at Los Angeles 105
Apr. 18—Los Angeles 107 at Boston *110

*—Denotes overtime period.

1962-63

SEMIFINALS

Mar. 19—Cincinnati 120 at Syracuse 123
Mar. 21—Syracuse 115 at Cincinnati 133
Mar. 23—Cincinnati 117 at Syracuse 121
Mar. 24—Syracuse 118 at Cincinnati 125
Mar. 26—Cincinnati 131 at Syracuse *127

EASTERN DIVISION FINALS

Mar. 28—Cincinnati 135 at Boston 132
Mar. 29—Boston 125 at Cincinnati 102
Mar. 31—Cincinnati 121 at Boston 116
Apr. 3—Boston 128 at Cincinnati 110
Apr. 6—Cincinnati 120 at Boston 125
Apr. 7—Boston 99 at Cincinnati 109
Apr. 10—Cincinnati 131 at Boston 142

Mar. 20—Detroit 99 at St. Louis 118
Mar. 22—Detroit 108 at St. Louis 122
Mar. 24—St. Louis 103 at Detroit 107
Mar. 26—St. Louis 104 at Detroit 100

WESTERN DIVISION FINALS

Mar. 31—St. Louis 104 at Los Angeles 112
Apr. 2—St. Louis 99 at Los Angeles 101
Apr. 4—Los Angeles 112 at St. Louis 125
Apr. 6—Los Angeles 114 at St. Louis 124
Apr. 7—St. Louis 100 at Los Angeles 123
Apr. 9—Los Angeles 113 at St. Louis 121
Apr. 11—St. Louis 100 at Los Angeles 115

*—Denotes overtime period.

FOR CHAMPIONSHIP

Apr. 14—Los Angeles 114 at Boston 117
Apr. 16—Los Angeles 106 at Boston 113
Apr. 17—Boston 99 at Los Angeles 119
Apr. 19—Boston 108 at Los Angeles 105
Apr. 21—Los Angeles 126 at Boston 119
Apr. 24—Boston 112 at Los Angeles 109

1963-64

EASTERN DIVISION SEMIFINAL SERIES

Cincinnati defeated Philadelphia 3 to 2

Mar. 22—Philadelphia 102 at Cincinnati 127
Mar. 24—Cincinnati 114 at Philadelphia 122
Mar. 25—Philadelphia 89 at Cincinnati 101
Mar. 28—Cincinnati 120 at Philadelphia 129
Mar. 29—Philadelphia 124 at Cincinnati 130

EASTERN DIVISION FINAL SERIES

Boston defeated Cincinnati 4 to 1

Mar. 31—Cincinnati 87 at Boston 103
Apr. 2—Cincinnati 90 at Boston 101
Apr. 5—Boston 102 at Cincinnati 92
Apr. 7—Boston 93 at Cincinnati 102
Apr. 9—Cincinnati 95 at Boston 109

WESTERN DIVISION SEMIFINAL SERIES

St. Louis defeated Los Angeles 3 to 2

Mar. 21—Los Angeles 104 at St. Louis 115
Mar. 22—Los Angeles 90 at St. Louis 106
Mar. 25—St. Louis 105 at Los Angeles 107
Mar. 28—St. Louis 88 at Los Angeles 97
Mar. 30—Los Angeles 108 at St. Louis 121

WESTERN DIVISION FINAL SERIES

San Francisco defeated St. Louis 4 to 3

Apr. 1—St. Louis 116 at San Francisco 111
Apr. 3—St. Louis 85 at San Francisco 120
Apr. 5—San Francisco 109 at St. Louis 113
Apr. 8—San Francisco 111 at St. Louis 109
Apr. 10—St. Louis 97 at San Francisco 121
Apr. 12—San Francisco 95 at St. Louis 123
Apr. 16—St. Louis 95 at San Francisco 105

CHAMPIONSHIP SERIES

Boston defeated San Francisco 4 to 1

Apr. 18—San Francisco 96 at Boston 108
Apr. 20—San Francisco 101 at Boston 124
Apr. 22—Boston 91 at San Francisco 115
Apr. 24—Boston 98 at San Francisco 95
Apr. 26—San Francisco 99 at Boston 105

1964-65

EASTERN DIVISION SEMIFINAL SERIES

Philadelphia defeated Cincinnati 3 to 1

Mar. 24—Philadelphia 119 at Cincinnati 117
Mar. 26—Cincinnati 121 at Philadelphia 120
Mar. 28—Philadelphia 108 at Cincinnati 94
Mar. 31—Cincinnati 112 at Philadelphia 119

EASTERN DIVISION FINAL SERIES

Boston defeated Philadelphia 4 to 3

Apr. 4—Philadelphia 98 at Boston 108
Apr. 6—Boston 103 at Philadelphia 109
Apr. 8—Philadelphia 94 at Boston 112
Apr. 9—Boston 131 at Philadelphia *134
Apr. 11—Philadelphia 108 at Boston 114
Apr. 13—Boston 106 at Philadelphia 112
Apr. 15—Philadelphia 109 at Boston 110

WESTERN DIVISION SEMIFINAL SERIES

Baltimore defeated St. Louis 3 to 1

Mar. 24—Baltimore 108 at St. Louis 105
Mar. 26—Baltimore 105 at St. Louis 129
Mar. 27—St. Louis 99 at Baltimore 131
Mar. 30—St. Louis 103 at Baltimore 109

WESTERN DIVISION FINAL SERIES

Los Angeles defeated Baltimore 4 to 2

Apr. 3—Baltimore 115 at Los Angeles 121
Apr. 5—Baltimore 115 at Los Angeles 118
Apr. 7—Los Angeles 115 at Baltimore 122
Apr. 9—Los Angeles 112 at Baltimore 114
Apr. 11—Baltimore 112 at Los Angeles 120
Apr. 13—Los Angeles 117 at Baltimore 115

CHAMPIONSHIP SERIES

Boston defeated Los Angeles 4 to 1

Apr. 18—Los Angeles 110 at Boston 142
Apr. 19—Los Angeles 123 at Boston 129
Apr. 21—Boston 105 at Los Angeles 126
Apr. 23—Boston 112 at Los Angeles 99
Apr. 25—Los Angeles 96 at Boston 129

*—Denotes overtime period.

1965-66

EASTERN DIVISION SEMIFINAL SERIES

Boston defeated Cincinnati 3 to 2

Mar. 23—Cincinnati 107 at Boston 103
Mar. 26—Boston 132 at Cincinnati 125
Mar. 27—Cincinnati 113 at Boston 107
Mar. 30—Boston 120 at Cincinnati 103
Apr. 1—Boston 112 at Cincinnati 103

EASTERN DIVISION FINAL SERIES

Boston defeated Philadelphia 4 to 1

Apr. 3—Boston 115 at Philadelphia 96
Apr. 6—at Boston 114, Philadelphia 93
Apr. 7—at Philadelphia 111, Boston 105
Apr. 10—at Boston 114, Philadelphia *110
Apr. 12—Boston 120 at Philadelphia 112

WESTERN DIVISION SEMIFINAL SERIES

St. Louis defeated Baltimore 3 to 0

Mar. 24—St. Louis 113 at Balitimore 111
Mar. 27—St. Louis 105 at Baltimore 100
Mar. 30—at St. Louis 121, Baltimore 112

WESTERN DIVISION FINAL SERIÉS

Los Angeles defeated St. Louis 4 to 3

Apr. 1—St. Louis 106 at Los Angeles 129
Apr. 3—St. Louis 116 at Los Angeles 125
Apr. 6—Los Angeles 113 at St. Louis 120
Apr. 9—Los Angeles 107 at St. Louis 95
Apr. 10—St. Louis 112 at Los Angeles 100
Apr. 13—Los Angeles 127 at St. Louis 131
Apr. 15—St. Louis 121 at Los Angeles 130

CHAMPIONSHIP SERIES

Boston defeated Los Angeles 4 to 3

Apr. 17—Los Angeles 133 at Boston *129
Apr. 19—Los Angeles 109 at Boston 129
Apr. 20—Boston 120 at Los Angeles 106
Apr. 22—Boston 122 at Los Angeles 117
Apr. 24—Los Angeles 121 at Boston 117
Apr. 26—Boston 115 at Los Angeles 123
Apr. 28—Los Angeles 93 at Boston 95

*—Denotes overtime period.

1966-67

EASTERN DIVISION SEMIFINAL SERIES

Boston defeated New York 3 to 1

Mar. 21—New York 110 at Boston 140
Mar. 25—Boston 115 at New York 108
Mar. 26—New York 123 at Boston 112
Mar. 28—Boston 118 at New York 109

Philadelphia defeated Cincinnati 3 to 1

Mar. 21—Cincinnati 120 at Philadelphia 116
Mar. 22—Philadelphia 123 at Cincinnati 102
Mar. 24—Cincinnati 106 at Philadelphia 121
Mar. 25—Philadelphia 112 at Cincinnati 94

EASTERN DIVISION FINAL SERIES

Philadelphia defeated Boston 4 to 1

Mar. 31—Boston 113 at Philadelphia 127
Apr. 2—Philadelphia 107 at Boston 102
Apr. 5—Boston 104 at Philadelphia 115

Apr. 9—Philadelphia 117 at Boston 121
Apr. 11—Boston 116 at Philadelphia 140

WESTERN DIVISION SEMIFINAL SERIES

St. Louis defeated Chicago 3 to 0

Mar. 21—Chicago 100 at St. Louis 114
Mar. 23—St. Louis 113 at Chicago 107
Mar. 25—Chicago 106 at St. Louis 119

San Francisco defeated Los Angeles 3 to 0

Mar. 21—Los Angeles 108 at San Francisco 124
Mar. 23—San Francisco 113 at Los Angeles 102
Mar. 26—Los Angeles 115 at San Francisco 122

WESTERN DIVISION FINAL SERIES

San Francisco defeated St. Louis 4 to 2

Mar. 30—St. Louis 115 at San Francisco 117
Apr. 1—St. Louis 136 at San Francisco 143
Apr. 5—San Francisco 109 at St. Louis 115
Apr. 8—San Francisco 104 at St. Louis 109
Apr. 10—St. Louis 102 at San Francisco 123
Apr. 12—San Francisco 112 at St. Louis 107

CHAMPIONSHIP SERIES

Philadelphia defeated San Francisco 4 to 2

Apr. 14—San Francisco 135 at Philadelphia *141
Apr. 16—San Francisco 95 at Philadelphia 126
Apr. 18—Philadelphia 124 at San Francisco 130
Apr. 20—Philadelphia 122 at San Francisco 108
Apr. 23—San Francisco 117 at Philadelphia 109
Apr. 24—Philadelphia 125 at San Francisco 122

*—Denotes overtime period.

1967-68

EASTERN DIVISION SEMIFINAL SERIES

Philadelphia defeated New York 4 to 2

Mar. 22—New York 110 at Philadelphia 118
Mar. 23—Philadelphia 117 at New York 128
Mar. 27—New York 132 at Philadelphia **138
Mar. 30—Philadelphia 98 at New York 107
Mar. 31—New York 107 at Philadelphia 123
Apr. 1—Philadelphia 113 at New York 97

Boston defeated Detroit 4 to 2

Mar. 24—Detroit 116 at Boston 123
Mar. 25—Boston 116 at Detroit 126
Mar. 27—Detroit 109 at Boston 98
Mar. 28—Boston 135 at Detroit 110
Mar. 31—Detroit 96 at Boston 110
Apr. 1—Boston 111 at Detroit 103

EASTERN DIVISION FINAL SERIES

Boston defeated Philadelphia 4 to 3

Apr. 5—Boston 127 at Philadelphia 118
Apr. 10—Philadelphia 115 at Boston 106
Apr. 11—Boston 114 at Philadelphia 122

Apr. 14—Philadelphia 110 at Boston 105
Apr. 15—Boston 122 at Philadelphia 104
Apr. 17—Philadelphia 106 at Boston 114
Apr. 19—Boston 100 at Philadelphia 96

WESTERN DIVISION SEMIFINAL SERIES

San Francisco defeated St. Louis 4 to 2

Mar. 22—San Francisco 111 at St. Louis 106
Mar. 23—San Francisco 103 at St. Louis 111
Mar. 26—St. Louis 109 at San Francisco 124
Mar. 29—St. Louis 107 at San Francisco 108
Mar. 31—San Francisco 103 at St. Louis 129
Apr. 2—St. Louis 106 at San Francisco 111

Los Angeles defeated Chicago 4 to 1

Mar. 24—Chicago 101 at Los Angeles 109
Mar. 25—Chicago 106 at Los Angeles 111
Mar. 27—Los Angeles 98 at Chicago 104
Mar. 29—Los Angeles 93 at Chicago 87
Mar. 31—Chicago 99 at Los Angeles 122

WESTERN DIVISION FINAL SERIES

Los Angeles defeated San Francisco 4 to 0

Apr. 5—San Francisco 105 at Los Angeles 133
Apr. 10—San Francisco 112 at Los Angeles 115
Apr. 11—Los Angeles 128 at San Francisco 124
Apr. 13—Los Angeles 106 at San Francisco 100

CHAMPIONSHIP SERIES

Boston defeated Los Angeles 4 to 2

Apr. 21—Los Angeles 101 at Boston 107
Apr. 24—Los Angeles 123 at Boston 113
Apr. 26—Boston 127 at Los Angeles 119
Apr. 28—Boston 105 at Los Angeles 119
Apr. 30—Los Angeles 117 at Boston *120
May 2—Boston 124 at Los Angeles 109

*—Denotes overtime period.

1968-69

EASTERN DIVISION SEMI FINAL SERIES

New York defeated Baltimore 4 to 0

Mar. 27—New York 113 at Baltimore 101
Mar. 29—Baltimore 91 at New York 107
Mar. 30—New York 119 at Baltimore 116
Apr. 2—Baltimore 108 at New York 115

Boston defeated Philadelphia 4 to 1

Mar. 26—Boston 114 at Philadelphia 100
Mar. 28—Philadelphia 103 at Boston 134
Mar. 30—Boston 125 at Philadelphia 118
Apr. 1—Philadelphia 119 at Boston 116
Apr. 4—Boston 93 at Philadelphia 90

EASTERN DIVISION FINAL SERIES

Boston defeated New York 4 to 2

Apr. 6—Boston 108 at New York 100
Apr. 9—New York 97 at Boston 112
Apr. 10—Boston 91 at New York 101
Apr. 13—New York 96 at Boston 97
Apr. 14—Boston 104 at New York 112
Apr. 18—New York 105 at Boston 106

WESTERN DIVISION SEMI FINAL SERIES

Los Angeles defeated San Francisco 4 to 2

Mar. 26—San Francisco 99 at Los Angeles 94
Mar. 28—San Francisco 107 at Los Angeles 101
Mar. 31—Los Angeles 115 at San Francisco 98
Apr. 2—Los Angeles 103 at San Francisco 88
Apr. 4—San Francisco 98 at Los Angeles 103
Apr. 5—Los Angeles 118 at San Francisco 78

Atlanta defeated San Diego 4 to 2

Mar. 27—San Diego 98 at Atlanta 107
Mar. 29—San Diego 114 at Atlanta 116
Apr. 1—Atlanta 97 at San Diego 104
Apr. 4—Atlanta 112 at San Diego 114
Apr. 6—San Diego 101 at Atlanta 112
Apr. 7—Atlanta 108 at San Diego 106

WESTERN DIVISION FINAL SERIES

Los Angeles defeated Atlanta 4 to 1

Apr. 11—Atlanta 93 at Los Angeles 95
Apr. 13—Atlanta 102 at Los Angeles 104
Apr. 15—Los Angeles 86 at Atlanta 99
Apr. 17—Los Angeles 100 at Atlanta 85
Apr. 20—Atlanta 96 at Los Angeles 104

CHAMPIONSHIP SERIES

Boston defeated Los Angeles 4 to 3

Apr. 23—Boston 118 at Los Angeles 120
Apr. 25—Boston 112 at Los Angeles 118
Apr. 27—Los Angeles 105 at Boston 111
Apr. 29—Los Angeles 88 at Boston 89
May 1—Boston 104 at Los Angeles 117
May 3—Los Angeles 90 at Boston 99
May 5—Boston 108 at Los Angeles 106

1969-70

EASTERN DIVISION SEMI FINAL SERIES

Milwaukee defeated Philadelphia 4 to 1

Mar. 25—Philadelphia 118 at Milwaukee 125
Mar. 27—Philadelphia 112 at Milwaukee 105
Mar. 30—Milwaukee 156 at Philadelphia 120
Apr. 1—Milwaukee 118 at Philadelphia 111
Apr. 3—Philadelphia 106 at Milwaukee 115

New York defeated Baltimore 4 to 3

Mar. 26—Baltimore 117 at New York **120
Mar. 27—New York 106 at Baltimore 99
Mar. 29—Baltimore 127 at New York 113
Mar. 31—New York 92 at Baltimore 102
Apr. 2—Baltimore 80 at New York 101
Apr. 5—New York 87 at Baltimore 96
Apr. 6—Baltimore 114 at New York 127

EASTERN DIVISION FINAL SERIES

New York defeated Milwaukee 4 to 1

Apr. 11—Milwaukee 102 at New York 110
Apr. 13—Milwaukee 111 at New York 112
Apr. 17—New York 96 at Milwaukee 101
Apr. 19—New York 117 at Milwaukee 105
Apr. 20—Milwaukee 96 at New York 132

WESTERN DIVISION SEMI FINAL SERIES

Atlanta defeated Chicago 4 to 1

Mar. 25—Chicago 111 at Atlanta 129
Mar. 28—Chicago 104 at Atlanta 124
Mar. 31—Atlanta 106 at Chicago 101
Apr. 3—Atlanta 120 at Chicago 131
Apr. 5—Chicago 107 at Atlanta 113

Los Angeles defeated Phoenix 4 to 3

Mar. 25—Phoenix 112 at Los Angeles 128
Mar. 29—Phoenix 114 at Los Angeles 101
Apr. 2—Los Angeles 98 at Phoenix 112
Apr. 4—Los Angeles 102 at Phoenix 112
Apr. 5—Phoenix 121 at Los Angeles 138
Apr. 7—Los Angeles 104 at Phoenix 93
Apr. 9—Phoenix 94 at Los Angeles 129

Los Angeles defeated Atlanta 4 to 0

Apr. 12—Los Angeles 119 at Atlanta 115
Apr. 14—Los Angeles 105 at Atlanta 94
Apr. 16—Atlanta 114 at Los Angeles *115
Apr. 19—Atlanta 114 at Los Angeles 133

CHAMPIONSHIP SERIES

New York defeated Los Angeles 4 to 3

Apr. 24—Los Angeles 112 at New York 124
Apr. 27—Los Angeles 105 at New York 103
Apr. 29—New York 111 at Los Angeles *108
May 1—New York 115 at Los Angeles *121
May 4—Los Angeles 100 at New York 107
May 6—New York 113 at Los Angeles 135
May 8—Los Angeles 99 at New York 113

INDIVIDUAL SCORING CHAMPIONS

Year	*Player, Team*	*Points*	*Ave.*
1947	Fulks, Philadelphia	1389	23.2
1948	Zaslofsky, Chicago	1007	21.0
1949	Mikan, Minneapolis	1698	28.3
1950	Mikan, Minneapolis	1865	27.4
1951	Mikan, Minneapolis	1932	28.4
1952	Arizin, Philadelphia	1674	25.4
1953	Johnston, Philadelphia	1564	22.3
1954	Johnston, Philadelphia	1759	24.4
1955	Johnston, Philadelphia	1631	22.7
1956	Pettit, St. Louis	1849	25.7
1957	Arizin, Philadelphia	1817	25.6
1958	Yardley, Fort Worth	2001	27.8
1959	Pettit, St. Louis	2105	29.2
1960	Chamberlain, Philadelphia	2707	37.6
1961	Chamberlain, Philadelphia	3033	38.4
1962	Chamberlain, Philadelphia	4029	50.4
1963	Chamberlain, San Francisco	3586	44.8
1964	Chamberlain, San Francisco	2948	36.9
1965	Chamberlain, San Francisco-Philadelphia	2534	33.5
1966	Chamberlain, Philadelphia	2649	33.5
1967	Barry, San Francisco	2775	35.6
1968	Bing, Detroit	2142	27.1
1969	Hayes, San Diego	2327	28.4
1970	West, Los Angeles	2309	31.2

CHAMPIONS IN MAJOR CATEGORIES

Season	FGM Pct.	Leaders	FTM Pct.	Leaders	Top	Rebounders
1946-47	.401	Bob Feerick (Wash.)	.811	Fred Scolari (Wash.)	....	
1947-48	.340	Bob Feerick (Wash.)	.788	Bob Feerick (Wash.)	....	
1948-49	.423	Arnie Risen (Roch.)	.859	Bob Feerick (Wash.)	....	
1949-50	.478	Alex Groza (Indpls.)	.843	Max Zaslofsky (Chi.)	....	
1950-51	.470	Alex Groza (Indpls.)	.855	Joe Fulks (Phil.)	1080	Dolph Schayes (Syr.)
1951-52	.448	Paul Arizin (Phil.)	.904	Bob Wanzer (Roch.)	880	Larry Foust (Fort Worth) Mel Hutchins (Milw.)
1952-53	.452	Neil Johnston (Phil.)	.850	Bill Sharman (Bos.)	1007	George Mikan (Mpls.)
1953-54	.486	Ed Macauley (Boston)	.844	Bill Sharman (Bos.)	1098	Harry Gallatin (N. Y.)
1954-55	.487	Larry Foust (Fort Worth)	.897	Bill Sharman (Bos.)	1085	Neil Johnston (Phil.)
1955-56	.457	Neil Johnston (Phil.)	.867	Bill Sharman (Bos.)	1164	Bob Pettit (St. Louis)
1956-57	.447	Neil Johnston (Phil.)	.905	Bill Sharman (Bos.)	1256	Maurice Stokes (Roch.)
1957-58	.452	Jack Twyman (Cinn.)	.904	Dolph Schayes (Syr.)	1564	Bill Russell (Boston)
1958-59	.490	Ken Sears (N. Y.)	.932	Bill Sharman (Bos.)	1612	Bill Russell (Boston)
1959-60	.477	Ken Sears (N. Y.)	.892	Dolph Schayes (Syr.)	1941	Wilt Chamberlain (Phil.)
1960-61	.505	Wilt Chamberlain (Phil.)	.921	Bill Sharman (Bos.)	2149	Wilt Chamberlain (Phil.)
1961-62	.513	Walt Bellamy (Chi.)	.896	Dolph Schayes (Syr.)	2052	Wilt Chamberlain (Phil.)
1962-63	.528	Wilt Chamberlain (S. F.)	.881	Larry Costello (Syr.)	1946	Wilt Chamberlain (S. F.)
1963-64	.527	Jerry Lucas (Cinn.)	.853	Oscar Robertson (Cinn.)	1930	Bill Russell (Boston)
1964-65	.510	Wilt Chamberlain (S. F.-Phil.)	.877	Larry Costello (Phil.)	1878	Bill Russell (Boston)
1965-66	.540	Wilt Chamberlain (Phil.)	.881	Larry Siegfried (Bos.)	1943	Wilt Chamberlain (Phil.)
1966-67	.683	Wilt Chamberlain (Phil.)	.903	Adrian Smith (Cinn.)	1957	Wilt Chamberlain (Phil.)
1967-68	.595	Wilt Chamberlain (Phil.)	.873	Oscar Robertson (Cinn.)	1952	Wilt Chamberlain (Phil.)
1968-69	.583	Wilt Chamberlain (L. A.)	.864	Larry Siegfried (Boston)	1712	Wilt Chamberlain (L. A.)
1969-70	.559	Johnn Green (Cinn.)	.898	Flynn Robinson (Mil.)	1386	Elvin Hayes (S. D.)

Season	No.	Most Assists	No.	Most Minutes	No.	Most Personals
1946-47	202	Ernie Calverly (Prov.)	....		208	Stan Miasek (Detroit)
1947-48	120	Howie Dallmar (Phil.)	....		231	Charles Gilmur (Chi.)
1948-49	321	Bob Davies (Roch.)	....		273	Ed Sadowski (Phil.)
1949-50	386	Dick McGuire (N. Y.)	....		297	George Mikan (Mpls.)
1950-51	414	Andy Phillip (Phil.)	....		308	George Mikan (Mpls.)

Season	Most Assists No.	Most Assists	Most Minutes No.	Most Minutes	Most Personals No.	Most Personals
1951-52	539	Andy Phillip (Phil.)	2939	Paul Arizin (Phil.)	286	George Mikan (Mpls.)
1952-53	547	Bob Cousy (Boston)	3166	Neil Johnston (Phil.)	334	Don Meineke (Ft. W.)
1953-54	578	Bob Cousy (Boston)	3296	Neil Johnston (Phil.)	303	Earl Lloyd (Syracuse)
1954-55	557	Bob Cousy (Boston)	2953	Paul Arizin (Phil.)	319	Vern Mikkelsen (Mpls.)
1955-56	642	Bob Cousy (Boston)	2838	Slater Martin (Mpls.)	319	Vern Mikkelsen (Mpls.)
1956-57	478	Bob Cousy (Boston)	2851	Dolph Schayes (Syr.)	312	Vern Mikkelsen (Mpls.)
1957-58	463	Bob Cousy (Boston)	2918	Dolph Schayes (Syr.)	311	Walt Dukes (Detroit)
1958-59	557	Bob Cousy (Boston)	2979	Bill Russell (Boston)	332	Walt Dukes (Detroit)
1959-60	715	Bob Cousy (Boston)	3338	Wilt Chamberlain (Phil.) Gene Shue (Detroit)	311	Tom Gola (Phil.)
1960-61	690	Oscar Robertson (Cinn.)	3773	Wilt Chamberlain (Phil.)	335	Paul Arizin (Phil.)
1961-62	899	Oscar Robertson (Cinn.)	3882	Wilt Chamberlain (Phil.)	327	Walt Dukes (Detroit)
1962-63	825	Guy Rodgers (S. F.)	3802	Wilt Chamberlain (S. F.)	316	Tom Gola (S. F.-N. Y.)
1963-64	868	Oscar Robertson (Cinn.)	3689	Wilt Chamberlain (S. F.)	325	Wayne Embry (Cinn.)
1964-65	861	Oscar Robertson (Cinn.)	3466	Bill Russell (Boston)	345	Bailey Howell (Balt.)
1965-66	847	Oscar Robertson (Cinn.)	3737	Wilt Chamberlain (Phil.)	344	Zelmo Beatty (St. Louis)
1966-67	908	Guy Rodgers (Chicago)	3682	Wilt Chamberlain (Phil.)	344	Joe Strawder (Detroit)
1967-68	702	Wilt Chamberlain (Phil.)	3836	Wilt Chamberlain (Phil.)	366	Bill Bridges (St. Louis)
1968-69	772	Oscar Robertson (Cinn.)	3695	Elvin Hayes (S. D.)	329	Bill Cunningham (Phil.)
1969-70	683	Lenny Wilkens (Seattle)	3665	Elvin Hayes (S. D.)	335	Jim Davis (Atlanta)

Most Disqualifications

Season	No.	Player
1946-47	....	
1947-48	....	
1948-49	....	
1949-50	....	
1950-51	19	Cal Christensen (Tri-City)
1951-52	18	Don Boven (Milwaukee)
1952-53	26	Don Meineke (Fort Wayne)
1953-54	12	Earl Lloyd (Syracuse)
1954-55	17	Charley Share (Milwaukee)
1955-56	17	Vern Mikkelsen (Minneapolis) Arnie Risen (Boston)
1956-57	18	Vern Mikkelsen (Minneapolis)
1957-58	20	Vern Mikkelsen (Minneapolis)
1958-59	22	Walt Dukes (Detroit)
1959-60	20	Walt Dukes (Detroit)
1960-61	16	Walt Dukes (Detroit)
1961-62	20	Walt Dukes (Detroit)
1962-63	13	Frank Ramsey (Boston)
1963-64	11	Zelmo Beaty (St. Louis) Gus Johnson (Baltimore)
1964-65	15	Tom Sanders (Boston)
1965-66	19	Tom Sanders (Boston)
1966-67	19	Joe Strawder (Detroit)
1967-68	18	John Tresvant (Det.-Cinn.) Joe Strawder (Detroit)
1968-69	14	Art Harris (Seattle)

ALL-TIME N.B.A. RECORDS

TEAM (SEASON)

Most games won—68, Philadelphia, 1966-67.
Highest Winning Percentage—.840, Philadelphia, 1966-67. (W-68, L-13).
Most games lost—67, San Diego, 1967-68.
Lowest Winning Percentage—.125, Providence, 1947-48. (W-6, L-42).
Most consecutive games won: 18, New York, Oct. 24-Nov. 28, 1969.
Most consecutive games lost: 17, San Francisco, Dec. 20, 1964-Jan. 26, 1965.
Most points per game scored: 125.4, Philadelphia, 1961-62.
Most points per game allowed: 125.1, Seattle, 1967-68.
Highest field goal percentage: .488, Milwaukee, 1969-70.
Highest free throw percentage: .794, Syracuse, 1956-57.

TEAM (ONE GAME)

Most points scored: 173, Boston (vs. Minneapolis, Feb. 27, 1959).
Most rebounds: 112, Philadelphia vs. Cincinnati, Nov. 8, 1959. Boston vs. Detroit, Dec. 24, 1960.

INDIVIDUAL (SEASON)

Most points scored: 4,029, Wilt Chamberlain, Philadelphia, 1961-62.
Most rebounds: 2,149, Wilt Chamberlain, Philadelphia, 1960-61.
Most Assists: 908, Guy Rodgers, Chicago, 1966-67.
Most disqualifications on personal fouls: 26, Don Meinke, Fort Wayne, 1952-53.
Highest field goal percentage: .683, Wilt Chamberlain, 1966-67.
Highest free throw percentage: .932, Bill Sharman, Boston, 1958-59.

INDIVIDUAL (GAME)

Most points scored: 100, Wilt Chamberlain, Philadelphia (vs. New York at Hershey, Pa., Mar. 2, 1962).
Most rebounds: 55, Wilt Chamberlain, Philadelphia (vs. Boston at Philadelphia, Nov. 24, 1960).
Most free throws attempted: 34, Wilt Chamberlain, Philadelphia (vs. St. Louis at Philadelphia, Feb. 22, 1962).
Most free throws made: 28, Wilt Chamberlain, Philadelphia (vs. New York at Hershey, Pa., Mar. 2, 1962).
Most assists: 28, Bob Cousy, Boston (vs. Minneapolis at Boston, Feb. 27, 1959) 28, Guy Rodgers, San Francisco (vs. St. Louis at San Francisco, Mar. 14, 1963).

EAST-WEST ALL-STAR GAMES

Date	*Attend.*	*Site*	*East Coach*	*Score*		*West Coach*	*MVP*
Mar. 2, 1951	10,094	Boston	Lapchick	W 111	94	Kundla	†Macauley
Feb. 11, 1952	10,221	Boston	Cervi	W 108	91	Kundla	†Arizin
Jan. 13, 1953	10,382	Fort Wayne	Lapchick	75	79 W	Kundla	Mikan
Jan. 21, 1954	16,487	N. Y. C.	Lapchick	W *98	93	Kundla	Cousy
Jan. 18, 1955	15,564	N. Y. C.	Cervi	W 100	91	Eckman	Sharman
Jan. 24, 1956	8,517	Rochester	Senesky	94	108 W	Eckman	Pettit
Jan. 15, 1957	11,178	Boston	Auerbach	W 109	97	Wanzer	Cousy
Jan. 21, 1958	12,854	St. Louis	Auerbach	W 130	118	Hannum	Pettit
Jan. 23, 1959	10,541	Detroit	Auerbach	108	124 W	Macauley	Baylor & Pettit
Jan. 22, 1960	10,421	Philadelphia	Auerbach	W 125	115	Macauley	Chamberlain
Jan. 17, 1961	8,016	Syracuse	Auerbach	131	153 W	Seymour	Robertson
Jan. 16, 1962	15,112	St. Louis	Auerbach	130	150 W	Schaus	Pettit
Jan. 16, 1963	14,838	Los Angeles	Auerbach	W 115	108	Schaus	Russell
Jan. 14, 1964	13,464	Boston	Auerbach	W 111	107	Schaus	Robertson
Jan. 13, 1965	16,713	St. Louis	Auerbach	W 124	123	Hannum	Lucas
Jan. 11, 1966	13,653	Cincinnati	Auerbach	W 137	94	Schaus	Smith
Jan. 10, 1967	13,972	San Francisco	Auerbach	120	135 W	Schaus	Barry
Jan. 23, 1968	18,422	New York	Hannum	W 144	124	Sharman	Greer
Jan. 14, 1969	12,348	Baltimore	Shue	W 123	112	Guerin	Robertson
Jan. 20, 1970	15,244	Philadelphia	Holzman	W 142	135	Guerin	Reed

† Not officially picked but generally hailed as top performers. * Overtime.

EAST LEADS IN SERIES, 13-6

HOME AND NEUTRAL COURT RECORDS

	Home			Neutral		Total
	Won	Lost	Pct.	Won	Lost	Games
1946-47	202	129	.610	..	..	331
1947-48	107	85	.557	..	..	192
1948-49	212	132	.616	16	16	360
1949-50	351	167	.678	43	43	561
1950-51	254	85	.749	15	15	354
1951-52	213	80	.727	37	37	330
1952-53	195	83	.701	73	73	351
1953-54	151	84	.643	89	89	324
1954-55	139	59	.702	90	90	288
1955-56	144	81	.640	63	63	288
1956-57	155	62	.714	71	71	288
1957-58	150	85	.638	53	53	288
1958-59	148	80	.649	60	60	288
1959-60	150	87	.633	63	63	300
1960-61	156	85	.647	75	75	316
1961-62	166	107	.608	87	87	360
1962-63	184	109	.628	67	67	360
1963-64	185	126	.595	49	49	360
1964-65	178	128	.582	54	54	360
1965-66	197	89	.689	74	74	360
1966-67	193	128	.601	84	84	405
1967-68	241	182	.529	69	69	492
1968-69	315	206	.605	54	54	575
1969-70	313	202	.608	59	59	574
Total	4699	2661	.638	1345	1345	8705

EVOLUTION OF N.B.A. SCORING

Year	*Games*	*Points Per Game Per Team*	*Shooting Average* *FG.*	*FT.*
1947	331	67.8	.279	.641
1948	192	72.7	.284	.675
1949	360	80.1	.327	.706
1950	561	80.0	.340	.714
1951	354	84.1	.358	.732
1952	330	83.7	.367	.735
1953	352	82.5	.370	.716
1954	324	79.5	.372	.709
1955	288	93.1	.385	.738
1956	288	99.0	.386	.744
1957	288	99.6	.380	.751
1958	288	106.6	.383	.783
1959	288	108.2	.394	.756
1960	300	115.3	.403	.734
1961	316	118.1	.415	.733
1962	360	118.8	.412	.728
1963	360	115.3	.439	.726
1964	360	110.0	.433	.722
1965	360	110.6	.425	.721
1966	360	115.5	.432	.727
1967	405	117.5	.441	.733
1968	462	116.7	.446	.721
1969	574	112.3	.441	.714
1970	574	116.7	.460	.751

ALL-N.B.A. FIRST AND SECOND TEAMS

FIRST	*1946-47* *SECOND*
Joe Fulks (Philadelphia)	Ernie Calverley (Providence)
Bob Feerick (Washington)	Frank Baumholtz (Cleveland)
Stan Miasek (Detroit)	John Logan (St. Louis)
Bones McKinney (Washington)	Chuck Halbert (Chicago)
Max Zaslofsky (Chicago)	Fred Scolari (Washington)

FIRST	*1947-48* *SECOND*
Joe Fulks (Philadelphia)	John Logan (St. Louis)
Max Zaslofsky (Chicago)	Carl Braun (New York)
Ed Sadowski (Boston)	Stan Miasek (Chicago)
Howie Dallmar (Philadelphia)	Fred Scolari (Washington)
Bob Feerick (Washington)	Buddy Jeannette (Baltimore)

FIRST	*1948-49* *SECOND*
George Mikan (Minneapolis)	Arnie Risen (Rochester)
Joe Fulks (Philadelphia)	Bob Feerick (Washington)
Bob Davies (Rochester)	Bones McKinney (Washington)
Max Zaslofsky (Chicago)	Ken Sailors (Providence)
Jim Pollard (Minneapolis)	John Logan (St. Louis)

1949-50

FIRST	*SECOND*
George Mikan (Minneapolis)	Frank Brian (Anderson)
Jim Pollard (Minneapolis)	Fred Schaus (Fort Wayne)
Alex Groza (Indianapolis)	Dolph Schayes (Syracuse)
Bob Davies (Rochester)	Al Cervi (Syracuse)
Max Zaslofsky (Chicago)	Ralph Beard (Indianapolis)

1950-51

FIRST	*SECOND*
George Mikan (Minneapolis)	Dolph Schayes (Syracuse)
Alex Groza (Indianapolis)	Frank Brian (Tri-Cities)
Ed Macauley (Boston)	Vern Mikkelsen (Minneapolis)
Bob Davies (Rochester)	Joe Fulks (Philadelphia)
Ralph Beard (Indianapolis)	Dick McGuire (New York)

1951-52

FIRST	*SECOND*
George Mikan (Minneaopils)	Larry Foust (Fort Wayne)
Ed Macauley (Boston)	Vern Mikkelsen (Minneapolis)
Paul Arizin (Philadelphia)	Jim Pollard (Minneapolis)
Bob Cousy (Boston)	Bob Wanzer (Rochester)
{Bob Davies (Rochester)	Andy Phillip (Philadelphia)
{Dolph Schayes (Syracuse)	

1952-53

FIRST	*SECOND*
George Mikan (Minneapolis)	Bill Sharman (Boston)
Bob Cousy (Boston)	Vern Mikkelsen (Minneapolis)
Neil Johnston (Philadelphia)	Bob Wanzer (Rochester)
Ed Macauley (Boston)	Bob Davies (Rochester)
Dolph Schayes (Syracuse)	Andy Phillip (Philadelphia)

1953-54

FIRST	*SECOND*
Bob Cousy (Boston)	Ed Macauley (Boston)
Neil Johnston (Philadelphia)	Jim Pollard (Minneapolis)
George Mikan (Minneapolis)	Carl Braun (New York)
Dolph Schayes (Syracuse)	Bob Wanzer (Rochester)
Harry Gallatin (New York)	Paul Seymour (Syracuse)

1954-55

FIRST	*SECOND*
Neil Johnston (Philadelphia)	Vern Mikkelsen (Minneapolis)
Bob Cousy (Boston)	Harry Gallatin (New York)
Dolph Schayes (Syracuse)	Paul Seymour (Syracuse)
Bob Pettit (St. Louis)	Slater Martin (Minneapolis)
Larry Foust (Fort Wayne)	Bill Sharman (Boston)

1955-56

FIRST	*SECOND*
Bob Pettit (St. Louis)	Dalph Schayes (Syracuse)
Paul Arizin (Philadelphia)	Maurice Stokes (Rochester)
Neil Johnston (Philadelphia)	Clyde Lovellette (Minneapolis)
Bob Cousy (Boston)	Slater Martin (Minneapolis)
Bill Sharman (Boston)	Jack George (Philadelphia)

1956-57

FIRST	*SECOND*
Paul Arizin (Philadelphia)	George Yardley (Fort Wayne)
Dolph Schayes (Syracuse)	Maurice Stokes (Rochester)
Bob Pettit (St. Louis)	Neil Johnston (Philadelphia)
Bob Cousy (Boston)	Dick Garmaker (Minneapolis)
Bill Sharman (Boston)	Slater Martin (St. Louis)

FIRST	*1957-58*	*SECOND*
Dolph Schayes (Syracuse)		Cliff Hagan (St. Louis)
George Yardley (Detroit)		Maurice Stokes (Cincinnati)
Bob Pettit (St. Louis)		Bill Russell (Boston)
Bob Cousy (Boston)		Tom Gola (Philadelphia)
Bill Sharman (Boston)		Slater Martin (St. Louis)

FIRST	*1958-59*	*SECOND*
Bob Pettit (St. Louis)		Paul Arizin (Philadelphia)
Elgin Baylor (Minneapolis)		Cliff Hagan (St. Louis)
Bill Russell (Boston)		Dolph Schayes (Syracuse)
Bob Cousy (Boston)		Slater Martin (St. Louis)
Bill Sharman (Boston)		Richie Guerin (New York)

FIRST	*1959-60*	*SECOND*
Bob Pettit (St. Louis)		Jack Twyman (Cincinnati)
Elgin Baylor (Minneapolis)		Dolph Schayes (Syracuse)
Wilt Chamberlain (Philadelphia)		Bill Russell (Boston)
Bob Cousy (Boston)		Richie Guerin (New York)
Gene Shue (Detroit)		Bill Sharman (Boston)

FIRST	*1960-61*	*SECOND*
Elgin Baylor (Los Angeles)		Dolph Schayes (Syracuse)
Bob Pettit (St. Louis)		Tom Heinsohn (Boston)
Wilt Chamberlain (Philadelphia)		Bill Russell (Boston)
Bob Cousy (Boston)		Larry Costello (Syracuse)
Oscar Robertson (Cincinnati)		Gene Shue (Detroit)

FIRST	*1961-62*	*SECOND*
Bob Pettit (St. Louis)		Tom Heinsohn (Boston)
Elgin Baylor (Los Angeles)		Jack Twyman (Cincinnati)
Wilt Chamberlain (Philadelphia)		Bill Russell (Boston)
Jerry West (Lost Angeles)		Richie Guerin (New York)
Oscar Robertson (Cincinnati)		Bob Cousy (Boston)

FIRST	*1962-63*	*SECOND*
Elgin Baylor (Los Angeles)		Tom Heinsohn (Boston)
Bob Pettit (St. Louis)		Bailey Howell (Detroit)
Bill Russell (Boston)		Wilt Chamberlain (San Francisco)
Oscar Robertson (Cincinnati)		Bob Cousy (Boston)
Jerry West (Los Angeles)		Hal Greer (Syracuse)

FIRST	*1963-64*	*SECOND*
Bob Pettit (St. Louis)		Tom Heinsohn (Boston)
Elgin Baylor (Los Angeles)		Jerry Lucas (Cincinnati)
Wilt Chamberlain (San Francisco)		Bill Russell (Boston)
Oscar Robertson (Cincinnati)		John Havlicek (Boston)
Jerry West (Los Angeles)		Hal Greer (Philadelphia)

FIRST	*1964-65*	*SECOND*
Elgin Baylor (Los Angeles)		Bob Pettit (St. Louis)
Jerry Lucas (Cincinnati)		Gus Johnson (Baltimore)
Bill Russell (Boston)		Wilt Chamberlain (S. F.-Phila.)
Oscar Robertson (Cincinnati)		Sam Jones (Boston)
Jerry West (Los Angeles)		Hal Greer (Philadelphia)

1965-66

FIRST	*SECOND*
Rick Barry (San Francisco)	John Havlicek (Boston)
Jerry Lucas (Cincinnati)	Gus Johnson (Baltimore)
Wilt Chamberlain (Philadelphia)	Bill Russell (Boston)
Oscar Robertson (Cincinnati)	Sam Jones (Boston)
Jerry West (Los Angeles)	Hal Greer (Philadelphia)

1966-67

FIRST	*SECOND*
Rick Barry (San Francisco)	Willis Reed (New York)
Elgin Baylor (Los Angeles)	Jerry Lucas (Cincinnati)
Wilt Chamberlain (Philadelphia)	Bill Russell (Boston)
Jerry West (Los Angeles)	Hal Greer (Philadelphia)
Oscar Robertson (Cincinnati)	Sam Jones (Boston)

1967-68

FIRST	*SECOND*
Elgin Baylor (Los Angeles)	John Havlicek (Boston)
Jerry Lucas (Cincinnati)	Willis Reed (New York)
Wilt Chamberlain (Philadelphia)	Bill Russell (Boston)
Oscar Robertson (Cincinnati)	Hal Greer (Philadelphia)
Dave Bing (Detroit)	Jerry West (Los Angeles)

1968-69

FIRST	*SECOND*
Billy Cunningham (Philadelphia)	John Havlicek (Boston)
Elgin Baylor (Los Angeles)	Dave DeBusschere (Det.-N.Y.)
Wes Unseld (Baltimore)	Willis Reed (New York)
Earl Monroe (Baltimore)	Hal Greer (Philadelphia)
Oscar Robertson (Cincinnati)	Jerry West (Los Angeles)

1969-70

FIRST	*SECOND*
Billy Cunningham (Philadelphia)	John Havlicek (Boston)
Connie Hawkins (Phoenix)	Bill Bridges (Atlanta)
Willis Reed (New York)	Lew Alcindor (Milwaukee)
Walt Frazier (New York)	Lou Hudson (Atlanta)
Jerry West (Los Angeles)	Oscar Robertson (Cincinnati)

OUTSTANDING PLAYERS AND ROOKIES OF THE YEAR

Year	*Outstanding Player*	*Rookie of Year*
1952-53	....	Don Meineke, Fort Worth
1953-54	....	Ray Felix, Baltimore
1954-55	....	Bob Pettit, Milwaukee
1955-56	Bob Pettit, St. Louis	Maurice Stokes, Rochester
1956-57	Bob Cousy, Boston	Tom Heinsohn, Boston
1957-58	Bill Russell, Boston	W. Sauldsberry, Philadelphia
1958-59	Bob Pettit, St. Louis	Elgin Baylor, Minneapolis
1959-60	Wilt Chamberlain, Philadelphia	Wilt Chamberlain, Philadelphia
1960-61	Bill Russell, Boston	O. Robertson, Cincinnati
1961-62	Bill Russell, Boston	Walt Bellamy, Chicago
1962-63	Bill Russell, Boston	T. Dischinger, Chicago
1963-64	Wilt Chamberlain, San Francisco	Jerry Lucas, Cincinnati
1964-65	Bill Russell, Boston	Willis Reed, New York
1965-66	Wilt Chamberlain, Philadelphia	Rick Barry, San Francisco
1966-67	Wilt Chamberlain, Philadelphia	Dave Bing, Detroit
1967-68	Wilt Chamberlain, Philadelphia	Earl Monroe, Baltimore
1968-69	Wes Unseld, Baltimore	Wes Unseld, Baltimore
1969-70	Willis Reed, New York	Lew Alcindor, Milwaukee

TEAMS (ACTIVE)

ATLANTA HAWKS

Entered N.B.A. in 1949-50 as the Moline or Tri-Cities Blackhawks in the merger of the B.A.A. and the National League. Principal owners: B. W. Grafton, Ben Kerner and Leo Ferris. Kerner took full control in 1950. Moved to Milwaukee and changed name to Hawks in 1951. Moved to St. Louis for the 1955-56 season. After 1967-68 season, sold for about $3,500,000 to an Atlanta group headed by Tom Cousins and Terry Saunders.

Home courts:

1949-51—Wheaton Field House, Moline, 6,000
1951-55—The Arena, Milwaukee, 11,000
1955-68—Kiel Auditorium, St. Louis, 10,000
(Also some games at St. Louis Arena, 15,000)

Year	*W.*	*L.*	*Pos.*	*Coach*	*Top Scorer*	*Pts.*	*Play-Offs*
				TRI-CITIES BLACKHAWKS			
1950	29	35	3	Potter-Auerbach	Eddleman	12.9	1-2
1951	25	43	5	McMillan-Logan-Todorovich	Brian	10.8	—
				MILWAUKEE HAWKS			
1952	17	49	5	Moore	Otten	12.0	—
1953	27	44	5	Levane	Nichols	15.8	—
1954	21	51	4	Levane-Holzman	Sunderlage	11.2	—
1955	26	46	4	Holzman	Pettit	20.4	—
				ST. LOUIS HAWKS			
1956	33	39	3	Holzman	Pettit	25.7	4-4
1957	34	38	1	Holzman-Martin-Hannum	Pettit	24.7	6-4
1958	41	31	1	Hannum	Pettit	24.6	8-3
1959	49	23	1	Phillip-Macauley	Pettit	29.2	2-4
1960	46	29	1	Macauley	Pettit	26.1	7-7
1961	51	28	1	Seymour	Pettit	27.9	5-7
1962	29	51	4	Seymour-Levane-Pettit	Pettit	31.1	—

1963	**48**	**32**	**2**	**Gallatin**	**Pettit**	**28.4**	**6-5**
1964	**46**	**34**	**2**	**Gallatin**	**Pettit**	**27.4**	**6-6**
1965	**45**	**35**	**2**	**Gallatin-Guerin**	**Beaty**	**16.9**	**1-3**
1966	**36**	**44**	**3**	**Guerin**	**Beaty**	**20.7**	**6-4**
1967	**39**	**42**	**2**	**Guerin**	**Hudson**	**18.4**	**5-4**
1968	**56**	**26**	**1**	**Guerin**	**Beaty**	**21.1**	**2-4**

ATLANTA HAWKS

1969	48	34	2	Guerin	Hudson	21.9	5-6
1970	48	34	1	Guerin	Hudson	25.4	4-5
Total	792	788					68-68

ATLANTA HAWKS' YEARLY LEADERS

Leading Scorer

Season—Player	*G.*	*Pts.*	*Avg.*
1949-50—Dwight Eddleman	64	826	12.9
1950-51—Frank Brian	68	1144	10.8
1951-52—Don Otten	64	767	12.0
1952-53—Jack Nichols	69	1090	15.8
1953-54—Don Sunderlage	68	760	11.2
1954-55—Bob Pettit	72	1466	20.4
1955-56—Bob Pettit	72	1849	*25.7
1956-57—Bob Pettit	71	1755	24.7
1957-58—Bob Pettit	70	1719	24.6
1958-59—Bob Pettit	72	2105	*29.2
1959-60—Bob Pettit	72	1882	26.1
1960-61—Bob Pettit	76	2120	27.9
1961-62—Bob Pettit	78	†2429	†31.1
1962-63—Bob Pettit	79	2241	28.4
1963-64—Bob Pettit	80	2190	27.4
1964-65—Zelmo Beaty	80	1351	16.9
1965-66—Zelmo Beaty	80	1656	20.7
1966-67—Lou Hudson	80	1471	18.4
1967-68—Zelmo Beaty	82	1733	21.1
1968-69—Lou Hudson	81	1770	21.9
1969-70—Lou Hudson	80	2031	25.4

Best Foul Shooter

Season—Player	*FTA*	*FTM*	*Pct.*
1949-50—Gene Englund	192	152	.792
1950-51—Frank Brian	508	418	.823
1951-52—Don Otten	418	323	.773
1952-53—John Payak	248	180	.726
1953-54—Don Sunderlage	337	252	.748
1954-55—Bob Pettit	567	426	.751
Charles Cooper	249	187	.751
1955-56—Bob Pettit	†757	†557	.736
1956-57—Slater Martin	291	230	.790
1957-58—Cliff Hagan	501	385	.768
1958-59—Clyde Lovellette	250	205	.820
1959-60—Clyde Lovellette	385	316	.821
1960-61—Clyde Lovellette	319	273	†.856
1961-62—Cliff Hagan	439	362	.825
1962-63—Cliff Hagan	305	244	.800
1963-64—Richie Guerin	424	347	.818
1964-65—Bob Pettit	405	332	.820
1965-66—Richie Guerin	446	362	.812
1966-67—Len Wilkens	583	459	.787
1967-68—Zelmo Beaty	573	455	.794
1968-69—Lou Hudson	435	338	.777
1969-70—Lou Hudson	450	371	.824

Top Playmaker

Season—Player	*G.*	*Ast.*	*Avg.*
1949-50—Marko Todorovich	65	207	3.2
1950-51—Frank Brian	68	266	3.9
1951-52—Mel Hutchins	66	190	2.9
1952-53—Mel Hutchins	71	227	3.2
1953-54—William Calhoun	72	189	2.6
1954-55—Robert Harrison	72	252	3.5
1955-56—Robert Harrison	72	277	2.5
1956-57—Jack McMahon	72	367	5.1
1957-58—Jack McMahon	72	333	4.6
1958-59—Slater Martin	71	336	4.7
1959-60—Slater Martin	74	330	4.5
1960-61—Jack McCarthy	79	430	5.4
1961-62—Cliff Hagan	77	370	4.8
1962-63—Len Wilkins	75	381	5.1
1963-64—Richie Guerin	80	375	4.7

Season—Player			
1964-65—Len Wilkens	78	431	5.5
1965-66—Len Wilkens	69	429	6.2
1966-67—Len Wilkens	78	442	5.7
1967-68—Len Wilkens	82	†679	†8.3
1968-69—Walt Hazzard	80	474	5.9
1969-70—Walt Hazzard	82	561	6.8

Most Minutes Played

Season—Player	*G.*	*Min.*	*Avg.*
1951-52—Mel Hutchins	66	2618	39.7
1952-53—Mel Hutchins	71	2891	40.7
1953-54—Lew Hitch	72	2452	34.1
1954-55—Frank Selvy	71	2668	37.6
1955-56—Bob Pettit	72	2794	38.8
1956-57—Ed Macauley	72	2794	38.8
1957-58—Bob Pettit	70	2528	36.1
1958-59—Bob Pettit	72	2873	39.9
1959-60—Bob Pettit	72	2896	40.2
1960-61—Bob Pettit	76	3027	39.8
1961-62—Bob Pettit	78	3182	40.8
1962-63—Bob Pettit	72	3090	†42.9
1963-64—Bob Pettit	80	†3296	41.2
1964-65—Zelmo Beaty	80	2916	36.5
1965-66—Zelmo Beaty	80	3072	38.4
1966-67—Bill Bridges	79	3130	39.6
1967-68—Bill Bridges	82	3197	38.9
1968-69—Bill Bridges	80	2930	36.6
1969-70—Bill Bridges	82	3269	39.9

Best Shooting Average

Season—Player	*FGA*	*FGM*	*Pct.*
1949-50—Dwight Eddleman	906	332	.366
Jack Nichols	898	310	.366
1950-51—Dwight Eddleman	1120	398	.355
1951-52—Mel Hutchins	633	231	.365
1952-53—Mel Mutchins	842	319	.379
1953-54—George Ratkovicz	501	197	.393
1954-55—Bob Pettit	1279	520	.407
Charles Share	577	235	.407
1955-56—Charles Share	733	315	.430
1956-57—Charles Share	535	235	.439
1957-58—Cliff Hagan	1135	503	.443
1958-59—Cliff Hagan	1417	646	.456
1959-60—Clyde Lovellette	1174	550	.468
1960-61—Clyde Lovellette	1321	599	.453
1961-62—Clyde Lovellette	724	341	.471
Larry Foust	433	204	.471
1962-63—Cliff Hagan	1055	491	.465
1963-64—Bob Pettit	†1708	†791	.463
1964-65—Zelmo Beaty	1047	505	.482
1965-66—Zelmo Beaty	1301	616	.473
1966-67—Zelmo Beaty	694	328	.473
1967-68—Zelmo Beaty	1310	639	.488
1968-69—Joe Caldwell	1106	561	.507
1969-70—Lou Hudson	1564	830	†.531

Top Rebounder

Season—Player	*G.*	*Reb.*	*Avg.*
1950-51—Cal Christensen	67	523	7.8
1951-52—Mel Hutchins	66	*880	*13.3
1952-53—Mel Hutchins	71	193	11.2
1953-54—Lew Hitch	72	691	9.6
1954-55—Bob Pettit	72	994	13.8
1955-56—Bob Pettit	72	1164	*16.2
1956-57—Bob Pettit	71	1037	14.6
1957-58—Bob Pettit	70	1216	17.4
1958-59—Bob Pettit	72	1182	16.4
1959-60—Bob Pettit	72	1221	17.0
1960-61—Bob Pettit	76	†1540	†20.3
1961-62—Bob Pettit	78	1457	18.7
1962-63—Bob Pettit	79	1195	15.1
1963-64—Bob Pettit	80	1224	15.3

Season—Player	G.	Pts.	Avg.
1964-65—Zelmo Beaty	80	966	12.1
1965-66—Zelmo Beaty	80	1086	13.6
1966-67—Bill Bridges	79	1190	15.1
1967-68—Bill Bridges	82	1102	13.4
1968-69—Bill Bridges	80	1132	14.2
1969-70—Bill Bridges	82	1181	14.4

Most Personal Fouls

Season—Player	*G.*	*PF*	*Avg.*
1949-50—Warren Perkins	60	260	4.3
1950-51—Warren Perkins	66	232	3.5
1951-52—Mel Hutchins	66	190	2.9
1952-53—George Ratkovicz	71	287	4.0
1953-54—Don Sunderlage	68	263	3.9
1954-55—Robert Harrison	72	291	4.0
1955-56—Charles Share	72	318	†4.4
1956-57—Charles Share	72	269	3.7
1957-58—Charles Share	72	279	3.9
1958-59—Cliff Hagan	72	275	3.8
1959-60—Cliff Hagan	75	270	3.6
1960-61—Cliff Hagan	78	286	3.7
1961-62—Bob Pettit	78	293	3.8
1962-63—Zelmo Beaty	80	312	3.9
1963-64—Bob Pettit	80	300	3.8
1964-65—Zelmo Beaty	80	328	4.1
1965-66—Zelmo Beaty	80	344	4.3
1966-67—Bill Bridges	79	325	4.1
1967-68—Bill Bridges	82	†*366	†*4.4
1968-69—Bill Bridges	80	290	3.6
1969-70—Jim Davis	82	335	4.1

Most Disqualifications

Season—Player	*G.*	*Disq.*
1950-51—Cal Christensen	67	†*19
1951-52—Don Boven	66	*18
1952-53—George Ratkovicz	71	16
1953-54—George Ratkovicz	69	11
1954-55—Charles Share	69	*17
1955-56—Charles Share	72	13
1956-57—Charles Share	72	15
1957-58—Charles Share	72	15
1958-59—Cliff Hagan	72	10
1959-60—Larry Foust	72	7
Al Ferrari	71	7
1960-61—Cliff Hagan	78	9
1961-62—Shellie McMillon	62	10
1962-63—Zelmo Beaty	80	12
1963-64—Zelmo Beaty	59	*11
1964-65—Zelmo Beaty	80	11
1965-66—Zelmo Beaty	80	15
1966-67—Bill Bridges	79	12
1967-68—Bill Bridges	82	12
1968-69—Zelmo Beaty	72	7
1969-70—Bill Bridges	82	6

* Led league. † Club record.

BALTIMORE BULLETS

Formed in 1961 as the Chicago Packers, by a syndicate headed by Dave Trager. Changed name to Chicago Zephyrs in 1962. Moved to Baltimore and became the Bullets in 1963 under the same ownership. Purchased in 1965 by a Washington syndicate headed by Abe Polin, Earl Foreman and Arnold Heft. Foreman sold his share in 1968.

Home courts and capacities:
1962—Chicago Amphitheater, 11,000
1963—Chicago Coliseum, 7,100
1963-64 on—Baltimore Civic Center, 12,348

Year	*W.*	*L.*	*Pos.*	*Coach*	*Top Scorer*	*Pts.*	*Play-Offs*
				CHICAGO PACKERS			
1962	18	62	5	Pollard	Bellamy	31.6	—
				CHICAGO ZEPHYRS			
1963	25	55	5	McMahon-Leonard	Bellamy	27.9	—
				BALTIMORE BULLETS			
1964	31	49	4	Leonard	Bellamy	27.0	—
1965	37	43	3	Jeannette	Bellamy	24.8	5-5
1966	38	42	2	Seymour	Ohl	20.6	0-3
1967	20	61	5 (E)	Farmer-Jeannette-Shue	Johnson	20.7	—
1968	36	46	6 (E)	Shue	Monroe	24.3	—
1969	57	25	1 (E)	Shue	Monroe	25.8	0-4
1970	50	32	3 (E)	Shue	Monroe	23.4	3-4
Total	322	415					8-16

(E) In Eastern Division

BALTIMORE BULLETS' YEARLY LEADERS

Leading Scorer

Season—Player	G.	Pts.	Avg.
1961-62—Walt Bellamy	79	†2495	†31.6
1962-63—Walt Bellamy	80	2233	27.9
1963-64—Walt Bellamy	80	2159	27.0
1964-65—Walt Bellamy	80	1981	24.8
1965-66—Don Ohl	73	1502	20.6
1966-67—Gus Johnson	73	1511	20.7
1967-68—Earl Monroe	82	1991	24.3
1968-69—Earl Monroe	80	2065	25.8
1969-70—Earl Monroe	82	1922	23.4

Best Foul Shooter

Season—Player	FTA	FTM	Pct.
1961-62—Robert Leonard	371	279	.752
1962-63—Terry Dischinger	522	402	.770
1963-64—Terry Dischinger	585	454	.776
1964-65—Bailey Howell	†629	†504	.801
1965-66—Kevin Loughery	358	297	.830
1966-67—Kevin Loughery	412	340	.825
1967-68—Jack Marin	314	250	.796
1968-69—Jack Marin	352	292	.830
1969-70—Kevin Loughery	298	253	†.849

Top Playmaker

Season—Player	G.	Ast.	Avg.
1961-62—Robert Leonard	70	378	5.2
1962-63—Sihugo Green	73	†422	†5.9
1963-64—Rod Thorn	75	281	3.7
1964-65—Kevin Loughery	80	296	3.7
1965-66—Kevin Loughery	74	356	4.8
1966-67—Kevin Loughery	76	288	3.8
1967-68—Earl Monroe	82	349	4.3
1968-69—Earl Monroe	80	392	4.9
1969-70—Earl Monroe	82	402	4.9

Most Minutes Played

Season—Player	G.	Min.	Avg.
1961-62—Walt Bellamy	79	3344	42.4
1962-63—Walt Bellamy	80	†3446	†43.2
1963-64—Walt Bellamy	80	3394	42.9
1964-65—Walt Bellamy	80	3301	41.3
1965-66—Don Ohl	73	2645	36.2
1966-67—Leroy Ellis	81	2938	36.3
1967-68—Earl Monroe	82	3012	36.7
1968-69—Kevin Loughery	80	3135	39.2
1969-70—Wes Unseld	82	3234	39.4

Best Shooting Average

Season—Player	FGA	FGM	Pct.
1961-62—Walt Bellamy	1895	†973	*.513
1962-63—Walt Bellamy	1595	840	.527
1963-64—Walt Bellamy	1582	811	.513
1964-65—Walt Bellamy	1441	733	.509
1965-66—John Green	668	358	†.536
1966-67—Don Ohl	1002	452	.451
1967-68—Leroy Ellis	800	380	.475
1968-69—Wes Unseld	897	427	.476
1969-70—Wes Unseld	1015	526	.518

Top Rebounder

Season—Player	*G.*	*Reb.*	*Avg.*
1961-62—Walt Bellamy	79	†1500	†18.9
1962-63—Walt Bellamy	80	1310	16.3
1963-64—Walt Bellamy	80	1361	17.0
1964-65—Walt Bellamy	80	1166	14.6
1965-66—Bailey Howell	79	773	9.8
1966-67—Leroy Ellis	81	970	12.0
1967-68—Ray Scott	81	1111	13.7
1968-69—Wes Unseld	82	1491	18.2
1969-70—Wes Unseld	82	1370	16.7

Most Personal Fouls

Season—Player	*G.*	*PF*	*Avg.*
1961-62—Walt Bellamy	79	281	3.4
1962-63—Walt Bellamy	80	283	3.5
1963-64—Gus Johnson	78	321	4.2
Terry Dischinger	80	321	4.1
1964-65—Bailey Howell	80	*†345	†4.3
1965-66—Bailey Howell	79	306	3.9
1966-67—Kevin Loughery	76	294	3.8
1967-68—Kevin Loughery	77	301	3.9
1968-69—Kevin Loughery	80	299	3.7
1969-70—Gus Johnson	78	269	3.4

Most Disqualifications

Season—Player	*G.*	*Disq.*
1961-62—Walt Bellamy	79	6
1962-63—Walt Bellamy	80	7
1963-64—Gus Johnson	78	*11
1964-65—Kevin Loughery	80	†13
1965-66—Bailey Howell	79	12
1966-67—Kevin Loughery	76	10
1967-68—Kevin Loughery	77	†13
1968-69—Jack Marin	82	4
1968-69—Wes Unseld	82	4
1969-70—Jack Marin	82	6
1969-70—Gus Johnson	78	6

* Led league. † Club record.

BOSTON CELTICS

Formed in 1946 by Boston Garden-Arena Corp. under Walter Brown. Became Boston Celtics under Brown and Lou Pieri as partners in 1951. Purchased in 1965 by Marvin Kratter and Jack Waldron of New York. Purchased in 1969 by Trans-National Communications in 1969.

Home court:
Boston Garden, 13,909 until 1969, then 15,128
(Also some games at Boston Arena, 5,000, and Providence Arena, 6,000)

Year	*W.*	*L.*	*Pos.*	*Coach*	*Top Scorer*	*Pts.*	*Play-Offs*
1947	22	38	6	J. Russell	Simmons	10.3	—
1948	20	28	3	J. Russell	Sadowski	19.4	1-2
1949	25	35	5	Julian	Ehlers	8.7	—
1950	22	46	6	Julian	Kinney	11.1	—
1951	39	30	2	Auerbach	Macauley	20.4	0-2
1952	39	27	2	Auerbach	Cousy	21.7	1-2
1953	46	25	3	Auerbach	Macauley	20.3	3-3
1954	42	30	2	Auerbach	Cousy	19.2	2-4
1955	36	36	3	Auerbach	Cousy	21.2	3-4
1956	39	33	2	Auerbach	Sharman	19.9	1-2
1957	44	28	1	Auerbach	Sharman	21.1	7-3
1958	49	23	1	Auerbach	Sharman	22.3	6-5
1959	52	20	1	Auerbach	Sharman	20.4	8-3
1960	59	16	1	Auerbach	Heinsohn	21.7	8-5
1961	57	22	1	Auerbach	Heinsohn	21.3	8-2
1962	60	20	1	Auerbach	Heinsohn	22.5	8-6
1963	58	22	1	Auerbach	S. Jones	19.7	8-5
1964	59	21	1	Auerbach	Havlicek	19.9	8-2
1965	62	18	1	Auerbach	S. Jones	25.9	8-4
1966	54	26	2	Auerbach	S. Jones	23.2	11-6
1967	60	21	2	W. Russell	S. Jones	22.1	4-5
1968	54	28	2	W. Russell	S. Jones	21.3	12-7
1969	48	34	4	W. Russell	Havlicek	21.6	12-6
1970	34	48	6	Heinsohn	Havlicek	24.2	—
Total	1080	675					119-78

BOSTON CELTICS' YEARLY LEADERS

Leading Scorer

Season—Player	*G.*	*Pts.*	*Avg.*
1946-47—Connie Simmons	60	620	10.3
1947-48—Ed Sadowski	47	910	19.4
1948-49—George Nostrand	60	589	9.8
1949-50—Sonny Hertzberg	68	693	10.2
1950-51—Ed Macauley	68	1384	20.4
1951-52—Bob Cousy	66	1433	21.7
1952-53—Bob Cousy	71	1407	19.8
1953-54—Bob Cousy	72	1383	19.2
1954-55—Bob Cousy	71	1504	21.2
1955-56—Bill Sharman	72	1434	19.9
1056-57—Bill Sharman	67	1413	21.1
1957-58—Bill Sharman	63	1402	22.3
1958-59—Bill Sharman	72	1466	20.4
1959-60—Tom Heinsohn	71	1629	21.7
1960-61—Tom Heinsohn	74	1579	21.3
1961-62—Tom Heinsohn	78	1742	22.3
1962-63—Sam Jones	76	1499	19.7
1963-64—John Havlicek	80	1595	19.9
1964-65—Sam Jones	80	†2070	†25.9
1965-66—Sam Jones	68	1577	23.2
1966-67—John Havlicek	81	1733	21.4
1967-68—John Havlicek	82	1700	20.7
1968-69—John Havlicek	82	1771	21.6
1969-70—John Havlicek	81	1960	24.2

Best Foul Shooter

Season—Player	*FTA*	*FTM*	*Pct.*
1946-47—Tony Kappen	161	128	.795
1947-48—Mike Bloom	229	160	.699
1948-49—Jim Seminoff	219	151	.689
1949-50—Tony Lavelli	197	168	.853
1950-51—Charles Cooper	270	223	.826
1951-52—Bill Sharman	213	183	.859
1952-53—Bill Sharman	401	341	*.850
1953-54—Bill Sharman	392	331	*.844
1954-55—Bill Sharman	387	347	*.897
1955-56—Bill Sharman	413	358	*.867
1056-57—Bill Sharman	421	381	*.905
1957-58—Bill Sharman	338	302	.893
1958-59—Bill Sharman	367	342	†*.932
1959-60—Bill Sharman	291	252	.866
1960-61—Bill Sharman	228	210	*.921
1961-62—Frank Ramsey	405	334	.825
1962-63—Tom Heinsohn	407	340	.835
1963-64—Tom Heinsohn	342	283	.827
1964-65—Sam Jones	522	†428	.820
1965-66—Larry Siegfried	311	274	*.881
1966-67—Sam Jones	371	318	.857
1967-68—Larry Siegfried	272	236	.868
1968-69—Larry Siegfried	389	336	*.864
1969-70—Larry Siegfried	257	220	.856

Top Playmaker

Season—Player	*G.*	*Ast.*	*Avg.*
1946-47—Connie Simmons	60	62	1.0
1947-48—Ed Sadowski	47	74	1.6
1948-49—Jim Seminoff	58	229	3.9
1949-50—Jim Seminoff	65	249	3.8
1950-51—Bob Cousy	69	341	4.9
1951-52—Bob Cousy	66	441	6.7
1952-53—Bob Cousy	71	547	*7.7
1953-54—Bob Cousy	72	518	*7.2
1954-55—Bob Cousy	71	557	*7.8
1955-56—Bob Cousy	72	641	*8.9

1056-57—Bob Cousy	64	478	*7.5
1957-58—Bob Cousy	65	463	*7.1
1958-59—Bob Cousy	65	557	*8.6
1959-60—Bob Cousy	75	†*715	†*9.5
1960-61—Bob Cousy	76	591	7.8
1961-62—Bob Cousy	75	584	7.8
1962-63—Bob Cousy	76	515	6.8
1963-64—K. C. Jones	80	407	5.1
1964-65—K. C. Jones	78	437	5.6
1965-66—K. C. Jones	80	503	6.3
1966-67—Bill Russell	81	472	5.8
1967-68—John Havlicek	82	384	4.7
1968-69—John Havlicek	82	441	5.4
1969-70—John Havlicek	81	550	6.8

Most Minutes Played

Season—Player	*G.*	*Min.*	*Avg.*
1951-52—Bob Cousy	66	2681	40.6
1952-53—Bob Cousy	71	2945	41.5
1953-54—Bob Cousy	72	2857	39.7
1954-55—Bob Cousy	71	2747	38.7
1955-56—Bob Cousy	72	2767	38.4
1956-57—Bill Sharman	67	2403	35.9
1957-58—Bill Russell	69	2640	38.3
1958-59—Bill Russell	70	2979	*42.5
1959-60—Bill Russell	74	3146	42.5
1960-61—Bill Russell	78	3458	44.3
1961-62—Bill Russell	76	3433	45.2
1962-63—Bill Russell	78	†3500	†44.9
1963-64—Bill Russell	78	3482	44.6
1964-65—Bill Russell	78	3466	44.4
1965-66—Bill Russell	78	3386	43.4
1966-67—Bill Russell	81	3297	40.7
1967-68—Bill Russell	78	2953	37.8
1968-69—Bill Russell	77	3291	42.7
1969-70—John Havlicek	81	3369	41.6

Best Shooting Average

Season—Player	*FGA*	*FGM*	*Pct.*
1946-47—Connie Simmons	768	246	.320
1947-48—Ed Sadowski	953	308	.323
1948-49—Gene Stump	580	183	.333
1949-50—Bob Kinney	621	233	.375
1950-51—Ed Macauley	985	459	.466
1951-52—Bob Donham	413	201	†.487
1952-53—Ed Macauley	997	451	*.452
1953-54—Ed Macauley	950	462	.486
1954-55—Bill Sharman	1062	453	.427
1955-56—Bill Sharman	1229	538	.438
1956-57—Bill Russell	649	277	.427
1957-58—Bill Russell	1032	456	.442
1958-59—Bill Russell	997	456	.457
1959-60—Bill Russell	1189	555	.567
1960-61—Sam Jones	1062	474	.446
1961-62—Sam Jones	1283	589	.459
1962-63—Sam Jones	1305	621	.476
1963-64—Sam Jones	1359	612	.450
1964-65—Sam Jones	†1818	†821	.452
1965-66—Sam Jones	1335	626	.429
1966-67—Bailey Howell	1242	636	.512
1967-68—Don Nelson	632	312	.494
1968-69—Bailey Howell	1257	612	.487
1969-70—Don Nelson	920	461	.501

Top Rebounder

Season—Player	*G.*	*Reb.*	*Avg.*
1950-51—Ed Macauley	68	616	9.1
1951-52—Bob Harris	66	631	8.0
1952-53—Ed Macauley	69	629	9.1
1953-54—Ed Macauley	71	571	8.0
1954-55—Ed Macauley	71	600	7.0
1955-56—Jack Nichols	60	625	10.4
1956-57—Bill Russell	48	943	19.6

1957-58—Bill Russell	69	1564	*22.7
1958-59—Bill Russell	70	1612	*23.0
1959-60—Bill Russell	74	1778	24.0
1960-61—Bill Russell	78	1868	23.9
1961-62—Bill Russell	76	1891	†24.9
1962-63—Bill Russell	78	1843	23.6
1963-64—Bill Russell	78	†1930	24.7
1964-65—Bill Russell	78	1878	*24.1
1965-66—Bill Russell	78	1779	22.8
1966-67—Bill Russell	81	1700	21.0
1967-68—Bill Russell	78	1451	18.6
1968-69—Bill Russell	77	1484	19.3
1969-70—John Havlicek	81	635	7.8

Most Personal Fouls

Season—Player	*G.*	*PF*	*Avg.*
1946-47—Connie Simmons	60	130	2.2
1947-48—Ed Sadowski	47	182	3.9
1948-49—Jim Seminoff	58	229	3.9
1949-50—Bob Kinney	60	251	4.2
1950-51—Kleggie Hermsen	71	261	3.8
1951-52—Bob Brannum	66	235	3.6
1952-53—Bob Brannum	71	287	4.0
1953-54—Bob Brannum	71	280	3.9
1954-55—Frank Ramsey	64	250	3.9
1955-56—Arnie Risen	68	300	†*4.4
1956-57—Tom Heinsohn	72	304	4.2
1957-58—Tom Heinsohn	69	274	4.0
1958-59—Jim Loscutoff	66	285	4.3
1959-60—Tom Heinsohn	75	275	3.7
1960-61—Frank Ramsey	79	284	3.6
1961-62—Tom Heinsohn	78	280	3.6
1962-63—Tom Heinsohn	77	267	3.5
1963-64—Tom Heinsohn	76	268	3.5
1964-65—Tom Sanders	80	†318	4.0
1965-66—Tom Sanders	72	317	†4.4
1966-67—Tom Sanders	81	304	3.8
1967-68—Tom Sanders	78	300	3.8
1968-69—Tom Sanders	82	293	3.6
1969-70—Henry Finkel	80	292	3.6

Most Disqualifications

Season—Player	*G.*	*Disq.*
1950-51—Kleggie Hermsen	71	8
Frank Kudelka	62	8
1951-52—Bob Donham	66	9
Bob Brannum	66	9
1952-53—Bob Brannum	71	17
1953-54—Bob Donham	68	11
1954-55—Frank Ramsey	64	11
1955-56—Arnie Risen	68	*17
1956-57—Tom Heinsohn	72	12
1957-58—Frank Ramsey	69	8
Lou Tsioropoulos	70	8
1958-59—Jim Loscutoff	66	15
1959-60—Frank Ramsey	73	10
Gene Conley	71	10
1960-61—Gene Conley	75	15
1961-62—Frank Ramsey	79	9
Tom Sanders	80	9
1962-63—Frank Ramsey	77	*13
1963-64—Frank Ramsey	75	7
1964-65—Tom Sanders	80	*15
1965-66—Tom Sanders	72	†*19
1966-67—K. C. Jones	78	7
1967-68—Tom Sanders	78	12
1968-69—Tom Sanders	82	9
1969-70—Henry Finkel	80	13

BUFFALO BRAVES

Formed in 1970, entering as expansion team for 1970-71 season. Carl Scheer, president. Eddie Donovan, general manager. Dolph Schayes, coach.

Home court: Memorial Auditorium, 12,500

CHICAGO BULLS

Formed in 1966 by a syndicate led by Dick Klein and Elmer Rich, Jr.

Home courts:
1966-67—Chicago Amphitheater, 11,002
1967-on—Chicago Stadium, 17,374

Year	*W.*	*L.*	*Pos.*	*Coach*	*Top Scorer*	*Pts.*	*Play-Offs*
1967	33	48	4	Kerr	Rodgers / Boozer	18.0	0-3
1968	29	53	4	Kerr	Boozer	21.5	1-4
1969	33	49	5	Motta	Boozer	21.7	—
1970	39	43	3 (T)	Motta	Walker	21.5	1-4
Total	134	193					2-11

CHICAGO BULLS' YEARLY LEADERS

Leading Scorer

Season—Player	*G.*	*Pts.*	*Avg.*
1966-67—Guy Rodgers	81	1459	18.0
1967-68—Bob Boozer	77	1655	21.5
1968-69—Bob Boozer	79	†1716	†21.7
1969-70—Chet Walker	78	1675	21.5

Best Foul Shooter

Season—Player	*FTA*	*PTM*	*Pct.*
1966-67—Guy Rodgers	457	383	.806
1967-68—Flynn Robinson	352	288	.818
1968-69—Bob Boozer	489	394	.806
1969-70—Chet Walker	†568	†483	†.850

Top Playmaker

Season—Player	*G.*	*Ast.*	*Avg.*
1966-67—Guy Rodgers	81	†908	†*11.2
1967-68—Keith Erickson	78	267	3.4
1968-69—Clem Haskins	79	306	3.9
1969-70—Clem Haskins	82	624	7.6

Most Minutes Played

Season—Player	*G.*	*Min.*	*Avg.*
1966-67—Guy Rodgers	81	3063	37.8
1967-68—Bob Boozer	77	†2988	†38.8
1968-69—Jerry Sloan	78	2939	37.7
1969-70—Clem Haskins	82	3214	39.2

Best Shooting Average

Season—Player	*FGA*	*FGM*	*Pct.*
1966-67—Bob Boozer	1104	538	.487
1967-68—Bob Boozer	1265	622	†.492
1968-69—Bob Boozer	†1375	†661	.481
1969-70—Chet Walker	1249	596	.477

Top Rebounder

Season—Player	*G.*	*Reb.*	*Avg.*
1966-67—Jerry Sloan	80	726	9.1
1967-68—Jim Washington	82	825	10.1
1968-69—Tom Boerwinkle	80	889	11.1
1969-70—Tom Boerwinkle	81	†1016	†12.5

Most Personal Fouls

Season—Player	*G.*	*PF.*	*Avg.*
1966-67—Jerry Sloan	80	293	3.7
1967-68—Jerry Sloan	77	291	3.8
1968-69—Tom Boerwinkle	80	†317	†4.0
1969-70—Bob Love	82	264	3.2

Most Disqualifications

Season—Player	*G.*	*Disq.*
1966-67—Jerry Sloan	80	7
1967-68—Keith Erickson	78	†15
1968-69—Tom Boerwinkle	80	11
1969-70—Tom Boerwinkle	81	4

* Led league. † Club record.

CINCINNATI ROYALS

Entered B.A.A. in 1948-49 as the Rochester Royals, owned by Lester and Jack Harrison. Moved to Cincinnati in 1957-58. Purchased by group headed by Frank Wood, Ambrose Lindhorst and Tom Grace in 1958.

Home courts:
- 1948-55—Edgerton Park Sports Arena, Rochester, 5,000
- 1955-56—Rochester War Memorial, 10,000
- 1956-on—Cincinnati Gardens, 11,438

Year	*W.*	*L.*	*Pos.*	*Coach*	*Top Scorer*	*Pts.*	*Play-Offs*
				ROCHESTER ROYALS			
1949	45	15	1	Harrison	Risen	16.6	2-2
1950	51	17	2	Harrison	Davies	14.0	0-2
1951	41	27	2	Harrison	Risen	16.3	9-5
1952	41	25	1	Harrison	Davies	16.2	3-3
1953	44	26	2	Harrison	Davies	15.6	1-2
1954	44	28	2	Harrison	Wanzer	13.3	3-3
1955	29	43	3	Harrison	Wanzer	13.1	1-2
1956	31	41	4	Wanzer	Stokes	16.8	—
1957	31	41	4	Wanzer	Twyman	16.3	—
				CINCINNATI ROYALS			
1958	33	39	2	Wanzer	Lovellette	23.4	0-2
1959	19	53	4	Wanzer-Marshall	Twyman	25.8	—
1960	19	56	4	Marshall	Twyman	31.2	—
1961	33	46	4	Wolf	Robertson	30.5	—
1962	43	37	2	Wolf	Robertson	30.8	1-3
1963	42	38	3 (E)	Wolf	Robertson	28.3	6-6
1964	55	25	2 (E)	McMahon	Robertson	31.4	4-6
1965	48	32	2 (E)	McMahon	Robertson	30.4	1-3
1966	45	35	3 (E)	McMahon	Robertson	31.3	2-3
1967	39	42	3 (E)	McMahon	Robertson	30.5	1-3
1968	39	43	5 (E)	Jucker	Robertson	29.2	—
1969	41	41	5 (E)	Jucker	Robertson	24.7	—
1970	36	46	5 (E)	Cousy	Robertson	25.3	—
Total	847	796					34-45

(E) In Eastern Division.

CINCINNATI ROYALS' YEARLY LEADERS

Leading Scorer

Season—Player	*G.*	*Pts.*	*Avg.*
1948-49—Arnie Risen	60	995	16.6
1949-50—Bob Davies	64	895	14.0
1950-51—Arnie Risen	66	1077	16.3
1951-52—Bob Davies	65	1052	16.2
1952-53—Bob Davies	66	1029	15.6
1953-54—Bobby Wanzer	72	958	13.3
1954-55—Bobby Wanzer	72	942	13.1
1955-56—Maurice Stokes	67	1125	16.8
1956-57—Jack Twyman	72	1174	16.3
1957-58—Clyde Lovellette	71	1659	23.4
1958-59—Jack Twyman	72	1857	24.8
1959-60—Jack Twyman	75	2338	31.2
1960-61—Oscar Robertson	71	2165	30.5
1961-62—Oscar Robertson	79	2432	30.8
1962-63—Oscar Robertson	80	2264	28.3
1963-64—Oscar Robertson	79	†2480	†31.4
1964-65—Oscar Robertson	75	2270	30.4
1965-66—Oscar Robertson	76	2378	31.3
1966-67—Oscar Robertson	79	2412	30.5
1967-68—Oscar Robertson	65	1896	29.2
1968-69—Oscar Robertson	79	1995	24.7
1969-70—Oscar Robertson	69	1748	25.3

Best Foul Shooter

Season—Player	*FTA*	*FTM*	*Pct.*
1948-49—Bobby Wanzer	254	209	.823
1949-50—Bobby Wanzer	351	283	.806
1950-51—Bobby Wanzer	273	232	.850
1951-52—Bobby Wanzer	417	377	*†.904
1952-53—Bobby Wanzer	473	384	.812
1953-54—Bobby Wanzer	428	314	.734
1954-55—Marion Spears	271	220	.812
1955-56—Don Meineke	232	181	.780
1956-57—Richie Regan	235	182	.774
1957-58—Jack Twyman	396	307	.775
1958-59—Jack Twyman	558	437	.783
1959-60—Jack Twyman	762	598	.785
1960-61—Oscar Robertson	794	653	.822
1961-62—Jack Twyman	435	353	.815
1962-63—Oscar Robertson	738	614	.832
1963-64—Oscar Robertson	†938	†800	*.853
1964-65—Oscar Robertson	793	665	.839
1965-66—Adrian Smith	480	408	.850
1966-67—Adrian Smith	380	343	* .903
1967-68—Oscar Robertson	660	576	*.873
1968-69—Oscar Robertson	767	643	.838
1969-70—Oscar Robertson	561	454	.809

Top Playmaker

Season—Player	*G.*	*Ast.*	*Avg.*
1948-49—Bob Davies	60	*321	*5.4
1949-50—Bob Davies	64	294	4.6
1950-51—Bob Davies	63	287	4.6
1951-52—Bob Davies	65	390	6.0
1952-53—Bob Davies	66	280	4.2
1953-54—Bob Davies	72	323	4.5
1954-55—Bobby Wanzer	72	247	3.4
1955-56—Maurice Stokes	69	328	4.8
1956-57—Maurice Stokes	72	331	4.6
1957-58—Maurice Stokes	68	403	5.9
1958-59—Johnny McCarthy	47	225	4.8
1959-60—Win Wilfong	72	265	3.7
1960-61—Oscar Robertson	71	690	*9.7
1961-62—Oscar Robertson	79	†*899	*11.4
1962-63—Oscar Robertson	80	758	9.5
1963-64—Oscar Robertson	79	868	*10.9

1964-65—Oscar Robertson	75	861	†*11.5
1965-66—Oscar Robertson	76	837	*11.1
1966-67—Oscar Robertson	79	845	10.7
1967-68—Oscar Robertson	65	633	9.7
1968-69—Oscar Robertson	79	*772	9.8
1969-70—Oscar Robertson	69	558	8.1

Most Minutes Played

Season—Player	*G.*	*Min.*	*Avg.*
1951-52—Bobby Wanzer	66	2498	37.8
1952-53—Jack Coleman	70	2625	37.5
1953-54—Bobby Wanzer	72	2538	35.3
1954-55—Jack Coleman	72	2482	34.5
1955-56—Maurice Stokes	67	2323	34.7
1956-57—Maurice Stokes	72	2761	38.3
1957-58—Clyde Lovellette	71	2589	36.5
1958-59—Jack Twyman	72	2713	37.7
1959-60—Jack Twyman	75	3023	40.3
1960-61—Oscar Robertson	71	3012	42.4
1961-62—Oscar Robertson	79	3503	44.3
1962-63—Oscar Robertson	80	3521	44.0
1963-64—Oscar Robertson	79	†3562	45.1
1964-65—Oscar Robertson	75	3421	†45.6
1965-66—Jerry Lucas	79	3517	44.5
1966-67—Jerry Lucas	81	3558	43.9
1967-68—Jerry Lucas	82	3619	44.1
1968-69—Oscar Robertson	79	3461	43.8
1969-70—Norm Van Lier	81	2895	35.7

Best Shooting Average

Season—Player	*FGA*	*FGM*	*Pct.*
1948-49—Arnie Risen	816	345	*.423
1949-50—Bobby Wanzer	614	254	.414
1950-51—Jack Coleman	749	315	.421
1951-52—Bobby Wanzer	772	328	.425
1952-53—Jack Coleman	748	314	.420
1953-54—Bobby Wanzer	835	322	.386
1954-55—Jack Coleman	866	400	.462
1955-56—Jack Twyman	987	417	.422
1956-57—Jack Twyman	1023	449	.439
1957-58—Jack Twyman	1028	465	.452
1958-59—Jack Twyman	†1691	710	.420
1959-60—Wayne Embry	690	303	.439
1960-61—Jack Twyman	1632	796	.488
1961-62—Jack Twyman	1542	739	.479
1962-63—Oscar Robertson	1593	†825	.518
1963-64—Jerry Lucas	1035	545	*.527
1964-65—Jerry Lucas	1121	558	.498
1965-66—Happy Hairston	814	398	.489
1966-67—Oscar Robertson	1699	838	.493
1967-68—Jerry Lucas	1361	707	.519
1968-69—Jerry Lucas	1007	555	.551
1969-70—Johnny Green	860	481	†*.559

Top Rebounder

Season—Player	*G.*	*Reb.*	*Avg.*
1950-51—Arnie Risen	66	795	12.0
1951-52—Arnie Risen	66	841	12.7
1952-53—Jack Coleman	70	774	11.1
1953-54—Arnie Risen	72	728	10.1
1954-55—Jack Coleman	72	729	10.1
1955-56—Maurice Stokes	69	1094	14.3
1956-57—Maurice Stokes	72	1256	*17.4
1957-58—Maurice Stokes	68	1142	16.8
1958-59—Jack Twyman	72	653	9.1
1959-60—Wayne Embry	73	692	9.5
1960-61—Wayne Embry	79	864	10.9
1961-62—Oscar Robertson	79	985	12.5
1962-63—Oscar Robertson	76	936	12.3
1963-64—Jerry Lucas	79	1375	17.4

1964-65—Jerry Lucas	66	1321	20.0
1965-66—Jerry Lucas	79	†1668	†21.1
1966-67—Jerry Lucas	81	1547	20.0
1967-68—Jerry Lucas	82	1560	19.0
1968-69—Jerry Lucas	74	1360	18.4
1969-70—Johnny Green	78	841	10.8

Most Personal Fouls

Season—Player	*G.*	*PF*	*Avg.*
1948-49—Arnie Johnson	60	247	4.1
1949-50—Arnie Johnson	68	260	3.8
1950-51—Arnie Risen	66	278	4.2
1951-52—Arnie Risen	66	258	4.0
1952-53—Arnie Risen	68	274	4.0
1953-54—Arnie Risen	72	284	3.9
1954-55—Arnie Risen	69	253	3.7
1955-56—Dick Ricketts	68	287	4.2
1956-57—Dick Rickets	72	307	†4.3
1957-58—Dick Rickets	72	277	3.8
1958-59—Jack Twyman	72	277	3.8
1959-60—Jack Twyman	75	275	3.7
1960-61—Wayne Embry	79	286	3.6
1961-62—Jack Twyman	80	315	3.9
1962-63—Bob Boozer	79	299	3.8
1963-64—Wayne Embry	80	325	*4.1
1964-65—Wayne Embry	74	297	4.0
1965-66—Wayne Embry	80	287	3.6
1966-67—Jerry Lucas	81	280	3.5
1967-68—Connie Dierking	81	315	3.9
1968-69—Connie Dierking	82	305	3.7
1969-70—Norm Van Lier	81	†329	4.1

Most Disqualifications

Season—Player	*G.*	*Disq.*
1950-51—Arnie Risen	66	9
1951-52—Bob Davies	65	10
1952-53—Jack Coleman	70	10
1953-54—Arnie Risen	72	19
1954-55—Arnie Risen	69	10
1955-56—Dick Ricketts	68	14
1956-57—Maurice Stokes-Dick Ricketts	72	12
1957-58—Maurice Stokes	68	9
1958-59—Wayne Embry	66	9
1959-60—Jack Twyman	75	10
1960-61—Arlen Bockhorn	79	9
1961-62—Hub Reed	80	9
1962-63—Bob Boozer	79	8
1963-64—Wayne Embry	80	7
Jack Twyman	68	7
1964-65—Wayne Embry	74	10
1965-66—Wayne Embry	80	9
1966-67—Connie Dierking	77	7
1967-68—Connie Dierking	81	6
1968-69—Connie Dierking	82	9
1969-70—Norm Van Lier	81	†*18

*** Led league. † Club record.**

CLEVELAND CAVALIERS

Formed in 1970, entering as expansion team for 1970-71 season. Nick J. Maleti, president and general manager. Bill Fitch, coach.

Home court: Cleveland Arena, 9,230

DETROIT PISTONS

Entered B.A.A. in 1948-49, as Fort Wayne Pistons, owned by Fred Zollner. Moved to Detroit for 1957-58 season.

Home courts:

1948-52—North Side H. S. Gym, Fort Wayne, 3,800
1952-57—Memorial Coliseum, 9,306
1957-61—Detroit Olympia, 14,000 (also some games at University of Detroit Gym, 9,000)
1961-on—Cobo Hall Convention Arena, 11,009

Year	*W.*	*L.*	*Pos.*	*Coach*	*Top Scorer*	*Pts.*	*Play-Offs*
				FORT WAYNE PISTONS			
1949	22	38	5	Bennett-Armstrong	Black	9.8	—
1950	49	28	3	Mendenhall	Schaus	14.3	2-2
1951	32	36	3	Mendenhall	Schaus	15.1	1-2
1952	29	37	4	Birch	Brian	15.9	0-2
1953	36	33	3	Birch	Foust	14.3	4-4
1954	40	32	3	Birch	Foust	15.1	0-4
1955	43	29	1	Eckman	Foust	17.0	6-5
1956	37	35	1	Eckman	Yardley	17.4	4-6
1957	34	38	3	Eckman	Yardley	21.5	0-2
				DETROIT PISTONS			
1958	33	39	2	Eckman-Rocha	Yardley	27.8	3-4
1959	28	44	3	Rocha	Shue	17.6	1-2
1960	30	45	2	Rocha-R. McGuire	Shue	22.8	0-2
1961	34	45	3	R. McGuire	Howell	23.4	2-3
1962	37	43	3	R. McGuire	Howell	19.9	5-5
1963	34	46	3	R. McGuire	Howell	22.7	1-3
1964	23	57	5	Wolf	Howell	21.6	—
1965	31	49	4	Wolf-DeBusschere	Dischinger	18.2	—
1966	22	58	5	DeBusschere	Miles	19.6	—
1967	30	51	5	DeBusschere-Butcher	Bing	20.0	—
1968	40	42	4 (E)	Butcher	Bing	27.1	2-4
1969	32	50	6 (E)	Butcher-Seymour	Bing	23.4	—
1970	31	51	7 (E)	Van Breda Kolff	Bing	22.9	—
Total	727	926					31-50

(E) Eastern Division.

DETROIT PISTONS' YEARLY LEADERS

Leading Scorer

Season—Player	G.	Pts.	Avg.
1948-49—Charles Black	58	567	9.8
1949-50—Fred Schaus	68	972	14.3
1950-51—Fred Schaus	68	1028	15.1
1951-52—Frank Brian	66	1051	15.9
1952-53—Larry Foust	67	958	14.3
1953-54—Larry Foust	72	1090	15.1
1954-55—Larry Foust	70	1189	17.0
1955-56—George Yardley	71	1233	17.4
1956-57—George Yardley	72	1547	21.5
1957-58—George Yardley	72	†2001	†*27.8
1958-59—Gene Shue	72	1260	17.6
1959-60—Gene Shue	75	1712	22.8
1960-61—Bailey Howell	77	1815	23.4
1961-62—Bailey Howell	79	1576	19.9
1962-63—Bailey Howell	79	1793	22.7
1963-64—Bailey Howell	77	1666	21.6
1964-65—Terry Dischinger	80	1456	18.2
1965-66—Eddie Miles	80	1566	19.6
1966-67—Dave Bing	80	1601	20.0
1967-68—Dave Bing	79	2142	*27.1
1968-69—Dave Bing	77	1800	23.4
1969-70—Dave Bing	70	1604	22.9

Best Foul Shooter

Season—Player	FTA	FTM	Pct.
1948-49—Bruce Hale	228	172	.754
1949-50—Fred Schaus	330	270	.818
1950-51—Fred Schaus	484	404	.835
1951-52—Frank Brian	433	367	.848
1952-53—Fred Scolari	327	276	.844
1953-54—Andrew Phillip	330	241	.730
1954-55—Frank Brian	255	217	.851
1955-56—Larry Foust	555	432	.778
1956-57—George Yardley	639	503	.787
1957-58—Gene Shue	327	276	.844
1958-59—Gene Shue	421	338	.803
1959-60—Gene Shue	541	472	†.872
1960-61—Gene Shue	543	465	.856
1961-62—Gene Shue	447	362	.810
1962-63—Bailey Howell	†650	†519	.798
1963-64—Bailey Howell	581	470	.809
1964-65—Terry Dischinger	424	320	.755
1965-66—Ray Scott	435	323	.743
1966-67—Tom Van Arsdale	347	272	.783
1967-68—Jimmy Walker	175	134	.766
1968-69—Jim Walker	229	182	.795
1969-70—Howard Komives	234	190	.812

Top Playmaker

Season—Player	G.	Ast.	Avg.
1948-49—Bruce Hale	52	156	3.0
1949-50—Fred Schaus	68	176	2.6
1950-51—Ken Murray	66	202	3.1
1951-52—Fred Schaus	62	247	4.0
1952-53—Andrew Phillip	70	397	5.7
1953-54—Andrew Phillip	71	449	6.3
1954-55—Andrew Phillip	64	491	†7.7
1955-56—Andrew Phillip	70	410	5.9
1956-57—Gene Shue	72	238	3.3
1957-58—Dick McGuire	69	454	6.4
1958-59—Dick McGuire	71	443	6.2
1959-60—Dick McGuire	68	358	5.3
1960-61—Gene Shue	78	530	6.8
1961-62—Gene Shue	80	465	5.8
1962-63—Don Ohl	80	325	4.1
1963-64—Ray Scott	80	244	3.1
Donnis Butcher	78	244	3.1

1964-65—Dave DeBusschere	79	253	3.2
1965-66—Ray Scott	79	238	3.0
1966-67—Dave Bing	80	330	4.1
1967-68—Dave Bing	79	509	6.4
1968-69—Dave Bing	77	†546	7.1
1969-70—Dave Bing	70	418	5.7

Most Minutes Played

Season—Player	*G.*	*Min.*	*Avg.*
1951-52—Frank Brian	66	2672	40.5
1952-53—Andrew Phillip	70	2690	38.4
1953-54—Mel Hutchins	72	2934	40.8
1954-55—Mel Hutchins	72	2860	39.7
1955-56—George Yardley	71	2353	33.3
1956-57—George Yardley	72	2691	37.4
1957-58—George Yardley	72	2843	39.5
1958-59—Gene Shue	72	2745	38.1
1959-60—Gene Shue	75	3338	*44.5
1960-61—Gene Shue	78	†3361	†44.8
1961-62—Gene Shue	80	3143	39.3
1962-63—Bailey Howell	79	2971	37.6
1963-64—Ray Scott	80	2964	37.1
1964-65—Dave DeBusschere	79	2769	34.8
1965-66—Eddie Miles	80	2788	34.9
1966-67—Dave DeBusschere	78	2897	37.1
1967-68—Dave Bing	79	3209	40.6
1968-69—Dave Bing	77	3039	39.5
1969-70—Jim Walker	81	2869	35.4

Best Shooting Average

Season—Player	*FGA*	*FGM*	*Pct.*
1948-49—Bruce Hale	585	187	.320
1949-50—Fred Schaus	996	351	.352
1950-51—Jack Kerris	689	255	.370
1951-52—Larry Foust	989	380	.394
1952-53—Andrew Phillip	629	250	.397
1953-54—George Yardley	492	209	.425
1954-55—Larry Foust	818	398	.487
1955-56—Larry Foust	821	367	.447
1956-57—Robert Houbregs	585	253	.432
1954-55—Larry Foust	818	398	.487
1958-59—Shellie McMillon	700	287	.439
1959-60—Bailey Howell	1119	510	.456
1960-61—Bailey Howell	1293	607	.469
1961-62—Bailey Howell	1193	553	.463
1962-63—Bailey Howell	1235	†637	.516
1963-64—Bailey Howell	1267	598	.472
1964-65—Terry Dischinger	1153	568	.493
1965-66—Eddie Miles	†1418	634	.447
1966-67—John Tresvant	585	256	.438
1967-68—Len Campbell	428	220	.514
1968-69—Terry Dischinger	513	264	.515
1969-70—Terry Dischinger	650	342	†.526

Top Rebounder

Season—Player	*G.*	*Reb.*	*Avg.*
1950-51—Larry Foust	68	681	10.0
1951-52—Larry Foust	66	*880	*13.3
1952-53—Larry Foust	67	769	11.5
1953-54—Larry Foust	72	967	13.4
1954-55—Larry Foust	70	700	10.0
1955-56—George Yardley	71	686	9.7
1956-57—George Yardley	72	755	10.5
1957-58—Walter Dukes	72	954	13.3
1958-59—Walter Dukes	72	958	13.3
1959-60—Walter Dukes	66	883	13.4
1960-61—Bailey Howell	77	†1111	†14.4
1961-62—Bailey Howell	79	996	12.6
1962-63—Bailey Howell	79	910	11.5
1963-64—Ray Scott	80	1078	13.5

1964-65—Reggie Harding	78	906	11.6
1965-66—Dave DeBusschere	79	916	11.6
1966-67—Dave DeBusschere	78	924	11.8
1967-68—Dave DeBusschere	80	1081	13.5
1968-69—Harold Hairston	81	959	11.8
1969-70—Otto Moore	81	900	11.1

Most Personal Fouls

Season—Player	*G.*	*PF*	*Avg.*
1948-49—Charles Black	58	247	4.3
1949-50—Howard Schultz	67	244	3.6
1950-51—Don Otten	67	255	3.8
1951-52—Jack Kerris	66	265	4.0
1952-53—Don Meineke	68	†334	†*4.9
1953-54—Larry Foust	72	258	3.6
1954-55—Larry Foust	70	264	3.8
1955-56—Larry Foust	72	263	3.7
1956-57—George Yardley	72	231	3.2
1957-58—Walter Dukes	72	311	*4.3
1958-59—Walter Dukes	72	332	*4.6
1959-60—Walter Dukes	66	310	4.7
1960-61—Walter Dukes	73	313	4.3
1961-62—Walter Dukes	77	327	*4.2
1962-63—Bailey Howell	79	301	3.8
1963-64—Ray Scott	80	296	3.7
1964-65—Reggie Harding	78	258	3.3
1965-66—Joe Strawder	79	305	3.9
1966-67—Joe Strawder	79	344	*4.4
1967-68—Joe Strawder	73	312	4.3
1968-69—Dave Bing	77	256	3.3
1969-70—Howard Komives	82	247	3.0

Most Disqualifications

Season—Player	*G.*	*Disq.*
1950-51—Don Otten	67	15
John Oldham	68	15
1951-52—Jack Kerris	66	16
1952-53—Don Meineke	68	†*26
1953-54—Don Meineke	71	6
1954-55—Larry Foust	70	9
1955-56—Larry Foust	72	7
1956-57—Larry Foust	72	7
1957-58—Walter Dukes	72	17
1958-59—Walter Dukes	72	*22
1959-60—Walter Dukes	66	*20
1960-61—Walter Dukes	73	*16
1961-62—Walter Dukes	77	*20
1962-63—Bailey Howell	79	9
1963-64—Bailey Howell	77	9
Jack Moreland	78	9
1964-65—Terry Dischinger	80	5
Dave DeBusschere	79	5
Ray Scott	66	5
Reggie Harding	78	5
1965-66—Joe Strawder	79	10
1966-67—Joe Strawder	79	*19
1967-68—Joe Strawder	73	*18
1968-69—Terry Dischinger	75	5
1969-70—Terry Dischinger	75	5

* Led league. † Club record.

LOS ANGELES LAKERS

Entered B.A.A. in 1948-49 as the Minneapolis Lakers, owned by Ben Berger and Max Winter. Sold in 1957 to Bob Short. Moved to Los Angeles for the 1960-61 season. Sold in 1965 to Jack Kent Cooke.

Home courts:

1948-60—Minneapolis Auditorium, 10,000 (Also some games at Minneapolis Armory, 9,500, and St. Paul Auditorium, 9,000)
1960-68—Los Angeles Sports Arena, 14,871
1969-on—The Forum, 17,500

Year	*W.*	*L.*	*Pos.*	*Coach*	*Top Scorer*	*Pts.*	*Play-Offs*
				MINNEAPOLIS LAKERS			
1949	44	16	2	Kundla	Mikan	28.3	8-2
1950	51	17	1	Kundla	Mikan	27.4	10-2
1951	44	24	1	Kundla	Mikan	28.4	3-4
1952	40	26	2	Kundla	Mikan	23.8	9-4
1953	48	22	1	Kundla	Mikan	20.6	9-3
1954	40	26	1	Kundla	Mikan	18.1	9-4
1955	40	32	2	Kundla	Mikkelsen	18.4	3-4
1956	33	39	2	Kundla	Lovellette	21.5	1-2
1957	34	38	2	Kundla	Lovellette	20.8	2-3
1958	19	53	4	Mikan-Kundla	Mikkelsen	17.3	—
1959	33	39	2	Kundla	Baylor	24.9	6-7
1960	25	50	3	Castellani-Pollard	Baylor	29.6	5-4
				LOS ANGELES LAKERS			
1961	36	43	2	Schaus	Baylor	34.8	6-6
1962	54	26	1	Schaus	West	30.8	7-6
1963	53	27	1	Schaus	Baylor	34.0	6-7
1964	42	38	3	Schaus	West	28.7	2-3
1965	49	31	1	Schaus	West	31.0	5-6
1966	45	35	1	Schaus	West	31.4	7-7
1967	36	45	3	Schaus	West	28.7	0-3
1968	52	30	2	Van Breda Kolff	Baylor	26.0	10-5
1969	55	27	1	Van Breda Kolff	Baylor	24.8	11-7
1970	46	36	2	Mullaney	West	31.2	11-7
Total	925	720					130-96

LOS ANGELES LAKERS' YEARLY LEADERS

Leading Scorer

Season—Player	*G.*	*Pts.*	*Avg.*
1948-49—George Mikan	60	1698	*28.3
1949-50—George Mikan	68	1865	*27.4
1950-51—George Mikan	68	1932	*28.4
1951-52—George Mikan	64	1523	23.8
1952-53—George Mikan	70	1442	20.6
1953-54—George Mikan	72	1306	18.1
1954-55—Vern Mikkelsen	71	1327	18.4
1955-56—Clyde Lovellette	71	1526	21.5
1956-57—Clyde Lovellette	69	1434	20.8
1957-58—Vern Mikkelsen	72	1248	17.3
1958-59—Elgin Baylor	70	1742	24.9
1959-60—Elgin Baylor	70	2074	29.6
1960-61—Elgin Baylor	73	2538	†34.8
1961-62—Jerry West	75	2310	30.8
1962-63—Elgin Baylor	80	†2719	34.0
1963-64—Jerry West	72	2064	28.7
1964-65—Jerry West	74	2292	31.0
1965-66—Jerry West	79	2476	31.4
1966-67—Jerry West	66	1892	28.7
1967-68—Elgin Baylor	77	2002	26.0
1968-69—Elgin Baylor	76	1881	24.8
1969-70—Jerry West	74	2309	31.2

Best Foul Shooter

Season—Player	*FTA*	*FTM*	*Pct.*
1948-49—George Mikan	689	532	.772
1949-50—George Mikan	728	567	.793
1950-51—George Mikan	717	576	.803
1951-52—George Mikan	555	433	.780
1952-53—George Mikan	567	442	.780
Slater Martin	287	224	.780
1953-54—George Mikan	546	424	.777
1954-55—Dick Schnittker	362	298	.823
1955-56—Dick Schnittker	355	304	.856
1956-57—Dick Garmaker	435	365	.839
1957-58—Vern Mikkelsen	471	370	.786
1958-59—Vern Mikkelsen	355	286	.806
1959-60—Elgin Baylor	770	564	.732
1960-61—Rudy LaRusso	409	323	.790
1961-62—Jerry West	926	712	.769
1962-63—Elgin Baylor	789	661	.838
1963-64—Jerry West	702	584	.832
1964-65—Jerry West	789	648	.821
1965-66—Jerry West	†977	†*840	†.860
1966-67—Jerry West	686	602	.878
1967-68—Jerry West	482	391	.811
1968-69—Johnny Egan	240	204	.850
1969-70—Jerry West	785	647	.824

Top Playmaker

Season—Player	*G.*	*Ast.*	*Avg.*
1948-49—George Mikan	60	218	3.6
1949-50—James Pollard	66	252	3.8
1950-51—Slater Martin	68	235	3.5
1951-52—Slater Martin	66	249	3.8
1952-53—Slater Martin	70	250	3.6
1953-54—Slater Martin	69	253	3.7
1954-55—Slater Martin	72	427	5.9
1955-56—Slater Martin	72	445	6.2
1956-57—Charles Mencel	72	201	2.8
1957-58—Robert Leonard	66	218	3.3
1958-59—Elgin Baylor	70	287	4.1
1959-60—Rod Hundley	73	338	4.6
1960-61—Elgin Baylor	73	371	5.1
1961-62—Jerry West	75	400	5.3
1962-63—Elgin Baylor	80	386	4.9
1963-64—Jerry West	72	403	5.6

NEW YORK KNICKERBOCKERS' YEARLY LEADERS

Leading Scorer

Season—Player	*G.*	*Pts.*	*Avg.*
1946-47—Sonny Hertzberg	59	515	8.7
1947-48—Carl Braun	47	671	14.3
1948-49—Carl Braun	57	810	14.2
1949-50—Carl Braun	67	1031	15.4
1950-51—Vince Boryla	66	982	14.9
1951-52—Max Zaslofsky	66	931	14.1
1952-53—Carl Braun	70	977	14.0
1953-54—Carl Braun	72	1062	14.8
1954-55—Carl Braun	71	1074	15.1
1955-56—Carl Braun	72	1112	15.4
1956-57—Harry Gallatin	72	1079	15.0
1957-58—Ken Sears	72	1342	18.0
1958-59—Ken Sears	71	1488	21.0
1959-60—Richie Guerin	74	1615	21.8
1960-61—Willie Naulls	79	1846	23.4
1961-62—Richie Guerin	78	†2303	†29.5
1962-63—Richie Guerin	79	1701	21.5
1963-64—Len Chappell	79	1350	17.1
1964-65—Willis Reed	80	1560	19.5
1965-66—Walt Bellamy	80	1820	22.8
1966-67—Willis Reed	78	1628	20.9
1967-68—Willis Reed	81	1685	20.8
1968-69—Willis Reed	82	1733	21.1
1969-70—Willis Reed	81	1755	21.7

Best Foul Shooter

Season—Player	*FTA*	*FTM*	*Pct.*
1946-47—Stan Stutz	170	133	.782
1947-48—Stan Stutz	135	113	.837
1948-49—Ray Lumpp	283	219	.774
1949-50—Vince Boryla	313	204	.764
1950-51—Vince Boryla	332	278	.837
1951-52—Harry Gallatin	341	275	.807
1952-53—Carl Braun	401	331	.825
1953-54—Carl Braun	429	354	.825
1954-55—James Baechtold	339	279	.823
1955-56—Carl Braun	382	320	.838
1956-57—Carl Braun	303	245	.808
1957-58—Carl Braun	378	321	.849
1958-59—Ken Sears	588	506	.861
1959-60—Ken Sears	418	363	†.868
1960-61—Ken Sears	323	268	.830
1961-62—Willie Naulls	455	383	.842
1962-63—Richie Guerin	†600	†509	.848
1963-64—John Egan	253	193	.763
1964-65—Howard Komives	254	212	.835
1965-66—Howard Komives	280	241	.861
1966-67—Dick Barnett	295	231	.783
1967-68—Cazzie Russell	349	282	.808
1968-69—Bill Bradley	253	206	.814
1969-70—Bill Bradley	176	145	.824

Top Playmaker

Season—Player	*G.*	*Ast.*	*Avg.*
1946-47—Ossie Schectman	54	109	2.0
1947-48—Carl Braun	47	61	1.3
1948-49—Carl Braun	57	173	3.0
1949-50—Dick McGuire	68	*386	*5.7
1950-51—Dick McGuire	64	400	6.3
1951-52—Dick McGuire	64	388	6.1
1952-53—Dick McGuire	61	296	4.7
1953-54—Dick McGuire	68	354	5.2
1954-55—Dick McGuire	71	542	7.6
1955-56—Dick McGuire	62	362	5.8
1956-57—Carl Braun	72	256	3.6

Season—Player	G.	Ast.	Avg.
1957-58—Carl Braun	71	393	5.5
1958-59—Richie Guerin	71	364	5.1
1959-60—Richie Guerin	74	468	6.3
1960-61—Richie Guerin	70	503	7.2
1961-62—Richie Guerin	78	539	6.9
1962-63—Richie Guerin	79	348	4.4
1963-64—John Egan	66	358	5.4
1964-65—Howard Komives	80	265	3.3
1965-66—Howard Komives	80	425	5.3
1966-67—Howard Komives	65	401	6.2
1967-68—Walt Frazier	74	305	4.1
1968-69—Walt Frazier	80	†635	7.9
1969-70—Walt Frazier	77	629	†8.2

Most Minutes Played

Season—Player	*G.*	*Min.*	*Avg.*
1951-52—Max Zaslofsky	66	2113	32.0
1952-53—Nat Clifton	70	2496	35.7
1953-54—Harry Gallatin	72	2690	37.4
1954-55—Harry Gallatin	72	2548	35.4
1955-56—Harry Gallatin	72	2378	33.0
1956-57—Ken Sears	72	2516	34.9
1957-58—Ken Sears	72	2685	37.3
1958-59—Richie Guerin	71	2558	36.0
1959-60—Richie Guerin	74	2420	32.7
1960-61—Richie Guerin	79	3023	38.3
1961-62—Richie Guerin	78	3346	†42.9
1962-63—Richie Guerin	79	2712	34.3
1963-64—Len Chappell	79	2505	31.7
1964-65—Willis Reed	80	3042	38.0
1965-66—Walt Bellamy	80	†3352	41.9
1966-67—Walt Bellamy	79	3010	38.1
1967-68—Willis Reed	81	2879	35.6
1968-69—Willis Reed	82	3108	37.9
1969-70—Willis Reed	81	3089	38.1

Best Shooting Average

Season—Player	*FGA*	*FGM*	*Pct.*
1946-47—John Palmer	521	160	.307
1947-48—Carl Braun	854	276	.323
1948-49—John Palmer	685	240	.350
1949-50—Ernie Vandeweghe	390	164	.421
1950-51—Harry Gallatin	705	293	.416
1951-52—Harry Gallatin	527	233	.442
1952-53—Harry Gallatin	635	282	.444
1953-54—Dick McGuire	493	201	.408
1954-55—Ray Felix	832	364	.438
1955-56—Ken Sears	728	319	.438
1956-57—Ken Sears	821	343	.418
1957-58—Ray Felix	688	304	.442
1958-59—Ken Sears	1002	491	*.490
1959-60—Ken Sears	863	412	*.477
1960-61—Dick Garmaker	933	415	.445
1961-62—Al Butler	756	350	.463
1962-63—Dave Budd	586	294	.502
1963-64—Bill McGill	936	456	.487
1964-65—John Egan	529	258	.488
1965-66—Walt Bellamy	†1373	695	.506
1966-67—Walt Bellamy	1084	565	.521
1967-68—Walt Bellamy	944	511	†.541
1968-69—Willis Reed	1351	†704	.521
1969-70—Walt Frazier	1158	600	.518

Top Rebounder

Season—Player	*G.*	*Reb.*	*Avg.*
1950-51—Harry Gallatin	66	800	12.1
1951-52—Nat Clifton	62	731	11.8
1952-53—Harry Gallatin	70	1098	*15.2
1953-54—Harry Gallatin	72	995	13.8
1954-55—Harry Gallatin	72	995	13.8

Season—Player	G.		
1955-56—Harry Gallatin	72	740	10.3
1956-57—Harry Gallatin	72	725	10.1
1957-58—Willie Naulls	68	799	11.8
1958-59—Willie Naulls	68	723	10.6
1959-60—Willie Naulls	65	921	14.2
1960-61—Willie Naulls	79	1055	13.4
1961-62—John Green	80	1061	13.3
1962-63—John Green	80	964	12.1
1963-64—John Green	80	799	10.0
1964-65—Willis Reed	80	1175	14.7
1965-66—Walt Bellamy	80	†1254	†15.7
1966-67—Willis Reed	78	1136	14.6
1967-68—Willis Reed	81	1073	13.2
1968-69—Willis Reed	82	1191	14.5
1969-70—Willis Reed	81	1126	13.9

Most Personal Fouls

Season—Player	*G.*	*PF*	*Avg.*
1946-47—Dick Fitzgerald	50	153	3.1
1947-48—Lee Knorek	48	171	3.6
1948-49—Lee Knorek	60	258	†4.3
1949-50—Harry Gallatin	68	215	3.2
1950-51—Nat Clifton	65	269	4.1
1951-52—Nat Clifton	62	227	3.7
1952-53—Carl Braun	70	287	4.1
1953-54—Carl Braun	72	259	3.6
1954-55—Ray Felix	72	286	4.0
1955-56—Ray Felix	72	293	4.1
1956-57—Ray Felix	72	284	3.9
1957-58—Ray Felix	72	283	3.9
1958-59—Ray Felix	72	275	3.8
1959-60—Charles Tyra	74	258	3.5
1960-61—Richie Guerin	79	310	3.9
1961-62—Richie Guerin	78	299	3.8
1962-63—Tom Gola	73	316	†*4.3
1963-64—Tom Gola	74	278	3.8
1964-65—Willis Reed	80	339	4.2
1965-66—Willis Reed	76	323	†4.3
1966-67—Willis Reed	78	293	3.8
1967-68—Willis Reed	81	†343	4.2
1968-69—Willis Reed	82	314	3.8
1969-70—Willis Reed	81	287	3.5

Most Disqualifications

Season—Player	*G.*	*Disq.*
1950-51—Nat Clifton	65	13
1951-52—Nat Clifton	62	8
Connie Simmons	66	8
Dick McGuire	59	8
1952-53—Carl Braun	70	†14
1953-54—Carl Braun	72	6
1954-55—Ray Felix	72	11
1955-56—Ray Felix	72	13
1956-57—Ray Felix	72	8
1957-58—Ray Felix	72	12
1958-59—Ray Felix	72	9
1959-60—Charles Tyra	74	8
1960-61—Ken Sears	52	6
Charles Tyra	59	6
1961-62—Darrall Imhoff	76	10
1962-63—Paul Hogue	50	12
1963-64—Tom Gola	74	7
1964-65—Willis Reed	80	†14
1965-66—Willis Reed	76	13
1966-67—Willis Reed	78	9
1967-68—Willis Reed	81	12
1968-69—Willis Reed	82	7
1969-70—Willis Reed	81	2
Dave DeBusschere	79	2
Dave Stallworth	82	2
Nate Bowman	81	2

* Led league. † Club record.

PHILADELPHIA 76ers

Entered N.B.A. in 1949-50 as the Syracuse Professional Basketball Club, Inc., in the merger of the B.A.A. and National League. Principal officer: John C. Johnson until 1956, then Jack Egan. Active direction under Dan Biasone. Sold in 1963 to Irv Kosloff and Ike Richman, and moved to Philadelphia as the 76ers.

Home courts:

1949-51—State Fair Coliseum in Syracuse, 7,500
1951-63—Onodaga County War Memorial, 8,000
1963-67—Convention Hall, Philadelphia, 12,000
Philadelphia Arena, 7,777
1967-on—The Spectrum, 15,244
(Also some games at the University of Pennsylvania's Palestra, 9,000)

Year	*W.*	*L.*	*Pos.*	*Coach*	*Top Scorer*	*Pts.*	*Play-Offs*
				SYRACUSE NATIONALS			
1950	51	13	1	Cervi	Schayes	16.8	6-5
1951	32	34	4	Cervi	Schayes	17.0	4-3
1952	40	26	1	Cervi	Schayes	13.8	3-4
1953	47	24	2	Cervi	Schayes	17.8	0-2
1954	42	30	3	Cervi	Schayes	17.1	9-4
1955	43	29	1	Cervi	Schayes	18.5	7-4
1956	35	37	3	Cervi	Schayes	20.4	4-4
1957	38	34	2	Cervi-Seymour	Schayes	22.5	2-3
1958	41	31	2	Seymour	Schayes	24.9	1-2
1959	35	37	3	Seymour	Schayes	21.3	5-4
1960	45	30	3	Seymour	Schayes	22.5	1-2
1961	38	41	3	Hannum	Schayes	23.6	4-4
1962	41	39	3	Hannum	Greer	22.8	2-3
1963	48	32	2	Hannum	Greer	19.5	2-3
				PHILADELPHIA 76ers			
1964	34	46	3	Schayes	Greer	23.3	2-3
1965	40	40	3	Schayes	Chamberlain	34.7	6-5
1966	55	25	1	Schayes	Chamberlain	33.5	1-4
1967	68	13	1	Hannum	Chamberlain	24.1	11-4
1968	62	20	1	Hannum	Chamberlain	24.3	7-6
1969	55	27	2	Ramsay	Cunningham	24.8	1-4
1970	42	40	4	Ramsay	Cunningham	26.1	1-4
Total	932	648					79-77

PHILADELPHIA 76ers' YEARLY LEADERS

Leading Scorer

Season—Player	*G.*	*Pts.*	*Avg.*
1949-50—Adolph Schayes	64	1072	16.8
1950-51—Adolph Schayes	66	1121	17.0
1951-52—Adolph Schayes	63	868	13.8
1952-53—Adolph Schayes	71	1262	17.8
1953-54—Adolph Schayes	72	1228	17.1
1954-55—Adolph Schayes	72	1333	18.5
1955-56—Adolph Schayes	72	1472	20.4
1956-57—Adolph Schayes	72	1617	22.5
1957-58—Adolph Schayes	72	1791	24.9
1958-59—Adolph Schayes	72	1534	21.3
1959-60—Adolph Schayes	75	1689	22.5
1960-61—Adolph Schayes	79	1868	23.6
1961-62—Hal Greer	71	1619	22.8
1962-63—Hal Greer	80	1559	19.5
1963-64—Hal Greer	80	1865	23.3
1964-65—Wilt Chamberlain	73	2534	†*34.7
1965-66—Wilt Chamberlain	79	†2649	*33.5
1966-67—Wilt Chamberlain	81	1956	24.1
1967-68—Wilt Chamberlain	82	1992	24.3
1968-69—Billy Cunningham	82	2034	24.8
1969-70—Billy Cunningham	81	2114	26.1

Best Foul Shooter

Season—Player	*FTA*	*FTM*	*Pct.*
1949-50—Al Cervi	346	287	.829
1950-51—Fred Scolari	331	279	.843
1951-52—Adolph Schayes	424	342	.807
1952-53—Adolph Schayes	619	512	.827
1953-54—Adolph Schayes	590	488	.827
1954-55—Adolph Schayes	587	489	.833
1955-56—Adolph Schayes	632	542	.853
1956-57—Adolph Schayes	691	625	†.904
1957-58—Adolph Schayes	696	629	†*.904
1958-59—Adolph Schayes	609	526	.864
1959-60—Adolph Schayes	597	533	*.892
1960-61—Adolph Schayes	†783	†680	.868
1961-62—Adolph Schayes	319	286	*.896
1962-63—Larry Costello	327	288	*.881
1963-64—Hal Greer	525	435	.829
1964-65—Larry Costello	243	277	*.877
1965-66—Hal Greer	514	413	.804
1966-67—Wally Jones	266	223	.838
1967-68—Wally Jones	202	159	.787
1968-69—Wally Jones	256	207	.809
1969-70—Wally Jones	226	190	.841

Top Playmaker

Season—Player	*G.*	*Ast.*	*Avg.*
1949-50—Al Cervi	56	264	4.7
1950-51—Fred Scolari	66	255	3.9
1951-52—George King	66	244	3.7
1952-53—George King	71	364	5.1
1953-54—Paul Seymour	71	364	5.1
1954-55—Paul Seymour	72	*483	*6.7
1955-56—George King	72	410	5.7
1056-57—Adolph Schayes	72	229	3.2
1957-58—Larry Costello	72	317	4.4
1958-59—Larry Costello	70	379	5.4
1959-60—Larry Costello	71	446	6.3
1960-61—Larry Costello	75	413	5.5
1961-62—Larry Costello	63	358	5.7
1962-63—Larry Costello	78	334	4.3
1963-64—Hal Greer	80	376	4.7

1964-65—Hal Greer	70	313	4.5
1965-66—Wilt Chamberlain	79	414	5.2
1966-67—Wilt Chamberlain	81	630	7.8
1967-68—Wilt Chamberlain	82	†*702	†*8.6
1968-69—Hal Greer	82	414	5.0
1969-70—Hal Greer	80	405	5.1

Most Minutes Played

Season—Player	*G.*	*Min.*	*Avg.*
1951-52—Red Rocha	66	2543	38.6
1952-53—Paul Seymour	67	2684	40.1
1953-54—Paul Seymour	71	2727	38.4
1954-55—Paul Seymour	72	2950	41.0
1955-56—Adolph Schayes	72	2517	35.0
1956-57—Adolph Schayes	72	2851	*39.6
1957-58—Adolph Schayes	72	2918	*40.5
1958-59—Larry Costello	70	2750	39.3
1959-60—Adolph Schayes	75	2741	36.5
1960-61—Adolph Schayes	79	3007	38.1
1961-62—John Kerr	80	2767	34.6
1962-63—Hal Greer	80	2619	32.7
1963-64—Hal Greer	80	3167	39.6
1964-65—Wilt Chamberlain	73	3301	45.4
1965-66—Wilt Chamberlain	79	3737	†*47.3
1966-67—Wilt Chamberlain	81	*3682	*45.4
1967-68—Wilt Chamberlain	82	†*3836	*46.8
1968-69—Billy Cunningham	82	3345	40.8
1969-70—Billy Cunningham	81	3194	39.4

Best Shooting Average

Season—Player	*FGA*	*FGM*	*Pct.*
1949-50—Adolph Schayes	903	348	.585
1950-51—George Ratkovicz	636	264	.415
1951-52—George King	579	235	.406
1952-53—George King	635	255	.402
1953-54—Adolph Schayes	973	370	.380
1954-55—John Kerr	718	301	.419
1955-56—John Kerr	935	377	.403
1956-57—John Kerr	827	333	.403
1957-58—Larry Costello	888	378	.426
1958-59—John Kerr	1139	502	.441
1959-60—Hal Greer	815	388	.476
1960-61—Dick Barnett	1194	540	.452
1961-62—Hal Greer	1452	644	.443
John Kerr	1220	541	.443
1962-63—John Kerr	1069	507	.474
1963-64—Paul Neumann	732	324	.443
1964-65—Wilt Chamberlain	*2083	*1063	*.510
1965-66—Wilt Chamberlain	1990	†*1074	†*.540
1966-67—Wilt Chamberlain	1150	785	*.683
1967-68—Wilt Chamberlain	1377	819	*.595
1968-69—Chet Walker	1145	554	.484
1969-70—Darrall Imhoff	796	430	.540

Top Rebounder

Season—Player	*G.*	*Reb.*	*Avg.*
1950-51—Adolph Schayes	66	*1080	*16.4
1951-52—Adolph Schayes	63	773	12.3
1952-53—Adolph Schayes	71	920	13.1
1953-54—Adolph Schayes	72	870	12.3
1954-55—Adolph Schayes	72	887	12.5
1955-56—Adolph Schayes	72	891	12.4
1956-57—Adolph Schayes	72	1008	14.0
1957-58—Adolph Schayes	72	1022	14.2
1958-59—John Kerr	72	1008	14.0
1959-60—Adolph Schayes	75	959	12.8
1960-61—Adolph Schayes	79	960	12.2
1961-62—John Kerr	80	1176	14.7
1962-63—John Kerr	80	1049	13.1

1963-64—John Kerr	80	1018	12.7
1964-65—Wilt Chamberlain	73	1673	22.9
1965-66—Wilt Chamberlain	79	*1943	†*24.6
1966-67—Wilt Chamberlain	81	†*1957	*24.2
1967-68—Wilt Chamberlain	82	*1952	*23.8
1968-69—Billy Cunningham	82	1050	12.8
1969-70—Billy Cunningham	81	1101	13.6

Most Personal Fouls

Season—Player	*G.*	*PF*	*Avg.*
1949-50—Alex Hannum	64	264	4.1
1950-51—Adolph Schayes	66	271	4.2
Alex Hannum	63	271	†4.3
1951-52—Red Rocha	66	249	3.8
1952-53—Adolph Schayes	71	271	3.8
1953-54—Earl Lloyd	72	303	*4.2
1954-55—Earl Lloyd	72	283	3.9
1955-56—Earl Lloyd	72	267	3.7
1956-57—Earl Lloyd	72	282	3.9
1957-58—Larry Costello	72	246	3.4
1958-59—Adolph Schayes	72	280	3.9
1959-60—Adolph Schayes	75	266	3.5
1960-61—Adolph Schayes	79	296	3.7
1961-62—John Kerr	80	282	3.5
1962-63—Hal Greer	80	278	3.5
1963-64—Hal Greer	80	291	3.6
1964-65—Dave Gambee	80	277	3.5
1965-66—Hal Greer	80	*315	3.9
1966-67—Hal Greer	80	302	3.8
1967-68—Hal Greer	82	289	3.5
1968-69—Billy Cunningham	82	*329	4.0
1969-70—Billy Cunningham	81	†331	4.1

Most Disqualifications

Season—Player	*G.*	*Disq.*
1950-51—Alex Hannum	63	†*16
1951-52—George Ratkovicz	66	8
Wally Osterkorn	66	8
1952-53—William Gabor	69	11
1953-54—Earl Lloyd	72	*12
1954-55—Adolph Schayes	72	6
1955-56—Adolph Schayes	72	9
1956-57—Earl Lloyd	72	10
1957-58—Adolph Schayes	72	6
1958-59—Adolph Schayes	72	9
1959-60—Adolph Schayes	75	9
1960-61—Adolph Schayes	79	9
Larry Costello	75	9
1961-62—Dave Gambee	80	10
1962-63—Lee Shaffer	80	5
Paul Neumann	80	5
1963-64—Hal Greer	80	6
Al Bianchi	78	6
Dave Gambee	41	6
1964-65—Larry Costello	64	10
Al Bianchi	60	10
1965-66—Bill Cunningham	80	12
1966-67—Lucious Jackson	81	6
Wally Jones	81	6
1967-68—Hal Greer	82	7
1968-69—Darrall Imhoff	82	12
1969-70—Billy Cunningham	81	15

* Led league. † Club record.

PHOENIX SUNS

Entered league as expansion team for 1968-69 season. Owned by syndicate with Richard Bloch as principal operator.

Home court: Arizona Veterans' Memorial Coliseum, 12,096

Year	*W.*	*L.*	*Pos.*	*Coach*	*Top Scorer*	*Pts.*	*Play-Offs*
1969	16	66	7	Kerr	Goodrich	23.8	—
1970	39	43	3 (T)	Kerr-Colangelo	Hawkins	24.6	3-4
Total	55	109					3-4

PHOENIX SUNS' YEARLY LEADERS

Leading Scorer

Season—Player	*G.*	*Pts.*	*Avg.*
1968-69—Gail Goodrich	81	1931	23.8
1969-70—Connie Hawkins	81	†1995	†24.6

Best Shooting Average

Season—Player	*FGA*	*FGM*	*Pct.*
1968-69—Dick Snyder	846	399	.472
1969-70—Jim Fox	788	413	†.524

Best Foul Shooter

Season—Player	*FTA*	*FTM*	*Pct.*
1968-69—Stan McKenzie	287	219	.763
1969-70—Gail Goodrich	604	488	†.808

Top Rebounder

Season—Player	*G.*	*Reb.*	*Avg.*
1968-69—Jim Fox	76	818	10.8
1969-70—Paul Silas	78	†916	†11.7

Top Playmaker

Season—Player	*G.*	*Ast.*	*Avg.*
1968-69—Gail Goodrich	81	518	6.4
1969-70—Gail Goodrich	81	†605	†7.5

Most Personal Fouls

Season—Player	*G.*	*PF*	*Avg.*
1968-69—Jim Fox	76	266	3.5
1969-70—Connie Hawkins	81	†287	3.5

Most Minutes Played

Season—Player	*G.*	*Min.*	*Avg.*
1968-69—Dick Van Arsdale	80	†3388	†42.4
1969-70—Connie Hawkins	81	3312	40.9

Most Disqualifications

Season—Player	*G.*	*Disq.*
1968-69—Jim Fox	76	6
1969-70—Jim Fox	81	†7

† Club record.

PORTLAND TRAILBLAZERS

Formed in 1970, entering as expansion team for 1970-71 season. Harry Glickman, president. Rolland Todd, coach.

Home court: Memorial Arena, 10,500.

SAN DIEGO ROCKETS

Entered N.B.A. in 1967-68. Principal owner and president, Robert Breitbard. Home court: San Diego International Sports Arena, 14,000

Year	*W.*	*L.*	*Pos.*	*Coach*	*Top Scorer*	*Pts.*	*Play-Offs*
1968	15	67	6	McMahon	Block	20.2	—
1969	37	45	4	McMahon	Hayes	28.4	2-4
1970	27	55	7	McMahon-Hannum	Hayes	27.5	—
Total	79	167					2-4

SAN DIEGO ROCKETS' YEARLY LEADERS

Leading Scorer

Season—Player	*G.*	*Pts.*	*Avg.*
1967-68—Don Kojis	69	1360	19.7
1968-69—Elvin Hayes	82	†*2327	†*28.4
1969-70—Elvin Hayes	82	2256	27.5

Best Foul Shooter

Season—Player	*FTA*	*FTM*	*Pct.*
1967-68—Dave Gambee	379	321	†.847
1968-69—Jim Barnett	310	233	.752
1969-70—Jim Barnett	366	289	.790

Top Playmaker

Season—Player	*G.*	*Ast.*	*Avg.*
1967-68—Art Williams	79	391	4.9
1968-69—Art Williams	79	†524	†6.6
1969-70—Art Williams	80	503	6.3

Most Minutes Played

Season—Player	*G.*	*Min.*	*Avg.*
1967-68—Don Kojis	69	2548	36.9
1968-69—Elvin Hayes	82	†*3695	†*45.0
1969-70—Elvin Hayes	82	*3665	*44.7

Best Shooting Average

Season—Player	*FGA*	*FGM*	*Pct.*
1967-68—Henry Finkel	492	242	†.492
1968-69—Elvin Hayes	2082	930	.447
1969-70—Elvin Hayes	2020	914	.452

Top Rebounders

Season—Player	*G.*	*Reb.*	*Avg.*
1967-68—Toby Kimball	81	947	11.7
1968-69—Elvin Hayes	82	†1406	†17.1
1969-70—Elvin Hayes	82	*1386	*16.9

Most Personal Fouls

Season—Player	*G.*	*PF*	*Avg.*
1967-68—Toby Kimball	81	273	3.4
1968-69—Don Kojis	81	†303	3.7
1969-70—John Block	82	275	3.4

Most Disqualifications

Season—Player	*G.*	*Disq.*
1967-68—Don Kojis	69	5
Dave Gambee	80	5
Henry Finkel	53	5
1968-69—Don Kojis	81	†6
Toby Kimball	76	†6
1969-70—Elvin Hayes	82	5

* Led league. † Club record.

SAN FRANCISCO WARRIORS

Formed in 1946 as the Philadelphia Warriors, owned by Pete Tyrell. Acquired by Eddie Gottlieb in 1952. Sold in 1962 to syndicate headed by Matty Simmons and Tom Gray and moved to San Francisco for 1962-63 season. Bought by Franklin Mieuli in 1964.

Home courts:

1946-52—Philadelphia Arena, 7,777
1952-62—Convention Hall, 9,200, and Arena
1962-64—Cow Palace, San Francisco, 13,862
1964-66—Civic Auditorium, 7,500, and Univ. of San Francisco Gym, 6,000
1966-67—Cow Palace, Civic Auditorium and Oakland Arena, 15,000

Year	*W.*	*L.*	*Pos.*	*Coach*	*Top Scorer*	*Pts.*	*Play-Offs*
				PHILADELPHIA WARRIORS			
1947	35	25	2	Gottlieb	Fulks	23.2	8-2
1948	27	21	1	Gottlieb	Fulks	22.1	6-7
1949	28	32	4	Gottlieb	Fulks	26.0	0-2
1950	26	42	4	Gottlieb	Fulks	14.2	0-2
1951	40	26	1	Gottlieb	Fulks	18.7	0-2
1952	33	33	4	Gottlieb	Arizin	25.4	1-2
1953	12	57	5	Gottlieb	Johnston	22.3	—
1954	29	43	4	Gottlieb	Johnston	24.4	—
1955	33	39	4	Gottlieb	Johnston	22.7	—
1956	45	27	1	Senesky	Arizin	24.2	7-3
1957	37	35	3	Senesky	Arizin	25.6	0-2
1958	37	35	3	Senesky	Arizin	20.7	3-5
1959	32	40	4	Cervi	Arizin	26.4	—
1960	49	26	2	Johnston	Chamberlain	37.6	4-5
1961	46	33	2	Johnston	Chamberlain	38.4	0-3
1962	49	31	2	F. McGuire	Chamberlain	50.4	6-6
				SAN FRANCISCO WARRIORS			
1963	31	49	4	Feerick	Chamberlain	44.8	—
1964	48	32	1	Hannum	Chamberlain	36.9	5-7
1965	17	63	5	Hannum	Thurmond	16.5	—
1966	35	45	4	Hannum	Barry	25.7	—
1967	44	37	1	Sharman	Barry	35.6	9-6
1968	43	39	3	Sharman	LaRusso	21.8	4-6
1969	41	41	3	Lee	Mullins	22.8	2-4
1970	30	52	6	Lee-Attles	Mullins	22.1	—
Total	847	903					55-64

SAN FRANCISCO WARRIORS' YEARLY LEADERS

Leading Scorer

Season—Player	*G.*	*Pts.*	*Avg*
1946-47—Joe Fulks	60	*1389	*23.2
1947-48—Joe Fulks	43	947	22.1
1948-49—Joe Fulks	60	1560	26.0
1949-50—Joe Fulks	68	965	14.2
1950-51—Joe Fulks	66	1236	18.7
1951-52—Paul Arizin	66	1674	*25.4
1952-53—Neil Johnston	70	1564	*22.3
1953-54—Neil Johnston	72	1759	*24.4
1954-55—Neil Johnston	72	1631	*22.7
1955-56—Paul Arizin	72	1741	24.2
1956-57—Paul Arizin	71	1817	*25.6
1957-58—Paul Arizin	68	1406	20.7
1958-59—Paul Arizin	70	1851	26.4
1959-60—Wilt Chamberlain	72	2707	*37.6
1960-61—Wilt Chamberlain	79	3033	*38.4
1961-62—Wilt Chamberlain	80	†4029	†*50.4
1962-63—Wilt Chamberlain	80	3586	*44.8
1963-64—Wilt Chamberlain	80	2948	*36.9
1964-65—Nate Thurmond	77	1273	16.5
1965-66—Rick Barry	80	2059	25.7
1966-67—Rick Barry	78	2775	*35.6
1967-68—Rudy LaRusso	79	1726	21.8
1968-69—Jeff Mullins	78	1775	22.8
1969-70—Jeff Mullins	74	1632	22.1

Best Foul Shooter

Season—Player	*FTA*	*FTM*	*Pct.*
1946-47—Joe Fulks	*601	*439	.730
1947-48—Joe Fulks	*390	*297	.762
1948-49—Joe Fulks	638	502	.787
1949-50—Vern Gardner	296	227	.767
1950-51—Joe Fulks	442	378	*.855
1951-52—Joe Fulks	303	250	.825
1952-53—Neil Johnston	794	556	.700
1953-54—Bob Zawoluk	230	186	.809
1954-55—Paul Arizin	585	454	.776
1955-56—Paul Arizin	626	507	.810
1956-57—Paul Arizin	†713	†591	.829
1957-58—Neil Johnston	540	442	.819
1958-59—Paul Arizin	922	587	.813
1959-60—Paul Arizin	526	420	.798
1960-61—Paul Arizin	632	532	.832
1961-62—Tom Meschery	262	216	.824
1962-63—Tom Meschery	313	228	.728
1963-64—Wayne Hightower	329	260	.790
1964-65—Paul Neumann	303	234	.772
1965-66—Rick Barry	660	569	.862
1966-67—Rick Barry	852	753	*.884
1967-68—Fred Hetzel	474	395	.833
1968-69—Jeff Mullins	452	381	.843
1969-70—Jeff Mullins	378	320	.847

Top Playmaker

Season—Player	*G.*	*Ast.*	*Avg.*
1946-47—Howie Dallmar	60	104	1.7
1947-48—Howie Dallmar	48	*120	*2.5
1948-49—George Senesky	60	233	3.8
1949-50—George Senesky	68	264	3.8
1950-51—Andrew Phillip	66	*414	*6.3
1951-52—Andrew Phillip	66	*539	*7.2
1952-53—George Senesky	69	264	3.7
1953-54—Jack George	71	312	4.3
1954-55—Jack George	68	302	4.4
1955-56—Jack George	72	457	6.3
1956-57—Jack George	67	307	4.5

Season—Player	G.		
1957-58—Tom Gola	59	327	5.5
1958-59—Tom Gola	64	269	4.2
1959-60—Guy Rodgers	68	482	7.1
1960-61—Guy Rodgers	78	677	8.7
1961-62—Guy Rodgers	80	633	7.9
1962-63—Guy Rodgers	78	825	*10.6
1963-64—Guy Rodgers	79	556	7.0
1964-65—Guy Rodgers	79	565	7.3
1965-66—Guy Rodgers	79	†846	†10.7
1966-67—Paul Neumann	78	342	4.4
1967-68—Al Attles	67	390	5.8
1968-69—Jeff Mullins	78	339	4.3
1969-70—Ron Williams	80	424	5.3

Most Minutes Played

Season—Player	*G.*	*Min.*	*Avg.*
1951-52—Paul Arizin	66	2936	*44.6
1952-53—Neil Johnston	70	3166	*45.2
1953-54—Neil Johnston	72	3296	*45.7
1954-55—Paul Arizin	72	2953	*41.9
1955-56—Paul Arizin	72	2724	37.8
1956-57—Paul Arizin	71	2767	38.9
1957-58—Neil Johnston	71	2408	33.9
1958-59—Paul Arizin	70	2799	39.8
1959-60—Wilt Chamberlain	72	3338	*43.3
1960-61—Wilt Chamberlain	79	3773	*47.9
1961-62—Wilt Chamberlain	80	†3882	†*48.5
1962-63—Wilt Chamberlain	80	3808	*47.6
1963-64—Wilt Chamberlain	80	3689	*46.1
1964-65—Nate Thurmond	77	3173	41.2
1965-66—Rick Barry	80	2990	37.4
1966-67—Rick Barry	78	3175	40.7
1967-68—Rudy LaRusso	79	2819	35.7
1968-69—Nate Thurmond	71	3208	45.2
1969-70—Jeff Mullins	74	2861	38.7

Best Shooting Average

Season—Player	*FGA*	*FGM*	*Pct.*
1946-47—Joe Fulks	1557	475	.305
1947-48—Howard Dallmar	781	215	.275
1948-49—Ed Sadowski	839	340	.405
1949-50—Vern Gardner	916	313	.342
1950-51—Paul Arizin	864	352	.407
1951-52—Paul Arizin	*1222	*548	*.448
1952-53—Neil Johnston	1114	504	*.452
1953-54—Neil Johnston	1317	591	.449
1954-55—Neil Johnston	1184	521	.440
1955-56—Neil Johnston	1092	499	*.457
1956-57—Neil Johnston	1163	520	*.447
1957-58—Neil Johnston	1102	473	.429
1958-59—Paul Arizin	1466	632	.431
1959-60—Wilt Chamberlain	2311	1065	.461
1960-61—Wilt Chamberlain	2479	1251	*.505
1961-62—Wilt Chamberlain	†3159	†1597	.505
1962-63—Wilt Chamberlain	2770	1463	†*.528
1963-64—Wilt Chamberlain	2298	1204	.524
1964-65—Paul Neumann	772	365	.473
1965-66—Al Attles	724	364	.503
1966-67—Jeff Mullins	919	421	.458
1967-68—Al Attles	540	252	.467
1968-69—Jeff Mullins	1517	697	.459
1969-70—Jerry Lucas	764	387	.507

Top Rebounder

Season—Player	*G.*	*Reb.*	*Avg.*
1950-51—Paul Arizin	65	640	10.0
1951-52—Paul Arizin	66	745	11.3
1952-53—Neil Johnston	70	976	13.9
1953-54—Neil Johnston	72	797	11.1
1954-55—Neil Johnston	72	1085	*15.1
1955-56—Neil Johnston	70	872	12.4

Season—Player	G.		
1956-57—Neil Johnston	69	855	12.4
1957-58—Neil Johnston	71	790	11.1
1958-59—Woody Sauldsberry	72	826	11.5
1959-60—Wilt Chamberlain	72	1941	*26.8
1960-61—Wilt Chamberlain	79	†2149	†*27.2
1961-62—Wilt Chamberlain	80	2052	*25.6
1962-63—Wilt Chamberlain	80	1946	*24.3
1963-64—Wilt Chamberlain	80	1687	21.1
1964-65—Nate Thurmond	77	1395	18.1
1965-66—Nate Thurmond	73	1312	18.0
1966-67—Nate Thurmond	65	1382	21.7
1967-68—Clyde Lee	82	1141	13.9
1968-69—Nate Thurmond	71	1402	19.7
1969-70—Clyde Lee	82	929	11.3

Most Personal Fouls

Season—Player	*G.*	*PF*	*Avg.*
1946-47—Joe Fulks	60	199	3.0
1947-48—Joe Fulks	43	162	3.5
1948-49—Ed Sadowski	60	273	*4.5
1949-50—Ron Livingstone	54	260	†4.8
1950-51—Paul Arizin	65	284	4.4
1951-52—Joe Fulks	61	255	4.2
1952-53—Joe Fulks	70	319	4.5
1953-54—Neil Johnston	72	259	3.6
1954-55—Paul Arizin	72	270	3.9
1955-56—Paul Arizin	72	282	3.9
1956-57—Paul Arizin	71	274	3.8
1957-58—Joe Graboski	72	249	3.4
1958-59—Woody Sauldsberry	72	276	3.8
1959-60—Tom Gola	75	311	4.1
1960-61—Paul Arizin	79	335	4.2
1961-62—Tom Meschery	80	320	4.0
1962-63—Guy Rodgers	78	296	3.8
1963-64—Wayne Hightower	79	269	3.5
1964-65—Tom Meschery	79	279	3.5
1965-66—Rick Barry	80	297	3.7
1966-67—Paul Neumann	78	266	3.4
1967-68—Rudy LaRusso	79	†337	4.3
1968-69—Rudy LaRusso	75	268	3.6
1969-70—Ron Williams	80	287	3.6

Most Disqualifications

Season—Player	*G.*	*Disq.*
1950-51—Paul Arizin	65	18
1951-52—Joe Fulks	61	13
1952-53—Joe Fulks	70	†20
1953-54—Walter Davis	68	9
1954-55—Joe Graboski	70	8
1955-56—Tom Gola	68	11
1956-57—Paul Arizin	71	13
1957-58—Tom Gola	59	11
1958-59—Woody Sauldsberry	72	12
1959-60—Tom Gola	75	9
1960-61—Tom Gola	74	13
1961-62—Paul Arizin	78	18
1962-63—Tom Meschery	64	11
1963-64—Gary Phillips	66	8
1964-65—Al Attles	73	7
1965-66—Nate Thurmond	73	7
Tom Meschery	80	7
Al Attles	79	7
1966-67—Al Attles	70	13
1967-68—Rudy LaRusso	79	14
1968-69—Joe Ellis	74	13
1969-70—Joe Ellis	76	13

* Led league. † Club record.

SEATTLE SUPERSONICS

Entered N.B.A. in 1967-68. Principal owners: Samuel Schulman and Eugene Klein.

Home court: Seattle Center Coliseum, 12,595

Year	*W.*	*L.*	*Pos.*	*Coach*	*Top Scorer*	*Pts.*	*Play-Offs*
1968	23	59	5	Bianchi	Hazzard	23.9	—
1969	30	52	6	Bianchi	Rule	24.0	—
1970	36	46	5	Wilkens	Rule	24.6	—
Total	89	157					0-0

SEATTLE SUPERSONICS' YEARLY LEADERS

Leading Scorer

Season—Player	*G.*	*Pts.*	*Avg.*
1967-68—Walt Hazzard	79	1894	23.9
1968-69—Bob Rule	82	†1965	24.0
1969-70—Bob Rule	80	†1965	†24.6

Best Foul Shooter

Season—Player	*FTA*	*FTM*	*Pct.*
1967-68—Walt Hazzard	553	428	†.774
1968-69—Len Wilkens	†710	†547	.770
1969-70—Bob Boozer	320	263	.822

Top Playmaker

Season—Player	*G.*	*Ast.*	*Avg.*
1967-68—Walt Hazzard	79	493	6.2
1968-69—Len Wilkens	82	674	8.2
1969-70—Len Wilkens	77	†*683	†*9.1

Most Minutes Played

Season—Player	*G.*	*Min.*	*Avg.*
1967-68—Tom Meschery	82	2857	34.8
1968-69—Len Wilkens	82	†3463	†42.2
1969-70—Bob Rule	80	2959	36.9

Best Shooting Average

Season—Player	*FGA*	*FGM*	*Pct.*
1967-68—Bob Rule	1162	568	.489
1968-69—Bob Rule	†1655	†776	.469
1969-70—Dick Snyder	863	456	†.528

Top Rebounder

Season—Player	*G.*	*Reb.*	*Avg.*
1967-68—Bob Rule	82	840	10.2
1968-69—Bob Rule	82	†941	†11.5
1969-70—Bob Rule	80	825	10.3

Most Personal Fouls

Season—Player	*G.*	*PF*	*Avg.*
1967-68—Tom Meschery	82	323	3.9
1968-69—Art Harris	80	†326	†4.0
1969-70—Tom Meschery	80	317	39.6

Most Disqualifications

Season—Player	*G.*	*Disq.*
1967-68—Tom Meschery	82	†14
1968-69—Art Harris	80	†*14
1969-70—Tom Meschery	80	13

* Led league. † Club record.

TEAMS (DEFUNCT)

ANDERSON PACKERS

Year	W.	L.	Pos.	Coach	Top Scorer	Pts.	Play-Offs
1950	37	27	2	Schultz-Duffey-Moore	Brian	17.8	4-4

(ORIGINAL) BALTIMORE BULLETS

Year	W.	L.	Pos.	Coach	Top Scorer	Pts.	Play-Offs
1948	28	20	2 (W)	Jeannette	Hermsen	12.0	8-3
1949	29	31	3	Jeannette	Simmons	13.0	1-2
1950	25	43	5	Jeannette	Hoffman	14.4	—
1951	24	42	5	Jeannette-Budko	Rocha	13.1	—
1952	20	46	5	Scolari-Reiser	Scolari	14.6	—
1953	16	54	4	Reiser-Bee	Barksdale	13.8	0-2
1954	16	56	5	Bee	Felix	17.6	—
1955	3	11	—	Bee-Barthelme	————		—
Total	161	303					9-7

(W)—in Western Division,

CHICAGO STAGS

Year	W.	L.	Pos.	Coach	Top Scorer	Pts.	Play-Offs
1947	39	22	1	Olsen	Zaslofsky	14.4	5-6
1948	28	20	3	Olsen	Zaslofsky	21.0	2-3
1949	38	22	3	Olsen-Brownstein	Zaslofsky	20.6	0-2
1950	40	28	4	Brownstein	Zaslofsky	16.4	0-2
Total	145	92					7-13

CLEVELAND REBELS

Year	W.	L.	Pos.	Coach	Top Scorer	Pts.	Play-Offs
1947	30	30	3	Dennert-Clifford	Sadowski	15.9	1-2

DENVER NUGGETS

Year	W.	L.	Pos.	Coach	Top Scorer	Pts.	Play-Offs
1950	11	51	6	Darden	Sailors	17.3	—

DETROIT FALCONS

Year	W.	L.	Pos.	Coach	Top Scorer	Pts.	Play-Offs
1947	20	40	4	Curtis-Sachs	Miasek	14.9	—

INDIANAPOLIS JETS

Year	W.	L.	Pos.	Coach	Top Scorer	Pts.	Play-Offs
1949	18	42	6	Hale-Friddle	Lumpp	12.3	—

INDIANAPOLIS OLYMPIANS

Year	W.	L.	Pos.	Coach	Top Scorer	Pts.	Play-Offs
1950	39	25	1	Barker	Groza	23.4	3-3
1951	31	37	4	Barker-Jones	Groza	21.7	1-2
1952	34	32	3	Schaefer	Graboski	13.7	0-2
1953	28	43	4	Schaefer	Barnhorst	13.6	0-2
Total	132	137					4-9

PITTSBURGH IRONMEN

Year	W.	L.	Pos.	Coach	Top Scorer	Pts.	Play-Offs
1947	15	45	5	Birch	Gunther	14.1	—

PROVIDENCE STEAMROLLERS

Year	W.	L.	Pos.	Coach	Top Scorer	Pts.	Play-Offs
1947	28	32	4	Morris	Calverly	14.3	—
1948	6	42		Soar-Hickey	Calverly	11.9	—
1949	12	48		Loeffler	Sailors	15.8	—
Total	46	122					—

ST. LOUIS BOMBERS

Year	W.	L.	Pos.	Coach	Top Scorer	Pts.	Play-Offs
1947	38	33	2	Loeffler	Logan	12.6	1-2
1948	29	19	1	Loeffler	Logan	13.4	3-4
1949	29	31	4	Lewis	Smawley	15.5	0-2
1950	26	42	5	Lewis	Macauley	16.1	—
Total	122	115					4-8

SHEBOYGAN REDSKINS

Year	W.	L.	Pos.	Coach	Top Scorer	Pts.	Play-Offs
1950	22	40	4	Suesens	Jorgensen	13.0	1-2

TORONTO HUSKIES

Year	W.	L.	Pos.	Coach	Top Scorer	Pts.	Play-Offs
1947	22	38	5	Sadowski-Hayman-Fitzgerald-Rolfe	Mogus	13.3	—

WASHINGTON CAPITOLS

Year	W.	L.	Pos.	Coach	Top Scorer	Pts.	Play-Offs
1947	49	11	1	Auerbach	Feerick	16.3	2-4
1948	28	20	4 (W)	Auerbach	Feerick	16.1	—
1949	38	22	1	Auerbach	Feerick	13.0	6-5
1950	32	36	3	Feerick	Scolari	13.0	0-2
1951	10	25	6	McKinney	———	——	—
Total	157	114					8-11

(W)—In Western Division.

WATERLOO HAWKS

Year	W.	L.	Pos.	Coach	Top Scorer	Pts.	Play-Offs
1950	19	43	5	Shipp-Smiley	Mehen	14.4	—

PERSONALITIES

LEW ALCINDOR——7′ 2″, U.C.L.A. 1969. After dominating college basketball throughout his career, he accepted a $1.4 million package from Milwaukee as the N.B.A.'s top draft choice and transformed a last-place team into a title contender. He was Rookie of the Year in 1970, finished second in scoring with 28.8 points a game, and third in rebounding.

PAUL ARIZIN——6′ 4″, Villanova 1950. One of the greatest jump-shot scorers. Led league in scoring in his second pro season (1951-52) and again in 1956-57. Played entire career with Philadelphia Warriors, averaged 22.8 points a game for ten seasons. Suffered from an asthmatic condition that made breathing difficult, but appeared tireless and possessed tremendous drive.

ARNOLD (RED) AUERBACH——Most successful coach in pro basketball history. Led Washington to Eastern Division titles in two of the first three years of the league, then built the Boston team that won eight straight play-off championships and nine out of ten. Born in Brooklyn, a graduate of George Washington University, he retired as coach of the Celtics in 1966 with 1,037 victories to his credit.

RICK BARRY——6′ 7″, Miami (Florida) 1965. Spectacular scorer from the corners, became the first player to outscore Wilt Chamberlain by leading the league in his second year (1966-67) with a 35.6 average. Rookie of the Year in 1965-66, when he averaged 25.7. His college coach, Bruce Hale, was his father-in-law, and Barry was the most prominent N.B.A. player to jump to the A.B.A. in 1967—to join an Oakland team coached by Hale.

ELGIN BAYLOR——6′ 5″, Seattle 1958. One of the greatest all-around players, an outstanding shooter, driver, rebounder. Known above all for "second effort" and strength near the basket. Scored at a better rate (28.6 per game for his first eight years) than anyone but Chamberlain and Robertson. All-league first team in nine of his first eleven seasons.

CARL BRAUN——6′ 5″, Colgate 1949. Exceptionally talented shooter of every variety of shot, set league record of 47 points in one game at age of twenty in 1947. Later in his career he developed into an outstanding playmaker, and was playing-coach of New York. Played most of his career with the Knicks, then one year with Boston (1961-62).

AL CERVI——5′ 11″, no college. A pro at the age of eighteen, Cervi epitomized the tough, smart, quick backcourt man with the Rochester Royals in the old National League and with Syracuse in the N.B.A. As player-coach at Syracuse, he had outstanding teams and in 1954-55, when no longer a player, coached the Nats to a league championship.

WILT CHAMBERLAIN——7′ 2″, Kansas 1959. The largest and most dominating player in basketball history. Scored 100 points in one game, averaged more than 50 for a full season (1961-62) and had a career total of more than 30,000 after his first eleven seasons. A native Philadelphian, Most Valuable Player in 1960, 1966 and 1967, he led the Philadelphia 76ers to the championship in 1967, ending Boston's string of titles.

BOB COUSY——6′ 1″, Holy Cross 1950. Hailed as "the greatest little man" among the pros, he was a spectacular passer, dribbler, shooter and clutch player. He was the quarterback in Boston's fast break. Most Valuable Player in 1957, first team all-league ten times in thirteen-year career in which he scored more than 18,000 points and made more than 6,900 assists. He became coach of Cincinnati in 1969.

BOB DAVIES——6′ 1″, Seton Hall 1942. Brilliant all-around backcourt man as driver, scorer and feeder for Rochester. Made all-league first string in both the old National League and the N.B.A. after the merger, helped lead Rochester to N.B.A. title in 1951.

BOB FEERICK——6′ 3″, Santa Clara 1942. Leading scorer of Washington's strong teams in 1947-49, all-league in 1947. Subsequently coached Washington and (after coaching at Santa Clara) San Francisco.

LARRY FOUST——6′ 9″, LaSalle 1950. One of the giant, mobile centers capable of battling Mikan on even terms while playing for Fort Wayne. Subsequently played for Minneapolis and St. Louis. All-league first team in 1955.

JOE FULKS——6′ 5″, Murray (Kentucky) State, 1943. First of the superscorers, a great jump shooter. Led league in the B.A.A.'s first season (1947), raised one-game record to the then incredible 63 points in 1949, all-league first team for the first three years of the B.A.A. Played entire career for Philadelphia Warriors.

HARRY GALLATIN——6′ 6″, Northeast Missouri 1949. "Ironman" of New York and Detroit, played 746 consecutive games. Top rebounder and defender in pivot, despite "small" size for center. Coach of the Year as rookie coach of St. Louis in 1962-63, later also coached New York.

TOM GOLA——6′ 5″, LaSalle 1955. One of the most admired college All-Americas, helped Philadelphia Warriors to league title as a rookie (1956). Top playmaker, strong defender and rebounder, reluctant shooter. Finished career with New York. At his peak, outstanding "ball hawk" as interceptor of passes.

HAL GREER——6′ 2″, Marshall 1958. Remarkable jump shooter and speedy backcourt man for Syracuse and Philadelphia 76ers. Key scorer for 76ers when they ended Boston's string of championships in 1967.

RICHIE GUERIN——6′ 4″, Iona, 1954. Versatile backcourt man who set New York's scoring record by averaging 29.5 points a game in 1962, then outstanding playmaker as player-coach for St. Louis Hawks in 1965-67, and Coach of the Year in 1968 as bench coach.

CLIFF HAGAN——6′ 4″, Kentucky 1953. High-scoring "small" forward for St. Louis Hawks during their domination of the Western Division, 1957-61. With Pettit and Lovellette, formed highest-scoring balanced front line in league history. Originally drafted by Boston, part of trade that brought Bill Russell to the Celtics.

ALEX HANNUM——6′ 7″. Southern California 1948. Journeyman player for six N.B.A. teams, then second most successful coach in league history. Led St. Louis (1958) and Philadelphia (1967) to championships, bracketing Boston's streak, and coached successfully at Syracuse and San Francisco (Western title in 1964) in between. Coached Oakland to A.B.A. Championship in 1969.

TOM HEINSOHN——6′ 7″, Holy Cross 1956. Highest-scoring forward of Boston's championship teams, Rookie of the Year in 1957, nicknamed "Ack-Ack" for willingness to fire at the basket from all angles with every type of shot. A leader of the players' struggle for a pension plan. Succeeded Bill Russell as Celtics' coach in 1969.

WILLAM (RED) HOLZMAN——Taking charge of the New York Knickerbockers as coach midway through the 1967-68 season after eight years as their scout, Holzman led the team to its first title in 1970. A graduate of C.C.N.Y., where he played for Nat Holman before World War II, he played on Rochester Royal championship teams and coached the N.B.A. Hawks in Milwaukee and St. Louis before joining the Knick organization. Coach of the Year in 1970.

NEIL JOHNSTON——6′ 8″, Ohio State 1949. Scoring champion in 1953, 1954 and 1955 as center for Philadelphia Warriors, pivotman with exceptional hook shot. Upon retirement, coached Warriors in 1960 and 1961. Made first team all-league four times.

JOHN KERR——6′ 9″, Illinois 1954. As center for Syracuse, Philadelphia and Baltimore, set league "iron man" record by playing 917 consecutive regular season and play-off games. As rookie coach of Chicago Bulls in 1967, performed the unprecedented feat of bringing an expansion club into the play-offs in its first year. Later coached Phoenix.

JOHN KUNDLA——Coach of Minneapolis Lakers when they dominated the league 1949-1954. Coached West All-Stars in first four games of the all-star series. A star player at the University of Minnesota, he returned there as coach after leaving the Lakers.

JOE LAPCHICK——One of the most famous of the Original Celtics as a player in the 1920s. Coached the New York Knicks for nine seasons, reaching the play-off finals three times in a row 1951-53. Coached East All-Stars in the first all-star game, and in three of the first four years. Coached championship college teams at St. John's before and after Knick career.

CLYDE LOVELLETTE——6′ 9″, Kansas 1952. A center with an exceptionally fine shooting touch from outside as well as inside. he was Mikan's successor at Minneapolis, then part of the Hagan-Pettit line that enabled the St. Louis Hawks to dominate the Western Division. Also played for Cincinnati and Boston.

JERRY LUCAS——6′ 8″, Ohio State 1962. Unanimous All-America as a collegian, held out a year before joining Cincinnati to form great combination with Oscar Robertson. Outstanding rebounder, playing center or corner; stong scorer, strong defender, good feeder. First team all-league in two of first three years.

ED MACAULEY——6′ 8″, St. Louis U. 1949. Super-smooth jump-shooter, ball-handler and fast-moving forward, too slight to be top-notch rebounder. Part of great scoring trio in Boston with Cousy and Sharman, then part of St. Louis team that won title in 1958 from Boston. Main consideration in trade that brought Bill Russell to Boston. Outstanding player of first All-Star Game, three times first-team all-league. Coached St. Louis to Western title in 1959 and 1960.

SLATER MARTIN——5′ 9″, Texas 1949. Smallest player of all-star calibre in league history, outstanding feeder and defender as backcourt man with championship teams for Minneapolis (feeding Mikan) and St. Louis (feeding Pettit).

DICK McGUIRE——6′ 0″, St. John's 1949. One of the greatest playmakers and passers in basketball history, but a poor shooter. Among assist leaders for New York and Detroit as a player, subsequently coach at Detroit and New York.

GEORGE MIKAN——6′ 10″, DePaul 1946. Huge, strong pivotman, most dominant figure in the league before the arrival of Bill Russell and Chamberlain, scoring and rebound champion. Led Minneapolis Lakers to five championships in six years, first team all-league six times, named by the Associated Press "Outstanding player of the first half-century" after 1950. After retirement as player, became coach and general manager of the Lakers, and in 1967 became Commissioner of the newly-formed American Basketball Association.

VERN MIKKELSEN——6′ 7″, Hamline, 1949. Powerful rebounder, defender and inside scorer who teamed with Mikan and Pollard to form the front line that enabled the Minneapolis Lakers to win their five championships.

BOB PETTIT——6′ 9″, Louisiana State 1954. First player to amass 20,000 points in an N.B.A. career, league scoring champion in 1956 and 1959, mainstay of the championship teams of the St. Louis Hawks, rookie of the year in 1955 and first-team all-league for ten straight years in eleven-year career. Good jump shooter, extraordinary rebounder, known for competitiveness and second-effort, strong defense. Most Valuable Player (by vote of N.B.A. players) in 1956 and 1959.

ANDY PHILLIP——6′ 2″, Illinois 1947. One of the prewar Illinois "Whiz Kids," one of the three top playmakers of his era (with McGuire and Cousy). Played for Chicago, Philadelphia, Fort Wayne and Boston. Led league in assists with Philadelphia in 1951 and 1952, helped Boston to its first league championship in 1957.

JIM POLLARD——6′ 5″, Stanford 1948. Strong scorer and rebounder, known for great jumping ability, alongside Mikan on the championship Minneapolis Laker teams. Coached Lakers in their last year in Minneapolis, and Chicago Packers in their first year in Chicago.

WILLIS REED——6′ 9″, Grambling 1964. Player of the year in 1970, when he was the key man of the champion Knicks, Reed swept all honors: Most Valuable Player, Outstanding Player of the All-Star Game, Most Valuable Player of the Playoffs. Originally a center, he made the all-star game as a forward twice before his switch back to center in 1968-69 helped transform the Knicks.

ARNIE RISEN——6′ 9″, Ohio State 1946. Skillful, rather than muscular, center who enabled Rochester to battle Mikan's Lakers on even terms and to win league title in 1951. High scorer from pivot. Helped Boston to its first title in 1957.

OSCAR ROBERTSON——6′ 5″, Cincinnati 1960. The "most complete" basketball player. In first eight seasons, averaged 30 points per game, made first-team all-league every year, led in assists five times, exceptional rebounder and defender as backcourt man, the most feared "take-charge" player at game's end, only "small" man besides Cousy to be named Most Valuable Player by vote of other players (in 1964). After the 1970 season he was traded to Milwaukee, joining Alcindor.

BILL RUSSELL——6′ 10″, San Francisco 1956. Most effective defensive center in basketball history, mainspring of Boston's string of championships, the man who revolutionized basketball by his goaltending and shot-blocking techniques. Named Most Valuable Player by other players five times, more than anyone else. Led league in rebounding four times. After the 1965-66 season, became playing coach of the Celtics, and led them to two more titles before retiring.

FRED SCOLARI——5′ 10″, San Francisco 1943. Outstanding backcourt man in early years of the league, helped Washington to two Eastern Division titles in the first three years of the B.A.A. Later played for Baltimore (serving as player coach), Syracuse, Fort Wayne and Boston.

DOLPH SCHAYES——6′ 8″, New York University 1949. Ranks third behind Chamberlain and Pettit in career scoring. Corner man with first-rate two-handed set shot from outside, also outstanding driver and rebounder, good ball-handler and defender. First-team all-league six times. When Syracuse moved to Philadelphia for 1963-64 season, became coach and won Eastern Title in 1966. Became supervisor of league referees for 1966-67 season, then coach of new Buffalo team in 1970-71.

FRED SCHAUS——6′ 5″, West Virginia 1949. Above average corner man for Fort Wayne and New York, became successful college coach at West Virginia, where he helped develop Jerry West. Became coach of the Lakers when they moved to Los Angeles for 1960-61 season, with West as top draft choice, and won four Western Division titles in seven years before moving up to become general manager.

PAUL SEYMOUR——6′ 2″, Toledo 1950. Tough, aggressive, hard-driving, strong defensive backcourt man for Syracuse before becoming successful coach. Coached Syracuse for three and a half seasons, then won Western Division title with St. Louis. Coached Baltimore Bullets to second place, their highest finish, in 1965-66.

BILL SHARMAN——6′ 2″, Southern California, 1950. Remarkable jump shooter and foul shooter, backcourt partner of Cousy on Boston's championship teams 1957-61. Led league in free-throw accuracy seven times, setting record of .932 in 1959. Coached Los Angeles Jets in American League in 1962, then became coach of San Francisco Warriors in 1966-67 and won Western Division title then coached Los Angeles in A.B.A.

JACK TWYMAN——6′ 6″, Cincinnati 1955. High-scoring cornerman for Royals in Rochester and Cincinnati, reaching a peak of 31.2 in 1960. Scored more than 15,000 points in eleven seasons.

BOB WANZER——6′ 0″, Seton Hall, 1948. Backcourt partner of Bob Davies on Rochester's strong teams which contested the Minneapolis Lakers, and which took the league title in 1951. Exceptional outside shooter, playmaker and ball-handler. Coached the Royals for three and a half seasons, covering their move to Cincinnati.

JERRY WEST——6′ 3″, West Virginia 1960. Spectacular backcourt scorer, teamed with Baylor to bring Los Angeles Lakers four Western Division championships. Averaged more than 30 points per game in four different seasons, set record by averaging more than 40 in 1965 play-offs. Jump shooter and exceptionally quick driver, also strong defensively and good playmaker. First-team all-league seven times in first nine years in league, and scoring champion in 1970.

GEORGE YARDLEY——6′ 5″, Stanford 1950. High-jumping corner man, first player to score 2,000 points in one season (1958 for Detroit Pistons, breaking season record set by Mikan). Later joined Schayes at Syracuse to make Nationals a powerful team.

MAX ZASLOFSKY——6′ 2″, St. John's 1949. Outstanding set-shooter and driver, first-team all-league during the first four seasons of the league while with the Chicago Stags, scoring champion in 1948. Helped bring New York Knicks to Eastern title in 1953, finished career with Fort Wayne.

INDEX